TOMORROW TO GOD IT BELONGS

Psychography by
Zibia Gasparetto

By the Spirit
Lucius

English Translation:
Roxana G. Arellano Bernabé
Lima, Peru, September 2023

Original Title in Portuguese:

"O AMANHÃ A DEUS PERTENCE"

© Zibia Gasparetto, 2006

Revision:

Karina Rodriguez

World Spiritist Institute
Houston, Texas, USA
E-mail: contact@worldspiritistinstitute.org

About the Medium

Zibia Gasparetto is a Brazilian spiritual writer. She was born in Campinas. She is married to Aldo Luis Gasparetto and has four children. According to her story, a night in 1950 she woke up and began to walk around the house speaking German, a language that she didn't know. The next day, her husband bought a book about Spiritism to study together.

Her husband assists the spiritual association Federação Espírita do Estado de São Paulo, but she has to stay at home. On one occasion, Gasparetto felt a severe pain in her arm which it begins to move around without control. After Aldo gives her a pencil and paper, she begins to write quickly. Writing her first novel "And Love Won" signed by a spirit called Lucius. The manuscript was typed. Gasparetto showed a Historian professor of São Paulo University, who was interested in Spiritism too. Two weeks later, she receives the confirmation that her book will be published by LAKE Editorial. In her late years, Gasparetto used her computer four times a week to write stories dictated by her spirits.

She wrote usually at night for one or two hours. "They [Spirits] are not available, to work many days per week", she explains. "I don't know why, but each one of them just appears once a week. I try to change but I couldn't" As a result, she used to have one night a week, which each spirit communicated with her.

Contents

Chapter I 5
Chapter II 10
Chapter III 16
Chapter IV 30
Chapter V 43
Chapter VI 55
Chapter VII 71
Chapter VIII 83
Chapter IX 92
Chapter X 109
Chapter XI 122
Chapter XII 135
Chapter XIII 147
Chapter XIV 159
Chapter XV 170
Chapter XVI 181
Chapter XVII 190
Chapter XVIII 200
Chapter XIX 211
Chapter XX 221
Chapter XXI 232
Chapter XXII 276
Chapter XXIII 314

Chapter I

Marcelo leaned back in his chair, frightened, and with the letter in his hands he dropped it without making any attempt to pick it up.

Nervously, he ran his hand across his forehead, as if to shake the unexpected news out of his head. beads of sweat broke out on his face and an unpleasant tightness in his chest suddenly appeared.

that couldn't be true. now that he managed to balance his expenses, he was earning well, he would buy a house furnished as a *capricho* , it was gone. Maybe I had misunderstood. He couldn´t believe it. He bent down picked up the paper from the floor with trembling hand, and read.

"Dear Marcelo

When you read this letter I Will be gone I've been trying to tell you the truth for a long time, but you don't give me a chance. I want to live, to be happy, to see the world, to make the most of my youth.

I have received a good job offer in another country and I have accepted it. A life by your side has become a routine and I don't want that life for myself. You are a good man and I am sure you will find another woman who will accept what you can offer her.

Don't look for me anymore. I am going to find my happiness and I hope you will be happy too. Goodbye.

Aline."

Marcelo sighed sadly. He needs to surrender to reality. That letter took him by surprise.

Aline will not show any lack of interest or dissatisfaction. He began to imagine that maybe something had happened that she had not wanted to tell him.

It could only be that. He got up quickly, grabbed his briefcase, the car key and decided to go to the airport to pick her up and try to prevent her from boarding the plane.

On the way he was remembering their relationship, their marriage, the moments of love they had enjoyed during their seven years together, he was convinced that something very serious had happened he stepped on the accelerator, he needed to get there as soon as possible to find out. what was going on there and keep her from leaving. Aline loved him, of that he was sure.

She was the great love of his life. He would not resign himself to losing her forever. Immersed in his thoughts he wanted to arrive soon, to shorten the way, he entered a road with little movement, without slowing down and he did not notice that a truck was coming around the corner.

He crashed head-on, his head hanging off the steering wheel and his legs caught in the wreckage, people tried to help him but it was too late. Marcelo was dead.

A policeman arrived, took the necessary measures. A policeman made the identification. picking up the driver's license read.

Marcelo Duarte. 29 years old, commented with a colleague. What a pity so young and strong.

The truck driver, pale, approached and said nervously:

It wasn't my fault! He went all the way into the track. I was turning, I assure you I looked, but I didn't see any car. Suddenly, there was a bang!

He's telling the truth, I saw everything. the guy came in at speed, I don't think he saw the truck, I don't think he saw the truck, he's fine.

It's okay. Sir could you testify. Did anyone else see how it went?

The people were leaving and the policeman reiterated:

- Collaborate in the death of the child. We will need their testimonies. A lady turned and said:

-It's okay. I saw him too. He was at the window, right in front. He was coming at full speed. I don't think he saw the truck. I saw that I was going to crash and I screamed, but it was useless. It was horrible. I'll never forget that. The police took their names, removed the body and everything went back to normal. But the people who were there continued to comment on the tragic event for a few days.

Aline boards the plane, places her carry-on suitcase on the luggage rack and gladly settles in. She picks up a magazine offered to her by a stewardess and starts leafing through it but she paid no attention to what was written. She could think of nothing else but the adventure that awaited him in Miami. Ever since she was a teenager, she had dreamed of going to the United States. She was making an effort to study English, which she spoke with some fluency. The second daughter of a middle-class married couple, she has dedicated herself to her studies from a very young age with the intention of getting a scholarship to a U.S. college. She went to the consulate and investigated the possibilities. Although there was a cultural exchange between the two countries, things were not easy. She was invited to fill out some forms and soon realized that the institution was not interested in receiving Brazilian students.

While going to high school, she did everything she could to get what she wanted, but it wasn't easy.

When she entered the Faculty of Letters, she met Marcelo, who was in his third year of architecture. From the first day he fell in love with her. Aine was not looking for a stable relationship. She had other projects. But Marcelo insisted, filling her with so much affection that she ended up giving in. Both Mário and Dalva, her parents, immediately sympathized with him and enjoyed their relationship. was a boy from a good family. well positioned in life, intelligent, friendly and soon to graduate.

Aline's father, Mario, came from a modest family. He worked for some years in a shoe factory but with a lot effort, sacrifice and economy he got make his dream. He became merchant: He opened a shoe store in the Santana neighborhood.

Are you going to quit your job? and if it doesn't work out, you were never a merchant. I think I am good at selling. then the girls are growing up and will be able to help us. Together we will prosper.

Marcelo was an attractive boy, handsome and full of life. At first, Aline was very proud to walk with him through the streets of the neighborhood and see the envious looks of the girls in the neighborhood.

But as time went by, she started to really like him and at that moment she put aside all her projects.

When he graduated, his father gave him money to open a law firm.

He partnered with a colleague and they went to work. Rodrigo, like him, came from a middle-class family. They became good and prosperous professionals and were successful.

Marcelo built a beautiful house and married Aline. She was fully committed to her new life, continued her studies and devoted herself to housework.

But as time passed, routine took over, making her return to her old goals.

Marcelo wanted to have children, but she avoided him, telling him that she would have them when she finished her studies and could fully dedicate herself to her role as a mother.

After graduating, she felt frustrated. She had nowhere to put her knowledge into practice. She thought about organizing a job, but Marcelo objected. However, Aline was becoming a sad and irritable person. She said she had studied so many years for nothing.

Then we will have children and you, as a mother, will be happier than working for others.

But she wouldn't get pregnant and was getting more bored every day. He couldn't bear to see her sad, not wanting to talk, and finally agreed to let her look for a job, making her promise that when she was pregnant she would quit her job.

Aline soon found a job in a foreign trade company and started working with enthusiasm.

Soon she was back to her old self and Marcelo was happy.

Chapter II

Aline leaned back in the airplane seat remembering her husband. An unpleasant feeling came over her by the time he would have read the letter. He must have been desperate.

He had thought long and hard before making that decision. She recognized that Marcelo was an ideal husband. That he loved her deeply, but on the other hand she felt that he had never reciprocated as he deserved. Many times, she felt irritated by the way he treated her, fulfilling all her wishes and being so passive.

On those occasions he behaved a little aggressively, provoking her reaction, but Marcelo did exactly the opposite of what she wanted. She would have preferred him to be in another position, to be more demanding. In a short time, Aline's admiration for him began to fade and her love for him began to fade.

On the other hand, she wanted to leave that graceless life and try her luck in the United States, which was making a strong comeback.

When she received an offer from a company to work in an office in Miami, she couldn't contain her excitement.

It was everything she wanted. She could not pass up this opportunity she had so longed for. She knew Marcelo would not accept and that to go she would have to end her marriage.

For her that marriage had ended a long time ago. She didn't want to continue pretending a feeling she didn't have. She knew he was going to suffer, but it seemed worse to continue deceiving him. At first she would despair. But in the end she would forget him and move on with her life, finding someone else who would offer her the love she could not give him.

At that moment she recognized that she had never really loved. Therefore, she herself knew that she could no longer take pills to avoid getting pregnant.

The stewardess held out the tray with dinner and Aline, overcome by her intimate thoughts, hurried to put it on the table. She felt hungry and began to eat pleasantly. She needed to chase away sad thoughts. She was realizing her greatest dream and living a special moment in her life. The past had to be left behind.

A movie was about to start on TV Aline felt satisfied, wishing she hadn't missed anything. It was a comedy she loved.

Then the lights dimmed and everyone tried to sleep. Aline straightened a small pillow and threw a blanket over her legs and tried to get comfortable.

I was tired, but not sleepy because I was excited about the adventure. She had barely slept the night before and the day had been exhausting, she had had to prepare everything on the sly.

She tried to relax and finally fell asleep. Sometime later, he dreamed that a plane was going through a storm and there was danger. The passengers were frightened and, suddenly, he saw among them the shadow of Marcelo, with his face beaten and blood dripping down his chest and legs.

He cried out her name in desperation, stood in front of her and said in anguish:

Aline I finally found you. Don't leave me anymore. Tell me you will stay by my side always.

- Aline gasped and woke up in a cold sweat with difficulty breathing. At the same time the plane's lights came on and a flight attendant came to her and told her

- Calm down. It's all right. It was a dream.

- What happened to Marcelo, he was full of blood, how did he end up there?

- Another flight attendant placed a glass of water in his hand saying:

- Calm down. You had a nightmare. You have no one here. Aline drank the water feeling her heart beat out of balance. She took a deep breath and said:

- And I think it was a nightmare, it was horrible, there was a storm, the passengers were afraid that the plane would crash.

- This usually happens with people who are afraid of flying. It's okay. You want a painkiller.

- No, thank you. I'm just afraid of flying.

- Whatever it is, you dreamt it. Look, it's quiet. People will go back to sleep, try to rest.

- Aline tried to calm down. It really had been a nightmare. A trip hidden from everyone. The separation from her husband. The whole thing had shaken her more than she could have imagined.

- Her heart was pounding, she tried hard to stay calm and succeeded to some extent. However, she was no longer sleeping.

When she closed her eyes trying to sleep. The figure of desperate Marcelo, his eyes wide open, his body full of blood, reappeared in front of her, making her startle.

She began to think that perhaps it would have been better to face the situation instead of running away.

She knew that Marcelo would not easily accept a separation, so she decided to act this way. She would suffer a blow, but since the situation was consummated. She would have no choice but to accept it and move on with her life.

Again, a memory of her dream reappeared in her and she saw Marcelo in despair in front of her.

She leaned restlessly back in an armchair. She had scheduled that trip a long time ago. She had not imagined she could be so frightened.

Yes, because it would just be a nightmare and even though she wouldn't realize it, she was scared.

She called the stewardess and told her she would take the painkiller. She took a pill and settled down trying to relax. Later she would be in Miami and this unpleasant moment would be forgotten.

Shortly after she fell asleep and this time in her dreams, but by her side all the time was Marcelo's spirit.

At that moment of the accident he felt himself being thrown away and lost consciousness. When he woke up in an unknown street, despite being dazed, he remembered that he had to stop Aline and prevent her from traveling.

Apparently, he had been in an accident and had been thrown out of the car.

He approached the tent and thought:

I'm glad they pulled me out of the car. Glad to be alive, need to get to the airport. He approached wanting to know if his car was in serviceable condition.

He felt dizzy, which forced him to sit on the sidewalk.

He took a deep breath trying to react. He couldn't pass out. Aline was leaving and he had to stop her. However, he couldn't get up. It was then that he saw a van approaching and a body being pulled out of the car.

He recognized himself and screamed at the top of his lungs:

- No! It can't be, I'm dead.

Marcelo was sitting on the stretcher. His body ached to move and blood was dripping from his open wounds.

Seeing his concern, the nurse told him

- If you don't stay still. I will be forced to give you a painkiller.

- I don't want anything. My life doesn't matter more than losing Aline. I need to find her.

- He said it with such force that he was thrown out of the vehicle. The nurse said to his colleague who was driving the ambulance:

- Let's go to Socorro Post. The patient does not accept our help. Immediately the vehicle changed course while they talked about the difficulties people have in accepting or disembarking. Marcelo found himself in a dark corridor, with seats and people sleeping. He walked past them looking for Aline.

He felt elated when he saw her sleeping. He had finally found her. He called out to her several times to get her up. But it was no use. She was asleep.

He decided to wait for her. Suddenly, he had a strange feeling. He saw her get on the plane and approach his sleeping body.

It was then that he faced her saying:

- Aline! At least, I have found you. Don't leave me anymore. Tell me that you will stay by my side forever.

- Aline gave a scream and threw herself on the sleeping body. The lights came on and the stewardesses came out.

To talk to her. While some of them woke up and looked scared.

Marcelo did not understand what was happening. Why she was screaming at the sight of him.

She was very frightened because of her injuries. However, he did not have time to explain it to her. He overheard a conversation from her and thought:

- I didn't make it to the airport and she boarded. We met on the plane. How did I end up here?

He felt his dizziness increasing and reacted in fear of blacking out again. It would be better not to try to find out what was wrong, at least not until she was stronger. When he thought about it, he felt bad. What mattered to him was being by her side. He watched her as she took a pill and fell asleep.

He waited for her to leave his body, but this time it didn't happen. He didn't notice anything. Then he settled down next to her. He felt calmer now. Aline would not leave him. He would go with her wherever she went.

After all, the most important thing was that they were together. Thinking. Like this. He managed to relax. Until he finally fell sleep.

Chapter III

Aline got off the plane, after passing through the identification controls pushing a trolley with the suitcases, she came out looking anxiously. She smiled when she saw a boy holding a card with her name on it.

She smiled when she saw a boy holding a card with her name on it. She approached.

Satisfied, introducing herself. He was a tall, elegant, blond-haired boy with blue eyes. They adjusted a little when he smiled.

He shook her outstretched hand saying:

- It's a pleasure my name is Michael, I work at the company. I'm in charge of welcoming you. And to take you to the place where you will be staying.

- Thank you.

- May I take your bags?

- My car is in the parking lot. Let's go Aline accompanied him with satisfaction. The day was beautiful and she watched curiously. Behind not wanting to miss any detail. At that moment she had completely forgotten the past with her husband was behind her.

- Her eyes sparkled with joy, as she walked to the car Michael watched her curiously. He noticed her euphoria and asked her.

- This is your first time in Miami.

- It's the first time I've left Brazil. Ever since I was a little girl I dreamed of seeing the United States.

- I thought I had already lived here. You speak our language well. Aline smiles happily.

- I have studied English since I was a child. It seems like a dream to be here. They got to the car and he opened the door for her to get in. Then he put the suitcases away and sat down next to her.

During the ride he smiled and looked at her curiously observing everything.

He talked a bit about the city, the company and finally stopped in front of a three-story building.

The company has rented an apartment for you. If you want to move in later, you can move in here.

- Let's take a look - Aline replied.

She loved the flower-filled garden and the simple but elegant houses. She tried to look natural, but she didn't want him to realize she was provincial. They entered the foyer, he introduced himself, took the key and they went upstairs. Michael opened the door and they entered a spacious and tastefully furnished living room. Then he noticed a balcony and a small kitchen.

Michael carried the suitcases into the room and placed them on a table. Aline looked at everything in delight. They returned to the living room and Michael asked

- Do you think everything will be all right here?

- Yes, thank you.

- You must be tired from the trip. I'll come early tomorrow morning to take you to the company.

- You don't need to come pick me up. I'll be there tomorrow at eight o'clock. She shook her head negatively.

- I'm still in charge of driving you and I will. Then you can get rid of me.

- Don't say that. I'm very grateful to you for taking me in and accompanying me. I thought it would make things easier for you.

- I didn't think otherwise. I'm self-sufficient to take care of myself.

- I'm sure I am.

- I have bought some things and put them in the fridge. I hope you like it. If you want anything else there is a market 3 blocks from here.

- Thank you.

After a handshake, he left. Aline sighed happily. Then she went to the kitchen. She opened the refrigerator. She looked curiously at the food. On the wall were key chains. Painted with culinary motifs, where there were two key rings with keys. On the other side was for the mail. Inside was a piece of paper that he picked up and read. It was a set of rules for the residents and instructions for the use of electrical appliances.

Aline was hungry, but she wanted to take a bath before eating. She went to the bedroom and opened the suitcases. She took what she needed and stepped into the shower. The perfume, the smell of the place and the novelties she observed gave her a great sense of freedom.

She seemed to be dreaming. At last she was free to live all her dreams. From then on. Everything would be different. New friends, new surroundings, new life. The water running down her body made her feel happy. When she came out of the bath, she felt refreshed. All the tiredness of the trip was gone. She went to the kitchen thinking:

-I'm going to eat something and take a walk.

There were rolls, cheeses and butter. She opened the cupboard drawers, arranged the plates and glasses, set the table with an American set, placed some delicacies and sat down to eat.

It was a simple appetizer, but for Aline it was as if it were a banquet. After eating, she took some money and went out. The day was hot and the sun was beating down hard. As she passed a store. Aline went in, thinking about buying some black glasses.

She had left hers in Brazil and was sure she could find better ones in Miami.

He noticed that people were dressed casually and in terms of fashion there was everything.

She passed by the market Michael had asked her to enter to get to know it. The heat was strong and she had an ice cream. Then she kept walking, going into the stores she liked.

Until she felt tired, bought some magazines and decided to go home.

The sun was high and she didn't know what time it was because she hadn't set her watch yet.

When she got to the lobby of her building, she saw that her watch had just been set. He saw that his watch had just struck seven. He took his own and went upstairs to the apartment.

He had bought some sandwiches to eat a little and had a soft drink and sat in the living room to watch television. He remembered Marcelo and felt an unpleasant sensation. She was really sad and unhappy.

She sighed thoughtfully. Although she didn't want to hurt him, she thought it was the best solution. She didn't love him and it wouldn't be fair to fake a feeling she didn't feel.

He would suffer at first, but since he didn't know where to find her, he would eventually forget her.

The spirit of Marcelo that had followed her all the time was approaching. She thought of him. Something she hadn't done for a whole day.

There were times when he felt dazed by pains that made him lie down again and rest. Images jumbled around in his head but he just thought about what was happening and he couldn't lose sight of it.

His priority was to be by her side. He hoped that at some point he would be able to hear.

The times he doubted he had died in that accident. She heard he was dead. But then why she wanted to take him to the hospital. Because he felt alive. He touched himself, feeling the musculature of his body.

He knew something different had happened, but he wasn't sure of anything.

Sensing that she was thinking about him, he moved closer to her in the hope that she might hear his thoughts.

I would rather talk to her to explain my motives. It was cruel to run away and leave only a letter. However, I would have talked to her or it would have been worse. He would not accept and would do everything possible to prevent her from leaving.

Why do you insist on wanting to leave me? You are mine. I will never let you. We will be together forever he hugged her. Aline did not hear what he said

However, she felt an unpleasant shiver.

It was better to forget the whole thing. He doesn't know where I am, he'll have to make do. Someday she'll thank me for being so honest.

- Never Aline. I will never settle for your abandonment. I will never leave you. Without hearing what he said Aline continued to think:

- I couldn't be living with him without love. When love is over it's better to separate. And it's over between us, there's no turning back.

Marcelo kissed her several times on the face saying anguished:

How can you say that. We don't love each other. We swear to belong to each other forever.

- He grabbed her and she felt a strong dizziness. She was breathing heavily. She got up in a panic, trying to take a deep breath. She went to the kitchen. Her hands and legs were shaking.

She grabbed a glass of water and took a few sips, trying to react. Maybe it was tiredness. He had experienced a lot of emotions in a short time. He decided to lie down when he saw that she was not feeling well. Marcelo let go of her and looked at her worriedly. She was feeling better now and went to bed. She needed to be well prepared for the next day. She put on her pajamas and slipped placidly into her wide bed. Despite being excited about the trip, the bed was soft, she was tired and soon fell asleep.

The next morning, she woke up in a good mood and got up in a hurry. Michael was punctual, when he rang the bell it was 8 o'clock and Aline was ready, they immediately went to the company. There Aline was introduced to Dr. Edward, her boss, and to some of her colleagues. With whom she would have more direct dealings.

It was a trading company that imported products from all over the world to supply the domestic market and export the surplus. Aline was hired. To be part of Doctor Edward's team. One of the directors and partner of the company. The personnel manager, led her to the room where she was to work.

- For the time being you will share the room with Rache. You have already been introduced.

- A tall girl. Slender. And very elegant approached smiling

- Welcome.

- Thank you - Aline replied.

- Janeth was the personnel manager and she handed her a brochure saying

- Here you will find all the information you need to know about our company if you don't understand something. You can call me. There are some benefits that our company offers to people like you.

Which ones?

Beyond what I was already informed, financing a car with low interest and a good payment term.

Satisfied with the new and interested in learning everything quickly and doing a good job. Aline was fully involved in the new tasks. It was an important company and with it the position she held.

The Board of Directors provided her with a salary, in addition to minimum wage, and some privileges. Aline liked Rachel from the very first moment. Besides being friendly, she looked her straight in the eye when she spoke, acted naturally and was very efficient.

Michael had told her that Rachel had been working in that position for over 5 years and that she was the trusted secretary who handled all the personal affairs of the president of the company.

The day passed quickly and on the way out Rachel offered her a ride.

Don't bother," Aline replied a little shyly, "I know how to get home.

- She noticed the other's embarrassment and explained:

- I live very close to you. Anyway, I had to stop by your house. It would be a good opportunity to get to know each other better.

- In that case, I accept. I'm looking forward to getting to know each other better. During the drive, Aline learned that Rachel was divorced and had an eight-year-old son, which she mentioned enthusiastically.

- And do you have children?

- No. I think I'm more comfortable, I was married for 7 years, but we separated. With a child everything would have been more complicated.

Rachel thought for a while and then answered

- It all depends on how you do it, John, he was a smart guy, he understood our reasons and accepted the situation well.

- I was fine with it because he was very close to me.

He was an excellent partner.

Aline sighed thinking about her family. How they would have received his departure.

Rachel looked at her and continued quickly:

- This is your first time in Miami.

- I have never traveled outside my country before.

- I admire your courage. And your radical change. You won't miss your family.

- Maybe I will. However, since I was a child I dreamed of going to work in the United States.

- And what did you hope to find here

- I don't know. There was a time when it became my goal. I didn't think about anything else. That's why I dedicated myself to study the language, the customs, etc.

- I know that in many countries young people have that dream. But do you think it is worth leaving your home country, where you have your family roots and an environment where you have been brought up? To go on an adventure to a strange place where you don't know anyone and you don't know what you are going to find.

- I think it's worth it. I have no illusions about a life here. I know you have to work hard. If I don't do my best I won't succeed. But at least I want to try. If I don't like it, I'll go back to my country.

You seem very determined to me. I think you're going to like living here.

- I love it so far. I needed a change. I was living in a rut. That eventually became unbearable. When I couldn't take it anymore, I turned my life around, got a job offer and came here.

I left and prepared everything without anyone knowing. I left a letter for my husband and went out

I thought I was brave, I am seeing that not so much.

- If I acted this way it was not for lack of courage, but of patience to deal with Marcelo's attachment. He would do nothing without me. He would never accept our separation. He dramatized, insisted, pursued me. So, I left without telling anyone. Since he couldn't find me, he would eventually accept the separation and, when that happened, we would divorce.

- Rachel listened seriously and reflected:

You should know what you're doing. I hope everything works out well for you.

We arrived. The car pulled up in front of the property and Aline invited her in.

Would you like to come in and have a drink?

Thanks now I don't need to pick John up from school. I can't be late. Aline didn't insist. She thanked him and said goodbye. She went up to her apartment thinking about the day's events.

It was almost seven o'clock, but the sun was up, not very bright. It had not yet gone into hiding. He entered the house cheerfully, wondering how he would spend the evening. He would like to go out, see the city, see new things, however, he thought better of it and resigned himself to strolling around and looking for a place to have dinner. He took a bath, got ready and went out. It was starting to get dark and he strolled through the streets, watching the people, looking at shop windows, and ended up entering a bookstore.

She was strolling along amused, thinking about buying a book, when she was approached by a girl saying:

- I can help you.

- Thank you. If I find something that interests me, I'll look for it.

- I'm not a salesperson. My name is Ruth, I'm in public relations at the Ferguson Institute. I thought you were here about Dr. William Morris' lecture.

Aline was interested.

- When is that lecture?

- Another time, nine o'clock in the second-floor auditorium.

- I've been in town for three days. I don't know that the Institute

What is studied there.

- The paranormal. Dr. Ferguson is a scientist who has been studying this subject for many years. He started researching since he lost his only daughter in an accident.

- I am Brazilian in my country this subject is much discussed. Some believe, others don't.

- And whose side are you on?

Neither. I never thought much about it. Ruth handed him a card that read.

- If someday you are interested and want to know about the Institute's research on the subject. Look us up. We have several courses on the subject and a lot of evidence of the continuity of life after death, obtained in years of work.

- I never thought there was anyone here who was seriously dedicated to this subject Ruth smiled and answered.

Why not. In the end we are all going to die one day and face the other side of life. With knowledge, everything would be easier.

- Well, I don't want to get involved in that. I smile trying to hide her feelings and ask:

- Today's class is about the topic.

- Life after death. There will be two very good mediums working with those present. If you want to go, I only have two places left. Aline hesitated and Ruth suggested.

- It might be helpful for you to attend. I feel that by coming here your life has changed radically. Much more than you think. You came for one reason and you may find another.

- Aline looked at her with admiration.

- How do you know I have changed my life? You don't know me.

- I feel you need spiritual help.

- No, and I am very happy here. I appreciate your interest, but I am not interested. Thank you for the invitation and good night.

- Aline turned her back on him and walked away.

- Ruth's eyes followed her and she thought

- Too bad, it would have been better if she had accepted my invitation. Aline left the bookstore uneasy; how did Ruth know what was going on in her life? It was not possible. She had said those words. Because she was interested in her attending that conference. And she had paid for the invitation.

- She must have been right by chance. She had never been so happy, she was sure she would work well, make a career, earn money, find friends. She kept walking and, as she passed a nice-looking restaurant, she saw that it was full and thought to herself.

- She went inside and settled in. People were chatting happily and Aline felt at ease.

- She ordered the food while waiting and looked around. Three boys at the next table were staring at her and she pretended not to notice. The waitress brought the food and she began to eat with an appetite. When she finished, one of the boys with a glass of wine in his hand approached her saying.

- My name is Robert, and yours? Aline smiled

- Aline.

- May I sit down?

- Yes, of course you can.

He had blond hair, blue eyes, wavy hair, a thin face and when he smiled he looked like a child.

- My friends and I often dine here and this is the first time we found her where she was hiding.

Aline smiled again:

- This is the first time I come here. I am Brazilian, I arrived a few days ago.

In that case, I offer to show you our city. He signaled to his two friends. They immediately approached with smiles on their faces. Robert made the introductions.

-Steve and Roy. This is Aline, from Brazil. After a handshake they sat down. Steve.

He was not as tall as Robert, long shoulders, brown eyes and straight hair. Roy was slim, somewhat dark, dark skin, thick lips and when he smiled he exhibited fine, gapped teeth.

Aline could tell they were polite and friendly guys. They invited her to go to a bar where there was music, but Aline declined the invitation:

It's late, I have to go home. I have to get up early for work tomorrow. The conversation was pleasant. They, talking about things in the city and asking questions about Brazil that they didn't know.

Aline asked for the bill, paid and got up.

It's early, stay a little longer, Robert asked.

- No, I can't.

We like him, said Steve. We'd like to show him around town.

- There'll be a chance, I promise.

They exchanged phones and Roy returned with a mysterious air:

Don't forget about us. This town is dangerous for pretty girls on their own. It's full of inveterate conquerors. We won't let you fall into their trap. We are proud to be your first friends and believe me we will take good care of you.

That's right," Robert nodded. We want to introduce you to some friends. Nice people you'll like.

- No introduction to the grown-ups," said Steve.

- Do you have a car? -asked Robert.

- No, I don't.

- In that case, we'll give you a ride home.

- I don't need a car. I live near here and I like to walk.

In exchange for letting, you out. Aline walked happily back home. Everything was going as she had wished. She was meeting people and making new friends.

She arrived and went to get ready for bed. It was after eleven o'clock and she was sleepy and Marcelo' spirit was looking at her angrily. She was overreaching herself by allowing other men to harass her.

She saw that the boys were looking at her with admiration. Mainly Roberto, who was very attracted to her.

As they talked, Marcelo was in the back keeping an eye on everything.

Ready to react if they tried to get close. Happily that didn't happen, but she was all giggly, enjoying being with them. As if she were a free woman, without a husband. Marcelo wanted to talk to her. Tell her how he felt. But she wouldn't listen to him. When that happened, it was desperate.

Because she wouldn't listen to him. He would be dead anyway. In that case because he felt regides in his body, the pains of his wounds.

He noticed that when he despaired, those pains increased unbearably. The times he wanted to go to the doctor, he imagined that he would get out of Aline's way, that he might lose sight of her, and he didn't want that. Aline fell asleep and he lay down beside her trying to calm down. It was then that he saw Aline's spirit.

She climbed out through the head of her sleeping body and stood beside the bed. Immediately Marcelo got up and called out to her in distress:

- Aline, Aline it's me Marcelo. I am here.

Aline's spirit looked at him in fright.

- Marcelo, what are you doing here, why are you so hurt?

- It was an accident. You left me, but I'm here again. I will never leave you, you are mine.

- He approached her wanting to hug her and Aline couldn't stand it. She threw herself on his sleeping body and woke up screaming in terror:

- How awful, it's not true. It was a nightmare. When she managed to move and lay back down.

Her heart was beating fast and he felt a shiver run through his body. She turned on the light, looked around and tried to calm down. It had been a nightmare. She went to the kitchen and got a glass of water. She went back to his room. She remembered his dream on the plane, where Marcelo was injured. Just like the one he had dreamt now.

- It was too much of a coincidence. Had something happened to him? She didn't want to leave any address or contact his family. She wanted to give him time to calm down and not come after her to ask her to come back. Aline was afraid to turn off the light and go to sleep. She left the lamp light on again.

- However, the memory of Marcelo's presence, wounded, full of blood, talking about an accident did not leave her in peace.

She tried to calm herself. Perhaps she was not as brave as she would have liked, she did not feel guilty for having run away like that. Those dreams could be the fruit of her own imagination, of her guilt. But when she thought of him she felt anguished, restless, distressed.

- I can't go on like this," she thought, "I need to know if everything is all right with him. Tomorrow I'll call mom to see how he's doing. But I'm not going to give her my address.

With this resolved, she felt calmer, but even so, the day was getting lighter when, overcome by fatigue, she fell asleep.

Chapter IV

Aline woke up late the next morning, having had little sleep. She intended to call her parents' house to find out if everything was all right. But she was running late and didn't want to be late for work.

The memory of the injured Marcelo would not leave her mind. She felt anxious, anguished. She wanted to call later, but she had to wait until lunchtime. She went to work and for her time did not pass. Raquel noticed her restlessness and asked her.

- Something has happened to you. You seem nervous.

- I can tell. I slept badly tonight. I had a horrible nightmare.

- You're very impressed.

- So much so that at lunchtime I'll call my parents' house to see if everything's all right.

- I have dreams that seem real.

- It was so real I was afraid it was happening now.

- Why don't you call now?

- I can't call from here.

- Tell the operator. She'll make the call and the fee will be deducted from your paycheck.

In that case I will request a call

He accepted the operator and gave him directions. A short time later, Aline recognized her mother's voice. Aline recognized her mother's voice

- Mom, it's Aline.

- Aline, my daughter, where are you? What have you done?

- I'm calling to tell you that I'm fine. I've been thinking a lot about you, especially about Marcelo, how he is.

For a few seconds Dalva was silent, Aline felt her fear growing.

So mom, Marcelo is well.

- No daughter, unfortunately something horrible happened. Ele had an accident in the car, Dalva's voice shook and she paused a little to take courage.

- An accident. Speak, mother, how is he?

- He was badly injured and did not resist. He was buried two days ago Aline turned pale the phone slipped from her hands and she collapsed on the table.

- Rachel ran to her and heard a voice on the other end of the receiver screaming

- Aline, Aline, my daughter , speak to me.

- Not understanding what she was hearing. Rachel stayed on the phone and said:

- Sorry, I don't speak Portuguese and hung up. She then called the personnel department for help. While waiting, She tried to revive her by tapping her face. Calling:

- Aline, Aline wake up come back.

- Shortly after. A company doctor appeared in the room.

- He was talking to a relative, gave a scream and fainted. He must have received some bad news.

- After a moment he sighed and came to. Remembering his mother's words, he couldn't hold back the tears.

- Rachel held his hand lovingly and asked her:

What happened, Aline?

It wasn't a nightmare Rachel, it was true. My husband died in a car accident.

The doctor who was watching her intervened:

She's very nervous, she'd better go home.

- I never thought this could happen - Aline said without holding back her tears - I have to call back to find out how it happened.

- The doctor intervened again:

You can do it another time. You'd better calm down. I'm going to give you a sedative. You're going home. And take this remedy. You're very agitated. You need to rest.

I'm very sorry, I didn't mean to disturb anyone.

In a case like yours the company offers a week off, I'll sign the order.

Thank you doctor, but it's not that I want to be so long I'm new to the company.

It is a general rule that you lost your husband, so you are entitled to that time off. Use that time to recover and feel better. Turning to Rachel, he continued.

Well, someone will see you home.

I'll go myself. I'll let Mari know so she can fill in for me, Mr. Morris.

No need to bother," Aline stammered. I'll make some arrangements, we'll be right there. Aline felt dizzy and nauseous in her stomach, and her legs were shaking.

She let herself go without saying anything. During the trip she cried softly and repeated from time to time:

- It was him, it was true, it was him My God what a horror. I need to call, to know how it was

- Calm down, when you get home you'll call again. Maybe I misunderstood.

- I heard very well. My mother said he was in a car accident and died.

If that happened you will have to accept it, death is irreversible.

- I didn't talk to him, I ran away, I left him, he went crazy, you'll see it wasn't an accident, maybe he did it on purpose.

- Don't exaggerate. His mother didn't say it was an accident. She didn't answer she was still crying when they got home she immediately called her mother who answered in grief.

- Daughter, where are you? You were desperate with all that. Not knowing where to find you was horrible. What happened to you for running away like that.

- Mother, you know that since I was a child I wanted to live abroad.

- But you couldn't do it. Abandoning a good husband, who loved you. Where was his head. Your father is not satisfied.

- Mother, I never thought this could happen. How was the accident?

- He turned a corner and did not see the truck crossing. He crashed head-on. Witnesses to the accident say he was speeding. He died on the spot. We still haven't recovered from the shock.

- Dona Ivone and João must be desperate.

- Both they and Marcio were not satisfied. When we found out I and your father went to the wake and were treated badly. They found your letter in Marcelo's pocket. Mainly Mr. João. He wasn't happy to lose his son.

Marcelo was his pride. Your father tried to talk, to tell him we didn't know why you left him. But they didn't believe us. They wanted me to call you. But I didn't know where to find you. Aline cried inconsolably.

Mother, I could never have imagined this misfortune.

Why didn't you come to tell me what happened? She did something that displeased you.

- I did nothing. I got tired of the routine, I wanted to change my life. A few times I tried to convince him to come, but he never took me seriously.

- But you married for love.

- That's true, but then I realized I didn't love him anymore.

- Do you have another one? That's why you ran away without saying anything.

- No, mother. I never had another one. I was offered a good job here in Miami, that's why I left.

- If you had told us, we could have avoided this madness.

- That's exactly why I didn't tell you.

- You'd better get your things in order and get back here as soon as possible.

- When I found out, I fainted. I was at the company working. The doctor gave me a painkiller. And a week off to recover.

- Your place is here, in your country, with your family. Take the first plane and go home.

- No, Mother. I'm going to rest as the doctor told me and I'll think about what to do.

- Come back. We need you very much.

- Now I'm going to cut. The painkiller I took is taking effect. I'm going to leave you and call you back.

- I want your phone number.

- I'm going to rest. When I feel better, I'll call again. I'm sorry about what happened. I'll see you tomorrow.

- He cut her off before Dalva had time to say anything else. Rachel looked at her and asked

- And how did it go? Aline recounted and concluded:

- I feel guilty. If I hadn't left him, none of this would have happened.

- How can you know. I think the death was caused by an accident. You are not to blame for anything. It was an accident.

- It was. I always drove carefully. Entering a street at high speed, without looking would never do it.

If he had been in a normal state. I was desperate.

- Now it is better to rest, to try to sleep, to forget. There is no point in suffering for something that has no remedy.

- I'm afraid he'll turn up, on the sleep plane, wounded, blood dripping from several places. How can that be? He's dead.

Rachel was silent, not knowing what to say. Aline would tell her about her dream before she knew the truth.

She couldn't doubt what she was saying. She tried to justify herself:

- It could be a coincidence. You're worried you left without saying goodbye and I can imagine that drama. The dead don't come back.

- It was him on the plane who said: "Aline, I finally found you. Don't leave me anymore. He told me you would always be by my side" Rachel felt a shiver run through her body and responded in fear:

- No importance can be attached to such a thought. We must not invoke the dead.

- I am not invoking him. I didn't even know he was dead. I repeat, his soul came after me.

- How awful! You shouldn't play with such things. It's better to sleep. Rest. And pull yourself together, try to forget. No attitude of yours will bring you back.

- I'd like at least not to feel so much guilt.

- You're very sad. What are you going to do? You're going back to Brazil.

- I don't think so. Now I have more reason to stay here. During the vacations I'm going to visit my family.

- How are you feeling?

- Sleepy.

- You're going to sleep. I'm retiring. If you need anything, you have all my phone numbers. You can call me anytime.

- Thank you.

She went out and Aline accompanied her to the door, went to her room, changed her clothes and went to bed.

Although she was sleepy, the figure of Marcelo, wounded, dripping with blood, would not leave her mind. And his spirit sat on the edge of the bed, depressed, sad, discouraged.

It was true. He was dead. For an unknown reason, he felt alive, his wounds burned, his body ached, and he moved with the wound though he slipped, he did not fall.

At first he wanted to beat it, thinking he would lose consciousness as he exhausted himself. But then he realized that although he was still leaking, he was not weakening.

Marcelo followed Aline the whole time. He saw when she called her mother and fainted.

Excited he thought:

She still loves me. She is suffering from the accident. Despite her sadness that she confirmed he was dead. Marcelo felt some satisfaction that she felt guilty.

It's true. She was to blame for everything. If she hadn't been so out of it she wouldn't have caused that accident. She is the only one to blame. Now she is going to realize that she will never be happy away from my love. It was necessary for me to die so that she could appreciate how much we loved each other and how much she will miss me in her life. She approached Aline, who was sleeping. He stroked her hair and said, "I will never leave her:

- I will never leave her. I will be by your side forever. One day you will die and I will be waiting for you.

He felt tired, lay down on the side of the wide bed, tried to hug her, but his hands could not go through her body. In spite of this, he moved closer so that he could be there, sad at the same time satisfied to be by her side.

- Aline slept soundly, her spirit calm, in the shadow of unconsciousness brought on by the strong painkiller the doctor gave her. Dalva hung up the phone in grief, letting tears run down her face. She was not satisfied with that misfortune.

- The news of Aline's escape and her son-in-law's accident fell like a bombshell on her family, which until then she had considered happy and well constituted. Aríete approached her nervously:

- It was Aline again

- If it was her.

- She told why she had done it

- If she did, she's in the United States. She is crazy. Always with this mania for living there. I thought after the marriage she would have forgotten that nonsense.

- She never did. I was afraid that one day something like that would happen. Where is she and with whom?

- Yesterday, Mr. João insinuated that she must have run off with someone else. That's not true. She went to work.

- Mrs. Ivone told me the same thing. They think she fell in love with someone else. They think that happened.

- I don't believe it. She went to work. Living there was always her dream since she was a child.

- In that case she should never have married.

- When she fell in love with Marcelo I thought she had given up that silly dream. But she hasn't. Now she is there crying, full of guilt, crying because she must have regretted what she did. But now it's too late. The disgrace is done. I told her to come now.

- She will come back, it will be for the best.

- I don't know. She would suffer more here. Her family, his family, her friends, they all blame her for his death. If I were her I would stay there at least for a while.

She told me she would think about it, but I that I would prefer her to come and be with her family, so she would be better off.

- She gave him her address, or phone number.

- No. She was stunned. Because when she talked to me the first time, she fainted. The company doctor saw her and knowing what had happened gave her a strong painkiller. He sent her home. A co-worker gave her a ride and agreed to call me when she was better.

- Tears were streaming down Dalva's face and Aríete hugged her emotionally, saying:

- Mother, we are in shock, but there is nothing we can do. We have to manage.

- She ruined her happiness, that's her punishment.

- Don't say that mother, she left because she no longer loved her husband. I don't think she ever really loved him. She was unhappy.

- I can't understand it. They have been married for seven years, he was always a wonderful husband.

- But she didn't love him.

- She shouldn't have run away like that.

- If she had told Marcelo what she planned to do, maybe it would have been worse. The way he clung to her. I even think it was that attachment of his that made her dislike his company. I wouldn't like to have a cloying man clinging to my lap.

- You don't know what you're saying. Life is not what you think it is. Love is not that wonderful dream of Prince Charming that never existed. Many women would like to have a husband as much in love as he is.

- What bothers me, Mother, is that now everything is going to be her fault. But now that I think about it, he was the one driving the car, she never imagined that could happen.

- I don't like it when you talk like that. I don't understand your coldness in the face of this tragedy.

- It is not coldness. Whenever an accident happens. Like this one. One instead of regretting what happened. People look for a culprit to throw the whole weight of the situation on him.

- But she is to blame. If she hadn't run away. Marcelo would be alive.

- Who can guarantee it, mother. If the time of his death had come, it would happen one way or another. I don't think Aline should go back. At least until all this is over for her. If I were her I would never go back.

- And you claim me when I tell you that you are cold, and have no feelings. You'd be able to abandon her parents and walk away from her family forever.

- Don't talk about abandonment. When I miss them, I send them tickets to stay with me for a while.

- I hope you're not thinking of abandoning us either.

- Not at the moment. However, I don't know what the future holds.

Don't even say it as a joke. Enough of this nonsense, daughter. Aríete smiled and answered:

- Well, I will marry a very rich man, my purpose is to travel all over the world, to know other countries, you will have to be happy. The doorbell rang and Aríete went to open the door. Rodrigo, Marcelo's partner, was at the entrance.

- We need to talk - he was serious.

- Rodrigo came in.

He led him into the living room and asked him to make himself comfortable.

- My father is not back from the store yet. I'm going to call mom

- Dalva came in, saw him and started crying. He got up and hugged her saying

I know we are very overwhelmed by what happened and that maybe I should have waited a little longer to talk to you. However, I'm a little lost, not knowing what to do. I haven't found a job. I thought maybe you guys could tell me something.

- I can't get my head around what has happened. Mario reopened the store today, but he's lost too. Dalva struggled to hold back tears.

- I read the look on Aline's face and was so surprised. They looked so happy. Marcelo lived for her. All he thought about was her. Everything he did was for her approval. Why did he take that attitude?

- It was Aríete who answered

- Since she was a child, Aline wanted to live in the United States. She studied English from a very young age. So much so that she speaks correctly and without an accent. When Marcelo fell in love with her and courted her, she was thrilled with him. We thought she had forgotten that teenage dream. But she hadn't.

- You mean she went to the United States.

- With whom? Who arranged for her to go.

- Aline went on her own. For all we know, she got a job offer and decided to take it.

Rodrigo plopped down on the couch and didn't answer. Then Dalva, who had stopped crying, intervened:

- She was doing everything alone and in secret. None of us knew what she intended to do.

- It's hard to believe that she did it all alone. Someone must have encouraged her to take the initiative.

- I know what you're thinking," said Aríete, holding back his deep anger. She was not cheating on her husband. Nor was she eloping with any man. She called us recently from a company where she works. When she heard about the accident, she fainted and needed to be seen by a doctor.

- That's not what Marcelo's parents say. I'm sorry, I didn't mean to imply anything. It's just that she acted strangely.

Aríete with a voice of firm indignation said:

- I'm sure Aline never imagined this could happen. She is devastated like all of us. Regretting that fact. I know you are judging her and blaming her for the accident. It is an injustice. She left because she no longer loved her husband. If she had told him, it would have been a disgrace. Despite what happened, I recognize that my sister has a right to who she wants to live with. Rodrigo listened to her as if he were seeing her for the first time. He did not know her well despite living with Aline and her partner.

- He sat back down, ran his hand through his hair and then said with a worried air.

- It's hard to accept this situation. I can imagine how Marcelo felt when he read that letter.

Dalva, calmer, intervened:

- And how we were when we found out. He hesitated for a moment and then said

- Well, I don't know what to say. Naturally after what's happened. Aline is going to leave that job and do you know when she's coming back?

- I'm afraid she's not coming back. When we talked I asked her to come back. She was very upset, tearful and told me she was going to think about it.

- I think she'd rather stay there. After all that effort to leave, why would she come back, Aríete asked.

- Well, Marcelo was my partner. Of everything we have in the company, half was his. I came because I need to talk to Aline about it. Mr. João wants me to turn everything over to him. But I can't do that. By rights, it belongs to Aline.

- They are angry with her and as her mother I feel very sad about that.- I'm in an uncomfortable situation. But I can't override Aline's rights and do what they want.

They don't believe it.

- After what happened, I want to stay out of it. They think Aline is guilty even of the accident, and that in a way it's an injustice. They can keep everything for me.

- It can't be like this, Mrs. Dalva. I want to do the right thing. I would like you to give me your phone number so we can talk.

- If I had the number I would gladly give it to you. But when she talked to me she told me that she was very sick and that the doctor had prescribed a very strong painkiller. She said she would call me when she was better.

- So please tell me if you know her phone number or address. As for the house where he lived, his parents have the key. A policeman also gave him his personal things.

- We will inform you as soon as we have news.

Are you going to continue with the company on your own - asked Aríete.

- I will for the time being. Marcelo was good at what he did, I'm afraid of putting someone else in and then regretting it.

- For a partnership to work there has to be a lot of seriousness and trust.

- So, I'm going to think about what to do.

- He got up and said goodbye to Dalva. He reiterated his promise to call as soon as he heard from Aline.

- That's another one that's left without an apartment - commented Dalva. where Aline's head was at when she decided to leave.

- There is no point in criticizing her now. She will know how to organize herself very well without Marcelo.

- You'll see. Little by little everything will come back to its place, in all this, the worst thing was Marcelo's death. That will never come back.

- That's right. That was forever.

Chapter V

A few days later Aline called Dalva and asked:

"How are you."

- More relaxed. I'm going back to work early tomorrow. How are things going over there?

- Bad, very bad. We went to Marcel's 7th day mass. Your father didn't want to go. He was very offended because his parents treated him badly. But I insisted. He was like another son to us.

- And they went.

- Yes, but they pretended they didn't know us and didn't greet us. And as soon as the mass was over we left. We didn't even go to pay our condolences.

- Don't be sad, they are in a state of shock. When they reflect better they will come back.

- Your father is very angry. For the time being it will be better if they don't show up and you don't come back.

- I thought long and hard and decided to stay here.

- You can't do that, at least you have to take care of your own things. Rodrigo was here and said that Mr. João has the keys to your house. Marcelo had assets; no doubt an inventory will have to be made. You will have to be present

Aline who was silent for a few seconds and then replied:

- I can't go back now. I have to think about my future. I don't want to lose my job. I want to talk to Aríete.

Dalva went to call her and she came right away. After greetings Aline told her:

I can't leave Brazil now. This job is very important to me. Then I have no head to argue with my in-laws. They won't understand me. You can help me.

- Yes, of course, I'm not working at the moment, I've been helping Dad in the store so I don't have to stay at home. I have all the time I can spare, what do you want me to do?

- I will draw up a power of attorney with full powers of attorney in your name for you to take care of all the legal formalities. I am sure you will do much better than me.

- Rodrigo mentioned that Marcelo's share now belongs to you. I will have to take care of that too. I was very worried. You know how Marcelo was that he took care of all the financial part. While he was on other projects. He doesn't want to hire another partner, he is afraid of making a mistake.

- If he came back I could work with him, I'm sure I would take care of him as well as Marcelo. He would take care of his own instead of working for others.

- I'm in no condition to go back. Why don't you take care of it for me? You know as much or more about management than I do. You have experience.

- You think he'd accept.

- I think he'd love it. I know your capabilities. Set up a meeting as if you were me. That money will be all for you. I'm earning very well. I don't need anything. Go find Rodrigo and tell him I'd like you to take my place in society until I return.

- You think he will accept.

- I think he will.

As for the problems with the house, everything there belongs to him by right.

- When I left, I left everything. I left the house. I have no right to anything.

- Anyway, I'm going to talk to Mrs. Ivone. And see what they plan to do with things.

- They'll speak ill of me, they'll say I'm to blame for Marcelo's death.

- It was an accident, you are not to blame for anything. Anyway, I want to have a conversation with them.

- Do as you see fit. I don't want them to be angry because of me.

- Stay calm. You know how I am. I don't want what they do or say to put me in a bad mood. I'm not scared of ugly faces and I don't care what other people think.

- I wish I could be like you. Even though we know it was an accident, there are times when I feel guilty. In the end, if I hadn't run away, maybe I would still be alive.

- I don't believe for me death has its moment. And he was destined for that day. If he had waited a little longer, he would have been widowed and left with everyone's approval.

- How could I imagine one of those things

- Only if you were psychic. By the way, you called because you dreamt that Marcelo was wounded. How did that happen?

I write to telling you the details. Our call is very long. I will leave you my address and phone number. Make a note.

- You can talk to me I have a pen and paper in my hand. After writing it down. Aline said goodbye.

- As soon as you have news let me know.

- Don't forget to write me a detailed account of the dream.

- I will send it to you, along with the power of attorney. Give my mother a kiss, and tell my father to forgive me. And not to be angry with me anymore.

She hung up and Dalva was not satisfied:

- She has to be here to defend herself. They accuse her of adultery.

- She has done nothing and someday they will find out. He wants her to take her place in Marcelo' office.

- At least that much. According to them, Marcelo invested a lot of money.

- I'm going to talk to him today. If he accepts my collaboration, we'll work together.

- It's a good solution. Your father will feel your absence in the store. In the end he got used to you, you did the accounting

- I can keep doing it for him. But I need to help Aline. He's right not to go back now. It doesn't make sense. It will overwhelm her more. Learning the details of the accident, seeing her house empty again. Face the problems with her family, friends. There at least no one would charge her anything.

- Dalva sighed sadly:

- I'm beginning to think you're right. If I could I would also travel for some time so I wouldn't hear comments even from people who claimed to be friends with her.

- Mom, you have to stop worrying about what other people say. It takes away your peace of mind and doesn't help you.

Translated with www.DeepL.com/Translator (free version)

You are cold I don't know who you got that way of being from.

- I am balanced. I have common sense. That doesn't mean I'm not sorry for what happened. But there is no sense in worrying about something that has no remedy. The most important thing now is to maintain the lucidity to face the situation that we have to resolve in the best possible way.

- I'm glad you feel that way. I don't have that courage. Aríete laughed, moving his head back slightly, in a gesture very much his own.

- Now I'm going to organize everything very well and I'm going to go to the office to talk to Rodrigo. I'm going to bring my résumé so he knows how I'm going to get in.

- He must already know that you are good at what you do.

- He doesn't know that. In fact, he was always distracted, he never needed to become close friends with our family. Marcelo always spoke very well of him. I just hope he's not annoying or bitter.

- At least they will understand each other, he will go back to work again.

- And well in those six months I lost my job. I didn't need another one because I wanted to rest a little. But now I was already thinking about going back to work.

- It's good that you're looking after your sister's interests. And the way things are going, she may not want anything, which is not fair. They were married in community of property, even if her in-laws don't want it, she is entitled to the assets.

- That's why I agreed to take over the situation. I'm going immediately to settle it. Shortly after. Aríete under the stairs, very elegant. With a leather briefcase as an executive's briefcase should be.

Dalva didn't hold back:

How beautiful.

Good looks are a must at work. I called Rodrigo, he's waiting for me.

- Good luck. If you find Mr. João or Ivone, put your foot down.

- Leave it to me. I know how to do it.

- Half an hour later she arrived elegantly at the office and a secretary immediately ushered her into Rodrigo's office.

- He was in front of a board reviewing a design when he saw her enter, approached her and asked her:

- Then, Aline arrived half an hour ago.

- Sit down, let's talk

- With a gesture he assigned her an armchair in front of the desk, then she sat down and he sat on the other side.

How is she?

- Very sorry

- She told me what she plans to do.

- For the moment she's not coming back from Brazil, she has sent me a power of attorney with full powers, asking me to represent her in everything.

- Rodrigo ran his hand through his hair, thoughtfully, and remained silent for a few seconds. Then he answered:

- And how is it going to be. You know that Marcelo's parents are not happy and blame her for the accident. It is a very delicate matter. I don't want to get into that discussion. I was counting on her to come back and settle the unfinished business with them directly.

- What unfinished business?

- They don't want him to receive anything that belonged to Marcelo. They are very indignant. On the other hand, she has her rights, but they don't want to accept it. Marcelo was more than a friend, he was like my brother. I don't want to stand in the way of his parents, who are suffering for their loss. Maybe if you explain it to them he would come back. If only to resolve this matter.

- Aline is assessing your situation and wants to cooperate so that you don't get hurt. She has asked me to make a proposal. If you accept everything will be resolved.

- Proposal? How so?

- Aline asked me that as long as she doesn't return from Brazil. I will replace her. Not only in legal proceedings, but also here in your company.

- You will.

- I do know that Marcelo was in charge of the administrative and financial part of the company, and that you didn't like that area. Well, I don't understand architecture, but I was trained in Business Administration, I have eight years of experience and I know I can handle that area very well.

- Aríete opened his leather briefcase, took out a folder and handed it to him saying:

- Here is my resume. You can look it over. You said you have no intention of hiring another partner. If you accept what I propose, you won't need him anymore.

- Aline will remain your partner, everything will be settled. When she decides to come back, you will decide if you want to continue with the partnership. Rodrigo listened to her thoughtfully.

- I am surprised. I was not expecting it. I was getting ready to do the inventory later, pay Aline her share as it would not be easy for me at this time because I might need to sell some goods.

Aríete smiled

- Our arrangement will be an emergency one. However, I am sure it will be of great help.

- For me it is a good solution, what worries me is the reaction of Marcelo's parents. They are going to fight with me and I wouldn't want that to happen.

- Anyway, they are going to fight. When a lawyer tells them that Aline is entitled to what Marcelo left, they won't be able to do anything to stop it. You will be in the middle of that fight whether you like it or not.

- I don't think I have a choice. I'm in it up to my neck anyway.

- Marcelo was a very capable boy and very dear to our family. We are all suffering because of what happened. However, Aline is slandered because her only sin was to stop loving her husband and end their marriage.

- They don't believe that.

- But I know they are wrong. And I intend to confront them, get the facts straight, tell them the truth. You don't need to get involved. It's a family problem and it's up to us to clear it up.

- If you succeed, I'll be quite relieved.

- You don't need to decide now. Think it over, check my resume and when you have an answer, call me.

- Okay, I'll think about it.

Aríete stood up and handed him a piece of paper that read:

- Here is Aline's phone number, but please don't give the number to anyone. Especially Marcelo's parents.

- Keep calm.

- It's good to avoid comments

- I understand, thank you for coming.

- When she left, he opened the folder she had left. He read the information and admired the level of knowledge Aríete had. Professionally she was very much on top of his needs.

- He was doing it to help his sister. He would be irresponsible not to accept her proposal.

- He saw a folder that the secretary put on the table where there were some rental contracts, bank statements. He hated to mess with that and did not want to learn. At that moment, he decided to call Aríete, accepting her proposal.

- If she is good as her resume says her situation would be solved. Aríete returned to the house satisfied. She was sure Rodrigo would accept. The agreement would be very convenient for him because he had no money to pay Aline's share.

- I saw you come in," asked Dalva:

- And how did it go?

- Very well, Rodrigo needs my help. He has no money to pay Marcelo's share. You knew his parents didn't want Aline to get anything.

- They are angry. I can imagine. To tell you the truth, I don't think Aline is going to demand anything.

- What's wrong mother. She is entitled to what he left her. She should not give up what belongs to him.

- They can claim abandonment on her part.

- Anyway, she was married, community property. Afterwards, they don't even know why Aline left and they slander her.

- The loss of a child is a hard blow.

- I agree. But also. It's not fair the way they are acting. After all they are rich, they don't need anything. They are only doing this lawsuit to punish Aline.

- In a way she deserved it. Where have you seen her do what she did?

- However, at first glance it is apparent that she acted badly. We don't know what her intimate life was like. Marcelo was very close to her. Everyone thought he was the ideal, loving husband. Attentive to her smallest desires. But I couldn't bear to live with such a man. He would suffocate me. Depriving me of my freedom.

- That's why she's single so far. A woman needs a partner. Someone who loves her. If Aline had had children she wouldn't have done what she did.

- Another deception. Children don't ensure a relationship, I think Aline got fed up with Marcelo's constant harassment.

- You're exaggerating. I wasn't.

- Isn't that right? Some time ago, when Aline had a few days off, I went to her house to return a book she had lent me. I stayed for two hours. In that time Marcelo called four times.

- Maybe he was worried about something.

- Nothing. He called to ask something unimportant. I think it was to find out if he was at home.

- He was very jealous.

- That shows he wasn't as good as he seemed. That's why I don't like to judge others. Who can know what is in people's hearts?

- Dalva sighed thoughtfully and then said.

Be that as it may. His attitude was irresponsible. If she didn't want to continue living with him, she should have spoken up, stood up to him.

- That was the way she found to free herself from the marriage she no longer wanted.

- The phone rang and Dalva answered

- Hello, this is Dalva. Yes, it's me. One moment - turning to Aríete, she continued:

- It's Rodrigo wants to talk to you.

- Aríete answered immediately

- Hello, yes.

- I am calling to tell you that I accept your proposal. First I must tell you that I may not be able to offer you a salary commensurate with what you are used to receiving for your work.

- I am sure we will understand each other. As to this point. I am doing this to help my sister.

- In that case, when can you have lunch?

- Tomorrow at eight o'clock would be fine. That would be fine.

- I'll be waiting. She hung up the phone satisfied.

- You know, Mom. I'm happy to take on that challenge.

- Why are you?

- Rodrigo is worried about Marcelo's parents. He knows they won't be able to do what they want with the inheritance. He knows they won't understand.

- They are very angry and their situation is delicate.

- I offered to help them solve this problem.

- Do you want to get into more trouble? It's not enough what Aline did.

- What Aline did wasn't that bad, so they're being very mean. Marcelo died in an accident. She's not to blame for that.

- If she hadn't left, he wouldn't have run after her like that.

Who can guarantee it. It could have happened even without him leaving home. No one dies before their time. One lady claims to be a person of Faith, she lives praying in church. She always goes to mass and does not believe that it is a force majeure that determines the moment of a person's death.

- You like to confuse me. One thing has nothing to do with the other. But be careful, think well what you are going to do so you don't get into trouble.

- You shouldn't get into that.

- I'm going to take a bath and get some things ready. Tomorrow I'll start working. I'm going to call Aline first. I'll let her know how things are going. The next morning, Aríete arrived at the office at eight o'clock sharp. A receptionist greeted her and she introduced herself.

- I am Aríete, sister of Aline, Marcelo's widow. Rodrigo has arrived.

- He should be here soon.

- Well, I don't know if he told you that I'm going to work here from today.

- Yes, he told me. Come with me. Aríete followed her to one of the areas.

- It was the office of Dr. Marcelo, who was in charge of administration. She shook her head negatively and continued in a sad voice - I find it unbelievable and I can't settle for it.

- It has not been easy.

- He was so young, so handsome, so educated. He was a man every woman would want to marry.

- From his tone. Aríete felt that behind his comment he was criticizing Aline's behavior.

- Too bad that when she met him he was already married, otherwise, who knows, maybe he would have chosen you.

- A bright blush appeared on her face and she hurried to answer:

- I didn't mean that. I don't want the lady to think that I was in love with him. Dr. Marcelo was always a very respectful and devoted man to his wife.

- That is fine. We are not here to evaluate anyone's qualities, but to work. You can go back to your place. If I need anything, I'll let you know. She left in a hurry. It was to be expected that she was angry about Aline. She had been at the funeral

With Marcelo's parents. She would have heard their opinion and it would have outraged her. She looked around. It was a spacious, elegant room. Nicely decorated. There were cards on the table that she began to open.

At that moment Rodrigo entered:

- You are punctual.

- I attach great importance to punctuality.

- I'm going to show you where things are. I'm out of time at the moment. We were working on a big project. And two days before the accident, we signed the contract. We have a deadline to finish the job and with everything that happened. I don't know where to start.

- Don't worry. I'm going to read the documents, I'm going to find out how things are going. Marcelo seemed very organized to me. I think you'll find everything in order.}

He sighed in relief.

- If you need anything, just let me know.

- Don't worry, I'll take care of everything.

- In that case I'll take care of our project.

- Good luck in the process. That's what I wish

- He smiled and she noticed two dimples forming on his face. She smiled too. In spite of everything. She was glad to be back at work. She sat down behind the desk and immediately began to open the letters.

Chapter VI

Aline got up, had a cup of coffee and went down to the garage to pick up her car.

It had been six months since she had worked and three months since her company had financed the car. During the week that she would be on leave, due to Marcelo's death, she had given a lot of thought to the sadness that she would decide to continue in Miami. She had no desire to return and face the comments of Marcelo's family and acquaintances.

They would never understand what she had done. Even her parents reproached her, telling her that she was to blame for her husband's death, what could she expect from others.

It was better to stay, work, adapt to his new life and try to forget that sad event.

Although she liked her job, the treatment she received from her colleagues and was making new friends, it was difficult for her to forget what had happened. During the day she devoted herself to her work and thought of nothing else, but at night, alone in her apartment, the memory of Marcelo never left her. There were moments when it seemed to her that she saw him hurt, asking for help, others when she remembered their love and their first years of marriage.

When that happened, she would come to taste the flavor of the kisses they exchanged or the moments of intimacy they had enjoyed, as if it were really happening at that moment.

Although at the time he would have felt happy, now remembering those moments gave him an unpleasant feeling.

As he remembered, he thought:

Why is this happening to me? Why can't I forget the past? Even if people judge me guilty. I don't feel that way. I never thought Marcelo could die like this. I never wished him any harm. My only weakness was believing I loved him and accepting that marriage. That was my fault. I should never have given up my plans because I married him.

That morning. On her way to work, the dream she had had with her husband the night before. She couldn't get it out of her mind.

She dreamed that they kissed passionately, while he repeated how much he loved her. And that he would never leave her, talking about the early days of their marriage although that time had been good, now, it wasn't being pleasant. Aline felt bad, nervous, she woke up weak, unwell. She felt that those dreams with Marcelo were not doing her any good. On the contrary. She wanted to forget, to erase from her life those years with him. But she couldn't. He was always in her thoughts. He was always in her thoughts.

He was always in her thoughts, reacting to every word she said or did, as if he were there.

This could not continue. She needed professional help. She believed it was shock brought on by the events that had traumatized her. She would seek a psychologist.

In the company cafeteria at lunch, she talked to Rachel about the problem. He offered to refer her to a friend of his who was a therapist.

- He's wonderful," she told her, "I'm sure he'll help you with it." Aline was relieved. Back at her desk, Rachel handed her a card with his phone number on it:

- Try calling him today.

- I don't know if he'll be able to get to you that quickly. He has a lot of clients.

I want to resolve this as soon as possible. I can't bear to think about what happened anymore.

- In that case. I'm going to intercede. Norman is my friend. I'll see what I can do.

- I'll be very grateful to him.

- Aline threw herself into her work with determination and steadfastness, ready to think no more of Marcelo. Two hours later, Rachel sought her out:

- Yes, I have now managed to talk to his secretary about him. Unfortunately. Norman is out of the country, at a conference. So he'll be back in ten days. I tried to make an appointment for when he returns. But she refused, claiming she didn't have time. Anyway, leave her your name, in case there are any cancellations.

- He must be really good.

- He's really great. If you could wait at least you would be sure to be seen by someone very competent.

- Thanks Rachel I will try.

- Look, why don't you try to distract yourself, go out, meet people, have fun. Staying home alone is not going to help you at all.

- I like to go out, I met some very nice guys near my house, however, every time I see them, I end up feeling bad.

- It's because he feels guilty, he doesn't accept what happened. I think I should insist on going out

Right now. I have many friends I can introduce you to in our area. They are cheerful people of our level. It becomes very pleasant when we meet.

- Maybe you are right. I need to react There is nothing I can do about the past. I need to look forward.

- That's right. So, whoever you talk to today will get you out of here. I'm meeting some friends at a bar. You can come with me.

- I slept so badly tonight, I don't know if I'll be good company.

- Stay there for a while and then go. At least you'll meet some interesting people.

- All right, I'll go.

At the end of working hours, Aline touched up her makeup, took the car and followed Rachel. She was ready to react. To forget the past, to turn the page of her life.

After parking next to her friend, Aline looked around. The place was very nice. The place was a bit out of the way, and there was a huge hall full of plants, nicely decorated. It was a hotel where there was a restaurant that overlooked the garden and a bar that was in a glassed-in area, full of plants and flowers.

It was full, and Aline liked the place.

- How nice! - she commented enthusiastically

- I'm glad to be here," Rachel replied cheerfully. My friends will be here soon, come, I'll introduce you to them.

- She waved her hand towards a table where there were two girls and two boys.

- This is Aline. Vivian, Vanessa, Robert and Nicolas. Aline greeted everyone and Rachel continued

- Aline is in town for a short time. She doesn't know this place.

- I am delighted. She said. They settled in and the waiter approached them and they placed an order. The conversation flowed easily. Vivian. She was a blonde girl, blue eyes, soft smile. Vanessa was tall, brown hair, slim, big eyes, firm voice. Robert was medium height, brown hair and eyes, flirtatious smile. Nicolas tall, slim, light skinned, but with dark hair, black eyes, full lips, strong jaw.

- Aline liked them all and felt encouraged. The theme revolved around her, because none of them knew Brazil. And they were curious to know what life was like in their country.

- Aline took the opportunity to clarify some rumors that were circulating in Brazilian society. The conversation was good, Aline stayed. Rachel saw her relaxed and got up:

- When it was after 9 o'clock. I have to go, I have to pick up John at Emily's house. Aline got up. Rachel continued:

- But you can stay

- The conversation is good. But I have to go they said goodbye. Aline exchanged phones with them and they left. Once outside, Rachel asked:

- What did you think of it?

- I liked it a lot. For a few moments I forgot all my problems. You're right. I need to go out and have fun.

- You're right. They liked you too. I think we can have a good time together.

- A little more cheerful, Aline went home. She turned on the radio and then the sound of a bolero invaded her and reminded her that this music was fashionable in Brazil.

- Marcelo's spirit, the irritated physiognomy, was beside her. How could she be walking, laughing, talking to those people, as if nothing had happened?

- If it was she who had died, he would be sad, dissatisfied, depressed. How could Aline be so indifferent to what was happening?

- He looked at her angrily. Aline felt an unpleasant sensation, she thought of Marcelo.

She felt she was screwing up, she told him:

- You want to forget me, you don't love me anymore I won't leave you because of you I'm in that state. You destroyed my life And everything I did to see you happy Your ingratitude has no excuse.

- Aline began to remember how Marcelo was, who showered her with attentions and a feeling of guilt invaded her. She reacted:

- I am not to blame for the accident. He exaggerates as usual. If he wasn't so dramatic and attached, he wouldn't have run away. I would have spoken; I would have told him that I didn't love him anymore and that I wanted to go on with my life as I had planned it since my childhood.

- Marcelo grew angrier and angrier. How could she be so cold? He had been a victim and she was to blame.

- Aline felt sick. She was nauseous, her head was dizzy and her body ached. She couldn't wait to get home.

Marcelo was still furious

- If you think I'm going to let her have fun with those bums. You're wrong. You have to go back to our house. And I want you to stay with me.

- Aline came into the house pale and with shaky legs, she went to take a bath and got a little better, but she was worried.

- Maybe she needed to seek help from another therapist. She couldn't go on feeling like this. If she wanted to progress in her work, she had to be well, clear-headed. Forget those unpleasant thoughts that were making her sick.

- She couldn't miss this opportunity she had worked so hard to get. Sitting on the bed, she remembered her family with nostalgia. She thought of her mother, remembered what she used to say:

- When you don't know what to do, ask God for help. His help never fails.

Dalva was a staunch Catholic. She went to Mass whenever she could and complained that her daughters were not like that.

- How do you want God to remember you if you never pray to him or talk to him?

- Aline believed in God in her own way, she had never been so attached to any religion, but at that moment her eyes filled with tears and she wanted to talk to God.

- Why was she being punished? In spite of everything, her conscience did not accuse her of anything. Why then did she feel so bad? And she could not forget the past. She was being punished for wishing for a better life. For no longer loving her husband, because she was now realizing her youthful dreams, did she feel bad?

Aline let her tears flow. When she felt calmer, she said quietly:

- My God, help me to understand what is happening to me, I want to get better. Please show me the way.

- Marcelo, comforted by her suffering, settled into a corner of the room. although he was sad, it seemed only fair that she should cry too. They were close, and what the other felt must also affect him.

- Aline sighed in relief. The discomfort disappeared and she decided to organize her clothes and arrange things for the next day:

- While rummaging through a bag, she dropped a card on the floor and picked it up."Ferguson Institute- Doctor William Morris- Paranormal Studies."

Aline remembered the girl she met at the bookstore who invited her to attend a lecture on the afterlife.

She sat on the bed thoughtfully. That girl said that maybe it was important to attend that lecture where she mentioned her life change. How was she to know?

A shiver ran through his body. He had never stopped to think about the afterlife. What happened to people when they died. It would be the end of everything. There was as some say another world where they would go.

If it were true, Marcelo would go somewhere else. That was not possible. The whole thing was making her nervous.

She threw the letter in her purse, trying to forget. But the girl's physiognomy did not leave her mind.

She was impressed by what he had told her, but that was just a coincidence. That girl did not know her. Therefore, she knew nothing of her life. He only said those words to convince her to attend the conference.

She turned on the television determined not to think about it anymore. The next morning, at the office. She was reading the newspapers and saw an advertisement that caught her eye. "Dr.

Wiliam Morris," or "Professor Morris," as he liked to be called. He presented some facts. Which according to him prove that life continues in other dimensions of the universe.

He claims, after twenty years of research that not only is it true, but that those who die can communicate with the living and interfere with their lives. Our reporter approached him after the lecture, questioning his claims to which he responded:

- The spirit world coexists with us. When someone dies, he leaves his body of flesh that served as his instrument to interact in this world. Although he retains his astral body that he possessed before he was born. Our eyes cannot see them, they vibrate in a space that our eyes cannot reach.

What is life like in these dimensions?

There are many directions in the universe. In the Bible you will find many quotes about them.

They have several levels, and each being who dies will live according to his spiritual level.

- The Lord says they can influence our lives.

- In a certain way. Whoever dies continues the same in this world. With the same feelings, affections, needs. Those who are attached to material goods, the people they love usually remain by their side influencing them. There is nothing to be afraid of because telling the truth makes people identify with what is happening to them and seek help.

- It will not be a form of proselytizing

- Let me invite you to visit our study group, where you can investigate and verify what I say. Then you will discover that it is better to know and take precautions. Bonds of affection are not easily broken, nor are bonds of hatred. Both can lead to situations that can lead to insanity. Therefore, I think the time has come to look into the matter.

- You can be sure I will be back. Thank you for the interview. People who were anxious to talk to Dr. Morris came to him and told him about their experiences. But he sent them to find him at the Institute during his daily shift to get more information.

There was a picture of Dr. Morris. A middle-aged man, elegant, energetic, but with a kindly face.

She closed the paper in shock. If this was true, Marcelo' spirit would be by her side and would never leave her.

Rachel approached.

- Something has happened. You look pale.

- Do you believe there is life after death? Do I believe that whoever dies can influence our lives?

- I don't know. There are many people who study that and believe. I, however, have never dwelled on such questions. Why do you ask?

- Aline showed Rachel the paper

- Read it.

The other obeyed and returned the paper saying. You were impressed by the interview. You still feel nervous about your husband's death.

- It wasn't that.

Aline told him about meeting a girl in a bookstore and continued:

- Yesterday, on the way home, I started to feel bad, anxious, desperate. I couldn't stop feeling bad and remembering the recommendations my mother made to me, I prayed, I asked God for help. I felt a little better. When I went to sort my clothes for today, I picked up a bag and the Institute's card fell to the floor.

I was shaking, Aline. What a thing. That might be a sign that I think you should go to the Institute.

- It will be. I've never been involved with anything like this before. I'm scared.

- I like to see the signs that life gives. That was amazing.

- I think so, too.

- See, now I'm curious. I'm going to investigate, I'm going to get information about that Institute. If it's a serious place you should go.

- I don't know about that. Just thinking about it makes me nervous.

- I'm going with you, I'm not afraid of anything.

- At the end of the afternoon, Rachel approached Aline and handed her some sheets of paper.

- Wow, I have information about that Institute. It's a serious place, run by some illustrious people. Dr. William Morris. In addition to being a psychiatrist, he is a doctor of philosophy. Author of several books, in the last twenty years he has devoted himself to research in parapsychology, at the side of Professor Rhine. In the classrooms of two famous universities, he is highly respected.

- I think I should go.

- I think I'm curious now. I'll go with you.

- I do not know. If I think about it. I'm scared. It seems that in that place something bad is going to happen to me.

- You are impressed. From the information, that institute is frequented by serious people, and there is no reason to be afraid. I know Dr. Morris is telling the truth, your husband's spirit may be near you. Aline felt a shiver run through her body:

- Don't tell me those things

- Tied up as you say he was. In that case he must still exist in another world, you think he wouldn't be by your side.

- That scares me. If that were true, it wouldn't do any good to have separated from Marcelo, I always swear he would never leave me.

- If I were you, I would go to that Institute today. Dr. Morris says that, although it can be scary, it's better to know than to ignore. And I think like him.

- Despite the fear I feel, I think he's right. It's better to go now, because if things are as I think they are, that whoever dies doesn't come back, I'll be done with that story.

- That's the way to talk. Facing our fears is always better. After Rachel left. Aline went to work. At lunchtime, she looked up the school's phone number and called.

- A receptionist informed her that the opening hours started at three o'clock in the afternoon and would run until eight o'clock in the evening.

- Aline took down the address and the definite time of the event and, as they were leaving, she told Rachel

- I'm with the management of the Institute. They will be attending until eight o'clock in the evening and I intend to go now. You will accompany me.

- Yes, I will call Beth to pick up my son from school. After calling, they went out. Rachel would go ahead, because she knew where the way to the high school was Aline would follow her.

- The high school was located in a very nice six-story building with parking in the basement. There were many people coming and going, and they went to the door.

- A receptionist greeted them and asked them what they wanted to do at the institute. And Aline. She said she had read an interview in the newspaper and was interested in studying the subject.

After filling out the form and answering a few questions, each was guided by an assistant.

Aline sat across from a young man who looked about twenty years old, blond, with curly, frizzy hair who smiled at her, looking into her eyes Aline smiled too and he asked her attentively.

It's your first time here

Aline told him in a few words that she had separated from her husband to come to work in Miami and that he had died in a car accident and she was done:

- I don't know if I was shocked by the news of his death, but I haven't been feeling well.

- And what do you feel

- Anguish, fear, it seems to me that something terrible is going to happen. I am a cheerful person, but now, I feel depressed, sleepy, but when I sleep I get sleepy and agitated. There are times when I feel pains in my body, sometimes on one side and sometimes on the other.

It is difficult to explain. I've always been a healthy person, I've never been sick. He heard her firm and asked her.

- Her husband was a dark, handsome, tall, brown-haired man with a dimple in his chin.

- Aline stirred uneasily in her chair:

- Yes, as you know.

- Their love was a denominator, that's why you ended up separating. It's hard to put up with a situation like that.

- It's true. You think his spirit can be close to me.

- Do not be afraid. He wishes you no harm.

- In fact, He always protects me. He always protects me. But now, he is dead. I don't think he can be here somehow.

- But he is. Dressed in a blue suit, face wounded, blood draining from his chest and legs. He needs help.

- Aline turned pale. The boy described Marcelo the same way she had dreamed him on the plane. Frightened, trembling, she couldn't hold back the tears streaming down her face. She felt the urge to run out of there. To get up.

The boy also got up and grabbed her arm, saying:

- Come with me

- I want to go, I can't stay here.

- Come, don't be afraid.

- He led her to a room where a group of people were meditating in silence. She sat down and at two signs two people approached, and a girl sat down in front of Aline, she held his hands while the man stood behind her chair, resting his hands on her, praying silently. Aline felt a gentle warmth invade her body and gradually a sense of relief enveloped her. She began to relax and felt much better. After a few minutes, the two of them moved away and the assistant led her back to her room and made her sit in his chair.

- Are you feeling better," he asked attentively.

- Yes, I feel relieved. What happened in that room

- You have received an energetic gift. You will feel stronger.

- I find it hard to accept that Marcelo still exists in another world. It scares me because I was very attached, so much so that I couldn't separate from him. I had to run away because he wouldn't accept it.

- He doesn't accept the separation and blames me for the accident.

- I never imagined that could happen. I never wished him any harm.

- I know he is not to blame for anything. It's good that you keep that in mind, because he wants you to feel guilty so he can dominate you.

- He may hate me.

- It is not that. On the contrary, he believes that you are love and that life only makes sense if you are by his side. He is deluded. People are free. No one belongs to anyone and everyone has the right to choose his or her own path. Therefore, don't give importance to the bad thoughts that go through his head. They are not yours. The thoughts that you pick up are yours or even from other discarnate spirits who want to take advantage of the situation.

- We are surrounded by beings from another dimension. Spirits who have lived in this world and after the death of the body refuse to move on to other destinies. They inspire us with depressive thoughts and we believe that they are ours because we feel them in the same way that our thoughts work.

- How can we differentiate ours from theirs? No, I think it's unfair and scary. We can't see them and we have no way to defend ourselves. Why would God allow such a situation?

- We have free will, common sense and we can choose to disregard destructive thoughts and nurture the good ones. That way, we will be free of those influences.

- Aline thought for a moment and then said, "It's a difficult situation.

- It's a difficult situation that I don't know how to deal with. It seems impossible to me that someone could haunt us like that after death.

- It is a reality that we have to face.

- That's what terrifies me. As hard as it is to accept, you described the event you saw in your dreams. How would I know.

- It's right next to you, I saw it.

- Aline shifted uneasily in her chair. Then she asked:

- What do you advise me?

- That I give you a spiritual treatment at our Institute.

- What does this treatment consist of?

- Donation of energy to make you feel stronger and at the same time help you to accept the separation.

I know and I know it won't be easy. He smiled softly and replied

- Everything is easy when God helps.

- That's true. I had forgotten. I think I could make him understand and accept it.

- Let's give it a try.

- Okay.

- He took a pad, a pencil. He handed it to her saying:

- Write here his full name, the day of his death. We also need a photo.

- For our team to be mentally prepared and to work. You'll have to come twice a week.

- Do you think I'll be okay?

- I think you will. Promise me you will help us, trying not to give importance to any sad and painful thoughts and not to feel guilty. You promise. He wrote on a piece of paper and handed it to her saying:

- When you come back bring that paper and try to be punctual. She said goodbye and thanked him and left. In the other room Rachel waited anxiously for her.

- And then

- It was unbelievable. Now I'm shaking.

- In short, tell all and then ask questions:

And how are you?

A girl attended me and told me nothing about those who died, however, she told me about the living.

- So, it's an old and complicated story. I'll tell it to you later:

- Excuse me I don't want to be indiscreet

- That's not the point. I need time to think about what he told me. How does he know so much about my life?

- You'll see that some spirit told him what happened to you.

- Come on, I need to find John. I'll tell you all about it another day.

- You don't have to. I just wanted to know if it was the same for you as it was for me.

- He's asked me to sign up for two courses. He says it will help me deal with my problem. I'll think about it. I'd like to do it. Now come on, they'll be leaving soon, they said goodbye and each picked up their car. During the drive. Aline could not forget the assistant's words. Marcelo was alive and by her side.

- At the thought, she recoiled in fright.

- In fact, he was there, sad, frightened. When Aline entered that room and the people began to pray, he felt anguished.

Those people wanted to separate her from him. Frightened, he left and waited for her near the car. He was determined not to let them separate him from her. He would resist. He would do anything to keep her. He was sitting next to her car. He realized his thoughts and said anxiously, "Don't be afraid of me:

Don't be afraid of me, do you think I'd hurt you? Aline felt shivers all over her body and shrugged even more. He walked away sadly and decided to keep his distance until she calmed down.

Chapter VII

Aline arrived home calmer. As much as the idea of Marcelo's spirit haunting her bothered her, she was comforted to know that she could count on the help of the Institute.

- They talked about the matter so naturally; they showed so much knowledge that they would undoubtedly find a way to solve her problem. He decided to do his part, avoiding sad thoughts. She turned on the television and a fashionable song filled the air. Satisfied, she prepared something to eat, sat down in front of the set, tray in hand, trying hard to forget her worries and pay attention to the program.

In a few moments, I forget everything, invaded by the music that bothered Marcelo.

- I did everything for her, I died for her, so little time ago and she doesn't call me. It seems that she is even happy with my death.

- At that moment, she saw a very clear light approaching and a woman of 40 years old, very pretty, with a beautiful dress down to her feet, entered the room.

Then he realized that she was not an incarnate person, because he saw her smile.

- Who are you?" he asked admiringly.

Your heart. A friend who wants to help you.

- I'm doing fine without your help.

- You're hurting. You need treatment.

- That was from the accident, but I'm getting better. In time I'll be fine.

- I came to find you to treat you.

- You want to separate me from Aline. I know that.

- I want you to get well. When you're well, I know you can come back.

- I can't go. I have to take care of her alone in this strange city.

- You know how to take care of yourself. Without care your condition may get worse.

- Don't try to insist. I don't want to go.

- It would be better for you. What do you expect from being with her like this? Every time she comes to you to transmit her anguish, her pains, her discomfort, her sadness. She feels bad.

- She feels this way because of guilt. She was the cause of my misfortune.

- It is not true. You were the cause of her death. I was upset:

- I know you came because you want to separate me from Aline. I heard that guy say I would be separated from her. I think you're part of the group. You can do whatever you want. But I'm not going. There's no way I'm getting out of here.

- He will only go with me if he wants to. However, you should warn him that it would be far better to go with me than to insist on staying in a place that is no longer his.

- Leave me alone. I'm not leaving here.

- He walked away and disappeared. Marcelo sighed in relief. A short time later, a tall, strong, dark-haired boy in a gray suit entered a room and Marcelo listened to him worriedly.

- Don't be afraid, my friend. Forgive the intrusion, but I think you need help.

- If you come to ask me to leave Aline. You can resign. She's my wife and I'm not leaving here.

- You are sure that your place is next to her. I came because I saw that you are being involved by people who do not wish you well.

- What do you mean

- That woman who was here recently. She is part of that group that your wife went to this afternoon.

- When I saw it that's what I thought.

- She is dangerous. With that quiet talk, she's enveloping and ends up getting what she wants.

- She wants to separate me from Aline, but she's not going to get it. He laughed wryly:

- She has strength if you don't prepare yourself. Soon she will come back with more strength and you will have to give up.

- Never! I would have nowhere else to go but Aline.

- You really like her.

- I adore her, I would never leave her.

- Those love stories move me. I too loved too much and suffered too much. I understand what you're going through. I even know what's going to happen. A young, beautiful, full of life woman like Aline will one day show up with someone else. She'll be interested and, when you least expect it, she'll be married again. Marcelo clenched his fists in anger:

- That will never happen. I will not allow it.

- I am here to help you. You need to get your wife to give you the courage you deserve. Notice that she is not uncomfortable with your death. You think she loves you!

- I never imagined she could do what she did. But I still don't want to lose her.

- She reached over and stroked Marcelo' back, saying, "You're not going to lose her:

- You're not going to lose her. I'm here to help you.

- Thank you. Until, at last, I found a friend.

- That's right. A friend for life. My name is Victor.

- I'm Marcelo.

- Of course. Do as I say. That power and much more. Marcelo listened in admiration.

- You must be very important

- The other raised his head haughtily and replied.

- I belong to a group that has a lot of power.

- I am very lost. Since my accident, I don't feel well. I feel pains from time to time, my head is spinning, I feel like I'm going to lose my senses.

- That's why I want to introduce you to my friends. They will take care of you and everything will be fine:

- I'd like to, but I can't get out of here.

- Look, she's already in bed. So as soon as she falls asleep we can go. Aline was tired and sleepy. She lay on her side and soon fell asleep. Marcelo saw when she left her body immediately he tackled her. But Victor stopped him saying:

- Don't do that. Let her go. She is accompanied by an assistant.

- I don't see anyone.

- Victor put his right hand. On his forehead. Who immediately saw a spirit of Aline.

- No Aline, you are just sleeping. That woman is protecting her, I advise you to stay away from her.

- Why? She works for the light. She works for the light. She works for the light.

- She works for the light.

- And who does she work for?

- For those of us who want to take care of our problems. The servants of the light are full of rules. They are soft-spoken, they take us in and arrest us. Then they force us to do everything they order us to do.

- God forbid.

- That's right, we don't want anyone to tell us what to do, we come together and we are able to take charge of our problems. Not only do they have the power, we have the power. Our group is powerful. Come on, now and we can go Marcelo doubt it:

- I don't know, what if they stop us too? Victor smiled incredulously:

- Don't think that. We are a democracy, we fight for our freedom. Come with me. I guarantee you won't regret it. We'll be back before Aline.

- In that case I'll go.

That's the way to talk.

Victor took Marcelo by the arm and they flew off in an unknown direction. Marcelo was dazzled. Since he had disincarnated he had never traveled through space.

He saw himself traveling to places, not knowing how he had been transported from a distance. Suddenly he thought 81

He could see himself in a place. Just as he would enter that plane and discover Aline's apartment. Victor should also be powerful enough to drive there. At first they drove through a sleepy city looking up at a sky full of stars. Then they entered a wave of fog. And Victor recommended.

This area is somewhat dangerous. But I'm not afraid. They can't see us Marcelo saw dark lumps, poorly dressed people who looked sick, he was frightened, but calmed down when he noticed they were moving unseen. The fog passed. And he saw a fortress, surrounded by high walls. Victor stood in front of a large gate saying.

- We have arrived

- Marcelo saw him and turned around worried. He seemed to have gone back in time and returned to the Middle Ages.

- Victor called a name and the door opened. They entered. Marcelo felt a shiver of fear as he saw the huge door close again.

- The place was anything but cheerful. There were men in uniform everywhere, looking very animated as they greeted them.

- Come, I want to introduce you to a friend. Mimo is one of the directors of this house.

- I am worried. He's sure we'll be back before Aline wakes up.

- Never doubt my word. I said I'd take him back and I'll keep it.

- I'm sorry. I'm sorry. I'm sorry. I'm sorry. I'm sorry. I'm sorry. It's just that we're so far away. I wouldn't know how to get back alone.

- I will take you there. I know the way well. Let's go. They walked down the immense courtyard to the two sides of the estate and stopped at the door that opened before climbing the next step.

- They entered a stone corridor, lit by torches to a room where there was a table and a

A man sitting at a computer-like machine saw them arrive. Victor greeted him, introduced Marcelo and asked:

Talk to Mimo.

- He's waiting for you. We can go in.

Victor led Marcelo through a handmade door, saying

Your room is here.

He didn't need to say anything. A door opened and they entered. The room was luxurious, full of upholstery and velvets. The heavy, neat wooden furniture, with dark colors, made the atmosphere so heavy that the light from some of the lamps seemed somewhat unreal.

Marcelo did not like what he saw. Sitting on a divan was a fat, balding, middle-aged man, dressed in a velvet robe, smoking on an opium-like device, releasing puffs into the air. In his round face, shrewd eyes held attention. Victor approached greeting and saying.

- I have brought a friend who needs help.

- Mimo noticed his face and became kind, almost tender as he responded:

- Take a good look at him. The friend is in great need. He moved closer. Encouraged by the gentle, almost affectionate tone. Marcelo approached. Mimo designated a place next to him saying.

- Sit here, my son. Let's see what I can do for you. Tell me everything.

Marcelo obeyed, and as soon as he sat down he was overcome with a strong emotion. He remembered everything that had happened to him. From the moment he found Aline's letter and was overcome with emotion, he cried in despair, as soon as Mimo put his hand on his head.

- Cry, my son. Unburden yourself. You are right to reveal yourself. What that woman did to you was terrible.

She had no pity for her pain. She paid with ingratitude for everything you did for her. I'm seeing what she went through. Poor boy. She doesn't deserve your love. She has to pay.

- No, I love her. I just want her to see me so she'll stay with me.

- But I can't live without her. I want her to stay with me.

- In that case we can have him come here.

- How can I do that?

- We can finish her body. Then she will come here and stay with you.

- Marcelo was frightened:

- But I love her. I can't want her to die.

- In that case we can't do anything. Only then will she come and stay with you.

- Marcelo sighed heavily, not knowing what to say. He wanted Aline to come with him, but at that price it would be fair.

- Was it fair what she was doing with him, he wondered. Marcelo realized that Mimo was reading his mind.

- Indeed, he was very powerful. He was afraid of what might happen to Aline. That's why he responded:

- I don't want to get to that point. I just want to stay by her side forever.

- In that case you will have to bide your time.

- Being by her side is all I want. If you want to help me don't let anyone separate us. And I will be eternally grateful to you.

- Mimo took a puff of opium and then said smiling:

- No one here needs your gratitude. We work by barter. We do favors and those people also do favors for us. It's all very serious and organized. If we don't admit it as treason. Here a word is worth more than everything. I can get you whatever you want, however you want.

However, it is good to know that in return you will have to provide us with a service.

- What kind of service?

- Whatever it takes. And a fair deal Marcelo hesitated for a moment and then agreed.

- It is, I think it is.

- We don't force anyone here. People are free to decide. If you accept our help, you know you'll have to reciprocate according to our deal.

- Marcelo accepted and Victor approached:

Thank you maestro. Marcelo still hasn't recovered from the accident. His wounds are bleeding, he is in pain, can I take him to the infirmary for treatment?

- They thanked him and left. Back in the courtyard, Marcelo breathed a sigh of relief. Victor drove to the side of the house where Marcelo was being attended to and taken by a nurse.

- Look at him. He's a friend Marcelo. He needs help. He turned around and became emotional:

- Renato, it's been a long time.

- Marcelo looked on in admiration. She was a woman in her thirties, fair skin, blue eyes and brown hair, very pretty. Her face rang a bell from where he met her, he couldn't remember.

- You're kidding yourself. My name is Marcelo. She hugged him trembling and answered:

- You still don't remember. But I never forgot.

- I tell you you're wrong. We don't know each other.

- I will not insist. Everything will happen in its own time. Come I will help you and take you to the next room saying:

- Lie down on the stretcher.

- He obeyed, looked around and saw that behind the stretcher there were several interlocking devices. Mirela pressed a button and the room lit up with blue light. Marcelo felt his head spinning and wanted to get up, but she assured him:

- Calm down. Don't be afraid. We're cleaning your wounds. Take it easy. You'll feel better later.

- Marcelo relived the moment of the accident. But little by little the feeling of panic passed.

- Take a deep breath, don't worry about anything. Just relax. He felt calmer and noticed that the burning in his wounds had passed. She turned on a green light and Marcelo began to feel a peace he had not felt in a long time. Mirela began to run her hands over his body, without touching him. An orange energy came from her hands. They penetrated his body, giving him a feeling of vigor.

- He didn't know how long the treatment lasted, but when she turned on the lights and asked him how he felt, he replied:

- It seems like a miracle. The pain, the discomfort disappeared. With a gesture from her, Marcelo sat up. He turned off some appliances and asked:

- Will you have to stay here?

- I have not only come to meet. I'm going back to my wife's side.

- Are you married?

- I am married. But my wife still lives in another world. I had a car accident and came here. But I'm not satisfied. Even if she can't see me. I'm going to stay with her.

- Mirela listened to him sadly:

- You have to accept the separation. It's not right to insist on something that has no way to continue. The day will come when you will have to let her go whether you want to or not. Marcelo gritted his teeth:

- That will never happen. Thanks for the help. I feel relieved. See, the wounds are healed. I will never forget what you did for me.

- I would like to do so much more. Unfortunately I can't.

- I have to leave. Victor is waiting for me. Let's go back to land. Mirela hesitated a little and then said:

- Beware of some people here. Have you made a deal?

- No. Why are you telling me that?

- Because things are not always what they seem.

Well, I have to go. Once again, thanks for everything. He was heading for the door, but Mirela took him by the arm:

- Please. Don't tell Victor what I told you. He can't like it.

- Stay calm. I won't say anything.

- Mirela became emotional and a tear glistened in her eyes as she said:

- In spite of everything I see that it was a gratifying emotion. Marcelo felt a wave of tenderness envelop him.

- And he embraced her with affection.

- I don't know how to explain it, but it seems that we have already lived other moments like this one.

- Yes, we have. Someday it will be remembered and then. Who knows, we will be able to talk about the past, relive our feelings.

- I feel this is true. Why don't I remember?

- Because your heart is still more attached to those who stayed on earth than to your astral life. When that happens, you will remember.

- Why don't you tell me everything?

- Because you need to recover your memory. It has to happen naturally. It's better not to force it.

- In that case, I'm going, thank you. I feel much better. I'd like to do something for you in gratitude.

- I need help too. Pray for me.

- I'm not much of a pray-er, but I'm going to try.

- He opened the door and Marcelo came out, Victor was waiting for him and when he saw him happy, he said:

- You have improved. You've lost that frightened face.

- That nurse works miracles. I feel very well. Victor was a little worried and asked

- Renato called you, said he knew you. Do you remember from where?

- No.

- He didn't tell you anything.

- No. I just thought it was funny, but if it were true I would have remembered. He must have been mistaken.

- That very thing could be

- Your treatment is powerful. What he did with me seems like a miracle.

- He has a gift for healing people. We have to go now. Let's go. Marcelo agreed. Victor took him by the arm and they flew away. It didn't take them long to reach Aline's apartment.

- They entered the room where she was sleeping peacefully. From the back of her neck a silver cord was coming out. It was lost in the distance.

- What is that? asked Marcelo in admiration;

- Nothing's wrong, it's just that the spirit hasn't returned to his body yet.

- He sleeps every night, but I've never seen that before.

- It's because he's better now, he's more sensitive. Well, but I have to go. Think well about what the master told you. I'll stay with you if you want to see me, call me and I'll come.

- Thank you for everything. It's very good to have a friend.

- You can count on me

He left and Marcelo sat on the side of the bed. That night's adventure had been fantastic. He remembered Mirela and felt a certain warmth. Who would she be?

Someday she would have been something in his life. He couldn't say. But a thrill came over him every time he remembered her. Suddenly his attention was focused on her. Aline was coming in through the closed window. She was beautiful, her spiritual body wrapped in light. Marcelo was fascinated. She looked like a goddess. But she passed him. And she settled into his sleeping body, sighing lightly. Then she turned on her side and slept on.

She was still under the strong emotion of the moment. Marcelo settled on the side of the bed, hugged her and fell asleep at the same time.

Chapter VIII

Rodrigo arrived at the office early and went to the project room. He had worked late the night before and had not been able to finish. He had to hurry because the deadline was approaching and the contractual penalty was high. It had been a month since Aríete had started working at his company and he was very satisfied. She took care of the administrative and financial side with competence and seriousness, leaving him free to carry out his work with peace of mind.

In addition, she put all the documentation in order. With effort and dedication. The company had never been as well managed as in her hands. Satisfied, Rodrigo sat down at his desk, reviewing what he had done the day before and got down to work.

Shortly after, the door opened, a man entered without knocking and Rodrigo looked at him in surprise:

- Mr. João What do you want here?

- First I want to know what that woman is doing here.

- Rodrigo did not understand and asked:

- Woman, what woman, the sister of that wicked Aline.

- The gentleman is nervous for no reason. Sit down, let's talk.

- I don't want anyone from that family in my son's company. Fire her now. Rodrigo looked at him seriously, sat down again and answered

- I can't do it.

- Of course, you can.

- First, like it or not, Aline is the sole heir to Marcelo's estate. Second, because Aríete offered to help me in her sister's place and she is very competent. And I can't do without her.

João ran his hands through his hair, nervous:

I can't believe what she says. She left him to his fate, she was to blame for my son's death, she cannot inherit his property.

- Marcelo died in a car accident and Aline was not present, the law does not recognize her guilt. Therefore, she is his sole heir.

- My wife and I will not believe that. There must be justice in this land. I will file a criminal complaint against her.

- Do what you want, Mr. João, but it will be useless to spend money for nothing.

- Whose side are you on? I thought you were Marcelo's friend. Now I see you never were.

- You're being unfair.

- If I were his friend I wouldn't accept that woman in this company. It's a betrayal of the highest order.

- I don't think so. I think the gentleman should reflect better before condemning Aline. We don't know the reasons why she decided to leave.

- Surely she ran away with someone else. What else could happen? Why would a woman married to a man who adored her, and gave her a queenly life, and indulged her in everything.

- Everything she loved would disappear. But for an unbridled passion, a madness.

- As far as I know, that's not what happened. Aline isn't living with anyone. She's working.

- That's what her relatives say to cover up their mistake. But at home we all know the truth.

- The man is being malicious.

- You are forgiving what he did.

You are preparing an apology so you can justify your attitude by giving the job to his sister.

Rodrigo tried to contain his indignation with her attitude. He didn't want to continue arguing. First because he was Marcelo's father and he was hurt by the loss of his son and second because he needed to keep a cool head to finish the job.

He took a deep breath and replied

- The gentleman thinks differently than I do. I respect his point of view. We are not going to argue. You still haven't said what you're here for.

- That's exactly what I've come to discuss about Marcelo' affairs.

- In that case, you'd better get a lawyer. Because as far as I know, Aline's family has already opened an inventory.

- They couldn't do it without consulting us. So much so that they did. Secondly the law is the sole heir to Marcelo' estate. If you do not accept it, I advise you to ask for information.

- You will realize that it was you who encouraged them to do so in the silence of the night, taking advantage of the fact that we were immersed in grief.

- Rodrigo was at the height of his irritation and answered him trying to control himself.

Look, Mr. João. I respect you a lot, I know you are suffering, but that does not give you the right to offend me.

Go home, try to calm down, and another day we'll talk again. João stood up, throwing a look of annoyance and said nervously:

- I thought I had found a friend, I was deceived. I have nothing more to say to you. From now on I will seek my rights through the law. You have nothing to lose.

He left with a stomp and a loud slam of the door. Rodrigo sat down in anguish. Aríete came in immediately:

- Excuse me, but you were talking very loudly and I couldn't stop listening to you.

- It was hard to control myself if I wasn't Marcelo...'s father.

It was better this way. Mr. João was beside himself. He never tried to find out what happened. He preferred to turn his pain into hate and judge everything about Aline and our family.

- He chose the worst way. It will only lead to more pain.

- They think only they are suffering. You don't know how much my parents are shocked and how much Aline suffers,

- Rodrigo looked her in the eyes and said seriously:

- I too have wondered why Aline did all this.

- Aline wanted to live in the United States since she was a child. She started studying English as soon as she got a job. She speaks English perfectly. She didn't want to fall in love or get married, but she went there. Marcelo fell in love and followed her everywhere. They began to fall in love after much insistence on his part. He filled her with so much affection that he conquered her. My parents did not want her to leave the country and did everything they could to get her to marry him.

- It always seemed to me that they were happy together.

- She liked him. I don't think it was enough to completely forget their previous plans.

- In the family he did not mention it. But with me he would open up, talk about his enthusiasm for everything related to that country.

- Maybe if they had had children she would have forgotten. The maternal institute was very strong

- From what I understand Marcelo wanted to have children, Aline always avoided them without telling him. I know he was taking pills.

- In that case Aline was not honest with him. I witnessed how much he wanted to be a father. Despite being married, I believe Aline never stopped thinking about realizing her childhood dreams.

That's why he did it. She got a job in a company in Miami, didn't say anything to anyone and left.

- Marcelo was very close to her. I imagine how surprised he must have been to find a letter. I suppose he might have tried to stop her from boarding. He took the car and that was the end of it. Maybe if Aline had talked to him, told him the truth, things would have gone better. -My sister always faced her problems head on. However, in Marcelo's case, not everything would be true. He called her several times a day. He wouldn't let her go free, he stayed close to her all the time. He never let her go alone.

- That's why I will never fall in love. I have a horror of dependence.

- Have you never fallen in love?

- I have never fallen in love. I'm not going to fall in love with anyone. A life of two is very difficult. A woman is very different from a man.

It's the opposite of marriage. There was a certain provocation in his eyes that he responded to with a smile:

- I am, but not against women.

- It shows in the number of calls from women.

- I have many friends and I like social life. However, you seem the opposite we have never seen each other in fashionable places.

- I prefer a good book or an intelligent conversation with friends. I don't frequent trendy places where there are superficial friendships. I tend to select my friends.

- Rodrigo listened thoughtfully.

I should have said that I have many acquaintances, because, in fact, true friends are rare. But back to our subject, do you think Aline regrets it?

- She is shocked by Marcelo's tragic death. In a way she feels guilty, but on the other hand she says that she no longer loved him and that it was not fair to continue living with him. She regrets what happened, but decides to continue living there. She likes her job, she likes the city. She wants to get on with her life.

- Maybe it's better that she doesn't go back. At least until Marcelo's parents forgive her.

- Not to mention my parents' recriminations. They are simple people, they liked Marcelo very much, they thought that married to Aline. With him they would be exempt from future problems. I can't understand why he did that.

- In time they will forget it. Marcelo's family will be the most difficult. They are the most indignant.

- I understand that losing a child is the greatest pain a human being can feel. Now let's forget and work. Life goes on, we have to move on.

- Rodrigo agreed and returned to the table to continue working. A conversation with Aríete had the gift of making him forget the anger that João's words had caused him.

- More willing, he resumed his project and began to work. Mr. João left his son's office grumbling with anger. Rodrigo was not the friend of Marcelo's he thought he was. Where had it become clear that he was on Aline's side?

- He could not forgive himself for that. Aríete, working in the room that was Marcelo's was humiliating. It was like putting his own enemy in his son's place. But he could not stay like that.

With nervous hands he rummaged through his wallet. He had found a lawyer's card he had been given and decided to look for it immediately. Unfortunately for him, the answer he got was not what he wanted. The lawyer's words confirmed what Rodrigo had told him. Marcelo was married in community of property. And Aline was his sole heir. João could do nothing and the lawyer advised him to forget the matter. João arrived home unhappy. Ivone was anxiously waiting for him. As soon as her husband entered, she asked:

- And then you can't imagine what happened.

- From the look on his face, I can see that everything has gone wrong.

- He sat down, took off his handkerchief, wiped his sweat and sighed nervously.

- Talk man, how did it go, he insisted.

- When I went into Marcelo's room, do you know who was there looking like a lady?

- Aríete

- The sister of that shameless woman

- That's her. She's working in our son's place, as if the office was hers.

- As Rodrigo accepted one of those things.

- That's what I went to ask him. But his answer left me with a lot of anger. She says that Aríete is very competent and that she has taken Aline's place because she is Marcelo's heir.

- So what. She gets everything that belonged to our son.

- She stayed.

- That's an insult. She must be squirming in her drawer.

- Rodrigo still wanted to defend that murderer and I came out of there very nervous.

- We can't let this go on. You have to get a lawyer.

- I already went and he told me we can't do anything. They were married in community property. Aline is the heir to everything.

Ivone was not satisfied. Tears of indignation ran down their faces and she exclaimed:

- God will not allow them to go unpunished and even with all that was theirs.

- According to the law we can do nothing.

- What is going on here? Why is mother crying?

- Marcio had come in and they hadn't noticed. Looking at her son, Ivone cried even more. It was João who answered:

- Aline's sister took possession of everything that was Marcelo's. And the lawyer says it's her right and we can't do anything about it.

- Marcio hugged his mother who listened to her saying:

- My son, now we only have you. You have to do something on behalf of your brother. This can't stay like this.

- Marcio was a brother two years younger than Marcelo and they looked alike physically. He lay in his mother's arms, feeling his heart clench. His brother had been his idol. He was shy, though. Marcelo was expansive, outgoing and often helped her with her personal problems.

His brother's death affected him deeply. A whole life depended so much on him that he now felt lost and aimless.

Gnashing his teeth, he responded angrily:

You're right mother this can't stay like this.

- We can't do anything - João interjected - the law is on his side.

- According to the law, we will try another way. Said Marcio, the two looked at him with interest and Ivone asked:

Which one?

- I have a friend who frequents the place where they perform miracles. João shook his head negatively:

That's just silly. I don't think it can work.

- I think it can. - Dora discovered that her husband had a mistress, she was about to leave home. She went to a garden, did everything she was told to do, soon after the other one had an accident, almost died, and she ended up leaving. Then her husband came home. With his tail between his legs. She told me.

- It may have been a coincidence," said João.

- It wasn't - Walter works at that center. Since he started going there, his life changed for the better. He was promoted, his salary increased. He is very satisfied. Some time ago he invited me to go there too. I never wanted to, but now. I think the time has come.

- I think it's better not to go to those places. I don't like those things. - João replied.

- Well, I think you should go. In the end, we are being robbed by the woman who killed our son. If the justice of men does nothing. We have to go to God's justice.

- That same mother. I will talk to him today and we will go there. I am sure we can turn this situation in our favor.

- That's right my son. We can't let that murderer keep everything that belonged to Marcelo.

- That same day. Marcio sought out a friend and told him what was going on and it ended:

- I thought about seeking help in your territory.

- I think that's a good idea. Father Jose is in great demand for solving those family cases. Tomorrow is Labor Day. Drop by the house at 7:30 and we'll go together. Marcio nodded in satisfaction. Until then he would suffer the events as a helpless victim. Now he had the opportunity to at least punish those guilty of his brother's death and justice would be done.

Chapter IX

- After Marcelo left the room. Mirela remained pensive. And some tears rolled down her face.

Remembering Renato, even if he did not remember her, brought her back to a great love she felt for him that the years had not been able to extinguish. In the 19th century, in a small town in the south of France, Mirela grew up in the midst of three siblings, on a family estate dedicated to viticulture.

At the age of 15, Mirela became a girl of rare beauty, with large blue eyes, fair skin, dark brown hair and a slender, well-built body. She attracted admiration wherever she went.

Then she was courted by an Italian nobleman, owner of a castle in Venice, who was in love and asked her in marriage. She refused because he was older, and also because her parents were ambitious, and forced her to marry. Although she did not love her husband, she ended up accepting that he loved her. Because she was surrounded by so much attention and affection, it was very difficult for her to refuse him. After her marriage, she went to live with him in his palace and for four years,

- As the years went by Mirela became more and more beautiful as she paraded around town with her husband and children. She was much admired.

- So, a gondolier madly in love with her who had never known passion, Renato, began to follow her everywhere, discreetly at first. Later with a certain insistence.

One afternoon when she was out for a walk with her two sons and an assistant, they entered the gondola where Renato works. Encouraged by having his beloved so close, he sang love songs so loudly that Mirela was left feeling a new emotion inside her.

From that day on, he began to notice her presence. And she discovered how he followed her everywhere. At first, Mirela liked him. He noticed her beauty, her passionate voice singing beautiful love songs. She felt that he loved her and his presence around her started to become indispensable.

One afternoon when she was out for a walk with her two children and an assistant, they entered the gondola where Renato worked. Encouraged by the fact that his beloved was so close, he sang love songs so loudly that Mirela felt a new emotion inside her.

From that day on, he began to notice her presence. And she discovered how he followed her everywhere. At first, Mirela liked him. She noticed his beauty, his passionate voice singing beautiful love songs. She felt that he loved her and her presence around him began to become indispensable.

On Mirela's anniversary, Giulio, her husband, wanting to please her, hired musicians for her party and Renato was among them.

When she saw him, she was moved and tried to control her feelings. When she went to take a break on the terrace, Renato passed by her, who was talking to a friend, and without anyone noticing, put a note in her hand.

Trembling with emotion, Mirela hid it in her lap as soon as she could. Then she went to her room, closed the door and read:

"Mrs.

I'm going crazy with love. I can't stand being near you anymore without being able to touch you I know how far away we are, but I long for a kiss from you. Then I can die, because I no longer feel like living.

Renato."

Mirela shuddered with pleasure imagining what that kiss would be like. This desire became part of her life.

So when Giulio traveled to Rome, she did not resist. She sent a note to Renato, meeting him at his house at midnight and, with the help of a maid, she prepared everything discreetly.

At the agreed time, Renato was taken to his room and they both threw themselves into each other's arms. With deep emotion they confessed their love to each other. Mirela had never felt anything like it and was frightened. She thought it was time to stop. However, she did not succeed. Every time her husband moved away, the two lovers loved each other more and more.

Mirela wanted to leave with Renato, she wanted to live by his side without having to hide, but there were the children and she didn't have the courage to leave them. Dragging them into this adventure would be impossible.

Giulio was a good man, but he would not accept his betrayal, much less take his children. He would surely kill Renato. It was then that the unexpected happened. One early morning, Giulio returned unexpectedly and upon entering his bedroom found Mirela in Renato's arms.

Seeing that scene Giulio flew into a rage, taking advantage of the traitors impression he took the revolver from the chest of drawers and pointed it at Renato saying:

- You damned traitor. In my absence you have taken advantage of my wife. I am going to finish you. Terrified, Mirela stood in front of Renato and said in sorrow:

- For God's sake don't do that

- Giulio's face contracted in a rite of pain:

- He wanted to believe that he had taken her against her will. That it had been an aggression. But now I see that it wasn't. You're defending him!

- Forgive me Giulio. Kill me, but please let him go.

Giulio felt dazed and for a few moments he staggered. It was enough for Renato to jump on him, grab the revolver and shoot him. Seeing his scream, Giulio fell and Renato fled out the window. He climbed down carefully without anyone seeing him.

The servants ran and tried to help him. But it was useless Giulio did not resist. Mirela told the police that it had been a burglar who had taken the revolver and fired. The police investigated, but did not find the murderer. A bellboy who knew about the affair with Renato, but was devoted to the bosses, kept silent, although he suspected the truth.

Mirela decided to return to the city to live with her family. She sold the castle, bought a villa in the south of France and moved there with her children. She was wealthy and could give her children a good education and provide well for the family. Renato later followed her and, in time, became friends with her family. They continued to see each other. And finally, with the full approval of her relatives, they married. And they lived together for many years. Remembering all that, Mirela thought that the happiness of those years cost them dearly as they returned to the spiritual world. Renato died at the age of sixty and Mirela, unhappy with widowhood, five years later, victim of pneumonia, left the physical life. When she awoke in the astral world, she was sheltered by two nurses and confined in a place of recovery. However, when she realized that death was nothing more than a change of state, she wanted to meet Renato.

- She asked everyone around her about him, but got no answer. No one knew where he was.

- That thought became a real obsession for her. She was sure that he was not in that place. She wanted to go, but they wouldn't give her permission to leave the hospital.

- You are not well. You have to continue treatment," a nurse told her.

We're too close to the Earth's crust," said another. You're not ready to go out there. It's too dangerous.

- Be patient. The hospital director told her that when she recovered we would help her locate the person she was looking for.

- But Mirela didn't want to wait. She would make any sacrifice to find Renato. She tried several times and, when she did not get permission, she became angry and furious. She began to do nothing she was asked to do.

- One night, he heard a male voice saying to him:

"I know where Renato is:

- Who is this? I don't see him.

- You can't see me because I'm outside. I can't come in or else they'll arrest me, like they did you.

- Yes, of course they will. Keep hesitating.

- They say that when possible they will help me find Renato.

- Mirela begins to cry inconsolably. The voice continues:

- I can't talk much now. But when everyone is resting, go to the garden and get as close to the wall as you can. I'll be waiting outside and I'll get in touch with you and tell you how to do.

- Okay, I'll go.

- Mirela felt the time passing. However, when she saw that everything was quiet, she went out to the garden next to the wall. At once a voice said softly

- Let's go now.

- As we go out, the wall is high and alarmed.

- Don't worry about that. I have everything prepared. You have to imagine you're on the other side. Do it with all your might. She obeyed and at that very moment she saw herself on the outside. the alarm light flashed and a figure pulled her along as the voice said.

- Let's go before they stop us. he wrapped his arms around her waist and they began to fly quickly. Mirela was breathless with excitement. When she calmed down a bit, she heard a man driving. He was tall, thin and his features were familiar.

- Who are you?

- Just a friend.

- Do you know where Renato is?

- Renato's fine.

He hasn't been very restless because you haven't given him peace.

- How so?

- I couldn't do anything but think about him.

- He was sorry he couldn't stop thinking about me.

- I can't say any more. We have to be calm. We're going through a very dangerous place. You have to cooperate. Imagine you're hiding so no one can see you.

- Mirela obeyed. Then she saw a group of people. With a disheveled and unpleasant physiognomy, she felt a great discomfort. Frightened, she closed her eyes and imagined that no one was watching her.

- Shortly afterwards, her companion said to her:

- You can be calm. We are far away from them, close to our destination.

- What is this place where Renato is?

- It's a group of people working for justice. You will see. After crossing this place where it was very foggy. They saw a medieval fortress. Surrounded by a high wall.

- We arrived

- he said.

- They approached the door. He said his name and a huge door opened and they entered a huge courtyard, where there were many uniformed men walking back and forth in various activities.

Where is Renato? - Mirela asked a little frightened.

He is here, but first we have to talk to Mimo, who is the director, and get permission to see him.

Mirela's heart felt anxious. But at the same time tense. She didn't like it there.

They went to a door that opened and walked down a stone corridor to Mimo's room, who was waiting for them sitting on a cushion.

Victor greeted him and introduced him to Mirela.

- She was Renato's wife and wished to see him. Mimo fixed her piercing eyes and said:

- Sit here beside me trembling she obeyed.

- He wishes to see Renato, but first I must tell him that he is in the custody of a colleague of ours who owes him obedience.

- As I do not understand

- I will refresh your memory. I have already forgotten the adultery you committed and which later ended the life of your first husband.

- Mirela shuddered and felt like running away. She got up in fright.

- Sit down - he ordered her in a firm voice.

- Our organization helps those who suffer injustice and claim their rights Giulio sought us out shortly after you killed him, asking for revenge. He was outraged by your betrayal. He always treated you with respect and did not deserve what you did to him. But you still took his life. So, we gave him our support. For a long time, he tried to do something against you, but he couldn't because the love he felt for his children and the happiness you had prevented him from getting any closer. The love that united you defended you from Giulio's hatred.

- He paused. While Mirela trembled with terror and could not manage to say anything. Then he continued:

- He knew how to wait. When Renato left his body. Giulio was waiting for him at the edge of the grave. We helped him bring him here, he was condemned to serve Giulio as a slave. Now he wants to see him, but we have to ask Giulio's permission.

- He won't let me... Mirela has to stammer.

- Maybe not.

She stood up exclaiming in anguish:

- I don't want to stay here. I have to leave now. I want to go back to where I was. Mimo laughed and snorted his device containing opium and, releasing the smoke, said:

- It's already late. You are already here. You too have a score to settle with Giulio.

Look at her, she tried to run away. But Victor held her back.

- Calm down, don't try to run away. It's better to face it at once. Mirela took a deep breath and answered:

- There's no point in talking to Giulio.

- Take her to him

- Mimo agreed.

- Victor took her by the arm and led her down a dark corridor, then they went down several steps until they reached a dark and fetid subway. They kept walking and little by little she began to make out the cells where there were some prisoners.

- Finally, they stopped in front of one of them. Mirela saw Giulio standing by the door, on the outside. As she realized that Renato was inside.

- In a second Giulio grabbed Mirela by the arm and they saw each other inside the cell, she saw Renato and cried out disconsolately.

- Renato my love. Until I finally find you. He came closer opening his eyes trying to see her.

- Look at her. Where are you? How did you come to this hell?

- I am here, my love.

He vanished into Giulio's arm and ran to embrace Renato - Giulio jumped on top of them separating them violently.

- How do you have the courage to go on facing me like this? It's time to pay for everything you did.

Mirela realized that Renato was in a bad way. Thin, pale, he looked like a shadow of his former self. Unable to contain herself, she screamed:

- Giulio I never imagined you could be so perverse.

- Perverse. You betrayed me, you ended my life. He took my place before you. And my two children. And you still defend him. And I'm the unjust one. He's the evil one. I only do justice.

- We didn't plan what happened. I fell in love with Renato and he fell in love with me. It was stronger than us. We couldn't avoid it.

- If I had known before I would have killed him. But in the end it was me who died with my own gun. But if men's justice has failed mine will not fail.

- It's been a long time since you arrested him. You don't think it's long enough. How far you intend to go with this.

- As far as I want to go. I say I have no desire to set him free. You're not going to make him happy. I guarantee you that. Mirela threw herself at him nervously:

- We love each other. You can't do anything with that.

- I can and I will

- Please, I implore you, let us go. I ask this in the name of the love you once felt for me.

- That love is long gone. It died that day. Today I feel only hate. A lot of hate. Come on, look at her. From now on you're going to serve me.

- I want to be with Renato

- He will stay with me. And on my side you'll have to stay. Come.

- Look at her, she's not leaving. Stay with me. Don't leave me. We have to talk, cried Renato in desperation.

- But Giulio didn't give her time to react, dragged her out and led her to his quarters.

- Here, you will stay with me. From now on you will take care only of me, of my comfort to rejoice in everything I want.

- Remembering all that. Mirela ran her hand over her head as if trying to forget what she had seen.

- During the first few days, she tried to see Renato, but she did not succeed. Then she turned from rebellion to the idea of conquering Giulio to try to get what she wanted. She began to pretend to forget Renato and to show more sympathy for Giulio, pretending to be more interested in his problems. There were times when Giulio was not feeling well. He would have crises of shortness of breath, of anguish when he was pale, he would break out in a cold sweat, he would fall into depression. At those times Mirela would try to help him in the hope that he would become less demanding. She began to notice that when she put her hands on him, rays of green light would come out and envelop him and soon after he would get better. People then discovered that particularity and she began to be asked to help those people. Satisfied that she could do something good, Mirela treated everyone with love and little by little she was seen with affection. Mimo, realizing this activity, allowed her to take charge of a ward and work with those who suffered. That was a great relief for him who received many complaints, many of the inhabitants suffered from some ailment and he did not know what to do. To relieve them. Mirela helped him to have fewer problems and Mimo began to appreciate her.

One afternoon, after having served a few people, Mirela sat thoughtfully, she had been there for a few days, years and during all that time she had felt a lot of remorse for everything she and Renato had done.

She still loved him as much as ever, however, the price they were paying for the crime they had committed was proving too high. If she could turn back time, she would have acted differently. He knew he had no strength to resist that love. But instead of committing adultery, she would have separated from her husband to have a relationship with Renato.

He was thinking about that when he saw a bluish light forming in the corner of the room and the figure of a woman appeared. He recognized her immediately:

Madame Gioconda. You too wish to take revenge on me.

- No, my child. I come in peace. I know you are sorry for what you did to my son Giulio. And you have helped him even though you were filled with hatred.

- Giulio was a good man. It was my fault that he changed so much. Gioconda shook her head negatively and answered:

- If he didn't have so much evil inside he wouldn't have thought of taking revenge. You have helped him a lot. Your hands have been able to heal him. And I am going to ask you to help me while I need to get Giulio out of here. And I could only do it if he wishes it. But he is still gripped by the two voices and if he can forgive or at least forget the revenge, he would agree to come with me.

Tears streamed down Mirela's face, and she responded emotionally:

- Madam, I will do my best to help you. I wish with all my heart that he manages to forgive me and go on his way. Giulio deserves to be happy. One day he will forget me and he will find a woman who will truly love him and be for him the wife that I did not know how to be.

- Thank you very much my daughter. I am sure that in this way you will also conquer your freedom and Renato's freedom.

She left and Mirela, moved, signed the resolution to dedicate herself to obtain Giulio's forgiveness.

From that day on, she began to treat him with more affection and little by little he began to accept her friendship. There were moments when he would forget the past and go back to the way he was before.

One morning when they were together in the classroom, Mirela was teaching Gioconda, she approached Giulio, putting her hands on him.

- Giulio, it's time for you to go your way and me mine. Enough of hatred and blame. I'm sorry for what I did, I won't make that mistake again. Wherever I am but we can't go back and do it differently. It is life that pushes us to move forward. We can't stand still in time. A few days ago your mother asked me for help.

- My mother asked you for help.

I thought you had come to collect from me, but no, you came because you felt my sorrow and she suffers because you got involved out of revenge. Your mother is an enlightened spirit and she suffers for seeing you in this place. She wishes to take you to a better place, where you can find peace, happiness.

- She said she could take you with her when you forget that revenge and forgive us and free yourself from the past.

Giulio remained thoughtful. Happy images of his childhood at his father's house flashed through his mind and he sighed wistfully.

- I'm tired Mirela. No more fights. But you can't get out of here; in the quest for revenge, I acquired obligations towards this group. I may not be able to free myself.

Before Mirela could answer, a bluish clearing formed and Gioconda appeared with outstretched arms.

Giulio threw himself into her arms sobbing like a child.

- Mother, forgive me, forgive me.

- My dear son. May God bless you.

I want to go with you. I am tired of this life.

- Say you don't want war anymore but peace. Free Renato and Mirela and you will be free to go on your way to a better world.

- Giulio looked at Mirela saying moved:

- I forgive you Mirela. I stopped hating you long ago. Now I want to go away and forget all that pain, that hatred that finished me.

- Forgive Renato. Free him too - Mirela asked.

- I forgive him after all the past is dead and I want to move on. At that very moment Renato entered the room and listened to her with admiration.

- Will you release me Giulio?

- Yes, I have forgiven him and I want to forget the past. My mother came to pick me up Gioconda hugged her son and said excitedly:

- At last, he learned to forgive. I thank you for your cooperation. From now on I will do what I can to help you. You can count on me. Now let's go. Stay with God.

She disappeared hugging her son. Renato threw himself into Mirela's arms, kissing her affectionately.

- At last, we are together. I can't imagine how I long for this moment.

- Yes, Renato. We are together. But we still can't get out of here, let's think

- At that moment. Victor appeared at the door saying:

- Mimo is waiting for them to talk. Renato saw Mirela fearful:

- He's not going to let us go:

- Calm down, Renato. He has nothing against us.

- Let's go.

- Said Victor

- Mimo doesn't like to wait.

- Mirela shook Renato's hand and they accompanied Victor.

- They entered the living room where Mimo was waiting for them in the usual place. Victor waved goodbye, designated a sofa in front of him saying:

- Come closer. Sit down. The two obeyed and waited in silence. Mimo

- He sniffed some opium, took a puff and answered aloud.

Giulio deserted and did not fulfill his obligations to our group and, as far as I know, you, Mirela, contributed to his departure. In that case you will have to serve us instead of him.

- You tricked me into bringing me here because of him. It was not I who made the commitment to you.

- But to get rid of him and help Renato, you encouraged him to side with the light. It is only fair that his debt should pass to you..

Renato intervened:

No, we already paid you for our mistakes. We want to take care of our lives.

- You can do that after you pay what you owe us. Renato was about to reply, but Mirela beat him to it:

- It is true that we can pay you that debt.

- Mimo took another drink, let out another puff and then said:

- You will continue some more time curing the ailments of our companions. Renato will go with one of us to do the work that Giulio had to do.

Before Renato answered, Mirela asked:

How long we have to stay here.

- It depends on the performance of each of you. However, it seems to me that you are very eager to get out of here. You do not know life outside these walls, you do not know the dangers you are in. We are surrounded by low vibrational spirits. You should be grateful for allowing them to stay here, protected, sheltered. What do you plan to do out of here?

Renato looked at Mirela without knowing what to say. It was she who answered:

- Maybe she is right. It is better to stay here until we know what to do.

- It's a sensible decision. I'm sure you want to be together. I will find a place for you in our community.

They both said thank you and left. At that moment it seemed like the best decision. From then on, they started living together in a room offered by Mimo and, despite the sadness of the place and the problems around, the two were happy together. Meanwhile, Renato did not like the job he had been assigned. He had to accompany two companions to the earth's crust, doing surveillance work and catching people in the name of justice.

Dissatisfied, he refused to continue this work. It was against his principles. He was threatened with imprisonment and Mirela feared that they would be separated again. She knew that whoever did not obey Mimo's orders was imprisoned and many mysteriously disappeared, terrified, she remembered a promise from Gioconda and mentally asked for help. Hours later she appeared in front of the two saying:

I heard your call. Before I came. I went to consult our major about your case. I heard that Renato is in danger staying here. I came to get him.

- I can't.

- He answered nervously

- I don't want to be separated from Mirela

- I can't take them both with me. Mirela needs to stay here a while longer. She's getting a lot out of the work she's doing here. She can do it from there. But, when the time comes, she can also leave here. Mirela listened to Renato and tried to hold back the tears that kept falling, took a deep breath and said, "Go to her, Renato:

- Go to her, Renato. I don't want anything bad to happen to you.

- The separation will be temporary- Gioconda looked at them and said:

- At the moment it is not possible for them to be together, but the day will come.

when, having overcome their challenges, they will finally be able to see each other. And stay by each other's side. Renato hugged Mirela tightly.

- You heard what Gioconda said. For the moment we can't be together. We have made many mistakes. We have to learn to act better. Today I know that when we become more aware of the true values of the spirit. We can be together and be happy. But now, go with her. Our love will overcome all barriers, don't be afraid.

- He still tried to oppose, but Mirela convinced him.

- Let's go - asked Gioconda

- Mimo sensed my presence. And Victor is on his way here. I can't wait any longer.

- She hugged Renato who with tear-filled eyes agreed to follow her and in a gesture of maro. She blew him an affectionate kiss with her fingertips. As soon as they disappeared, Victor entered saying:

- I'm here to pick up Renato.

- I'm late Victor. He left.

- Victor uttered a few mumbled threats and mumbled. Mirela shrugged her shoulders. She knew Mino wouldn't do anything against her because he needed her badly to keep helping people, which would allow him to have more peace. Some time later, Gioconda sought her out to tell her that Renato had been reincarnated. She felt sad, worried about how long she would have to wait to get him back. To which Gioconda replied:

- He will be back sooner than you think. Due to circumstances, he will not remain in that body for long.

- She was sure Renato would come back, but it was as if he was still far away. She did not remember the past or the love that united them.

- Remembering all that, Mirela wondered anxiously.

- Had she lost Renato forever?

To find an answer, she would have to wait for some time, only the future could tell her.

Chapter X

The following night, a few minutes before the beginning of the work on Father Joseph's land, Márcio entered with his friend.

- Wait here and, when it is time, I will call you - he said.

- Márcio agreed, listened and looked around curiously. It was not the first time he had been on the land and he admired the number of people around him. He could not wait. He was not satisfied with Marcelo's death. He had always dreamed of doing something to avenge him. The time had come and he could not wait.

- Only an hour later Walter called:

- Let's go. Father José is waiting.

- With a pounding heart, Marcio accompanied him. To the sound of drums, several mediums sang while some led by their guides attended to the people.

- Marcio was led to a separate room. Walter had said that Father Jose only attended to cases that other mediums had not resolved, but Walter had asked that he attend to him out of special deference, and the spirit had agreed.

The room was lit by some colored candles and in a corner there was an altar with several images, some herbs and some objects that he did not know. He was standing, dressed in dark clothes, smoking a cigar and as he saw him enter he said to him:

Marcio obeyed and continued:

- How can I help you?

- My brother's wife ran away and left a letter saying she was going to another country. He arrived home without knowing anything, he read the letter, he was so desperate that he went out to see if he could save him, he almost did, he had an accident and died. Marcio felt tears running down his face, but he didn't care. He took a deep breath and continued:

- It was a suffering for my whole family. But Aline, Marcelo's wife, didn't care. She still lives in Miami as if nothing had happened. My brother had a company that was doing very well. He put his sister there to take over what was his. That is not fair. It was because of her that he died. If she hadn't left, he wouldn't have died.

- Why do you need me?

- By law we can't do anything, but you can. My brother was a wonderful husband, he did everything for that woman and she was ungrateful. I want him to realize the mistake he made, to acknowledge his guilt and pay for what he did. I also want Marcelo's assets to return to our family.

Father José took a puff on his cigarette, took a few puffs and remained silent. After a few minutes he said

- Your brother loves that woman very much, but she didn't love him.

- That's the way it is.

- But he is there, by her side. He doesn't care about anything else; he just wants to be with her.

To tell you the truth, we can't do anything against her. He is not going to leave her.

There is no anger for what she did, only sadness.

- It's not fair. He can't love a woman who left him for sure for another man, and who caused his death.

- She is not with another man. She left because she no longer loved him. Marcio ran his hands through his hair, nervous:

- There is no way out. She will remain in good graces and we will continue to suffer for her death.

- With him by her side, she won't be able to be happy, find another man or get ahead in life. He wants her to be just for him. I don't think she should worry. His brother is doing everything, but we can catch his sister in the company. That's doable.

- Then do it Father Joseph.

- Well, you're going to have to bring some things for work. Walter approached with a pad of paper and Father Joseph said:

- What he wanted. Then he put a price on it. Marcio said nervously:

- It's a lot of money. We are facing great difficulties.

- In this case it's better to do nothing. Either we do it right or we don't do it at all.

- I think it will work.

- What I promise I keep. But you have to trust.

- I'll see if I can get the money.

- He left thoughtfully. Father Joseph was describing Marcelo's situation and if life continued even after death, his brother could be at Aline's side. He would never abandon her. However, he did not believe she would suffer. Marcelo would do anything to make her happy. Since he had met her, he had done nothing else. But, on the other hand, Aríete would feel the weight of his anger. That filled him with joy.

Then he arrived home, Ivone was anxiously waiting for him.

- And then, my son in a few words he told her everything and finished:

- Can you believe that despite everything, that fool Marcelo is still by her side, ¿protecting her?

- Ivone shook her head negatively:

- Because if he is conscious in the other world, why would he do the same, do you still think it's worth spending so much money?

Is it worth spending so much money?

- I think in the end it's not fair for that murderer and her family to keep what belonged to Marcelo.

- This is true. However, that Father Joseph is good. We won't spend money in vain.

- Well, Walter says we will. But I don't know.

His father won't want him. You know how he is with money.

- But if we do nothing, everything will stay as it is.

- That's true. But I know his father won't give the money, we don't have the means to pay.

- In fact, we have to convince him.

- Later, when João comes home. They tried to convince him to give him the money. But João refused

- That holy father is trying to exploit us. Marcio objected

- But dad, that's nothing compared to what Marcelo's signature is worth.

- You talk as if they can change the laws. I don't think that man will get what he promises.

- Well, I think it's worth a try," Ivone interjected. Money is never too much. Then it will be a way to punish those people who disgraced our son.

- I don't know, it sounds crazy to me. The lawyer assured me that nothing could be done. I'm definitely not going to give that money. It's better to give up these superstitions.

- They wanted to insist, but João cut them off:

- I'm not going to give in on this matter. I don't want to hear any more about it. The next day, when Marcio met Walter, he went and asked him immediately.

Then they raised the money.

- No, my father won't give me any. He says it's useless, that it won't work.

- He says that because he doesn't understand these things. I, who have gone there, I can say that people are very happy with what they have received there.

- I know if I had that money. I would do it all, but I am a student, I depend on my father.

- And his mother can't get a loan. From some friend. In the end, it's not such a big amount.

- I'll talk to her. I know my aunt will lend me. Let's see.

- You do it. When you get the money back. You can pay it back with interest. In the meantime. Aline continued to work hard at her position in the organization, trying to regain her joie de vivre.

- Three months ago, she and Rachel were attending a paranormal course at the Ferguson Institute and studying psychotic phenomena. Ferguson and studying psychotic phenomena. Considering the claim that life continues after death, she had become very frightened because she knew that if Marcelo was still living. on the other side of life, he would not be separated from her.

- One night, at the end of class. She was very distressed and went to talk to the professor.

- Can you spare me a few minutes of your time?

- I can do it. Let's go to another room.

- Aline accompanied him in silence. Once seated in the room across from him, she said nervously:

- Dr. Morris, today's class made me very nervous.

- Why?

- In a few words Aline told her story. And she finished

- I'm sure Marcelo is still by my side. I'm afraid. I don't know how to face it. attachment.

- It has always bothered me, it was the same when he was alive, now it scares me. Dr. Morris smiled, showing a row of nice, straight teeth. He was an elegant older man, with lively eyes, gray hair and a lot of sympathy.

- Calm down. You can do no wrong.

- He showed up on the plane, he was horrible, saying he was never going to leave me again. I thought it was a nightmare, now I think it was himself. Wounded from the crash, dripping blood. He was horrible.

I tried to remember him as when he was here and well I didn't feel that image. Surely the spirit of him. He must be better by now.

- But I don't want him near me. What can I do to avoid him.

- Keep doing energetic treatments. I am sure our spiritual friends who help us at eta Institution will talk to him, making him see that it is time for him to take care of himself and that he must accept the separation.

Aline shook her head, dejected.

- He won't accept it, he's too stubborn.

- But you can help us a lot by having the right attitude.

- What can I do?

- Talk to your spirit. When you feel something different, like chills, sadness, pain, anger, without any justifiable reason, imagine that your husband is in front of you and have a conversation, explain to him why you have left him, talk to him about your feelings, ask him to follow his own path and let you follow yours. People are free to follow what life wants from them and when the time comes they have to leave him and there is nothing that can stop it.

- It would be very good for Marcelo to understand that.

- He speaks sincerely. I think the same when I think that even if people like to be together, there will come a time when they will have to stop.

- It would be very good for Marcelo to understand that

- He speaks sincerely. I thought the same thing about people. I think that even though people like to be united, there will come a time.

In that each one will have to go to one side, learn new things, renew energies, develop his potential. happy of the one who loves and at that moment manages to release the loved one freeing him so that both can mature.

- I will do it with all my heart so that Marcelo may continue in peace. I thank him for his affection as he always treated me, I wish him to be very happy, however, I confess that I did not know how to love him as he deserved.

- Don't blame yourself, everyone is as he is. Her spirit longed to grow, she was not satisfied with living a life as her husband wanted.

- It's true, he smothered me, trying to guess what I was thinking, what I wanted, he called me several times during the day and I didn't feel free to do what I wanted. I didn't want big adventures, but I wanted to enjoy the pleasure of taking a walk, without having to say what I was doing. Explaining where I was, the schedule or what to eat, where to go.

- I know what that's like. Excessive attachment cripples the chance you have to be happy next to him.

- I am relieved, thank you for listening to me. I'm going to take your advice.

- You do that. I would like to accompany you in that case. Anything different that happens, look me up.

- Aline said goodbye and left the room calmer. She found Rachel in the bookcase:

- Where was she? I looked for her everywhere.

- She was talking to a professor to clear up some doubts.

- About the class.

- No, about my personal problem. Knowing that life continues after death made me uneasy. The presence of Marcelo's spirit at my side frightened me. Dr. Morris listened to me, taught me how to deal with the situation. I feel more relieved.

- That's a good thing. The opposite happened to me. It was gratifying to know that death is not the end and that we will still be alive somewhere when our time comes. In the end, we will all, someday, have to face that fatality. The two left the Institute talking animatedly. On the street they separated and each went to her car.

- That night they had not arranged to go out and Aline decided to stop at the supermarket because her grocery store was empty.

- She left the car in the parking lot, went inside, grabbed a shopping cart and started to choose some products. the immense variety and the neat layout caught her attention. He ended up buying more than he needed.

Satisfied, she paid the cashier and headed for the parking lot. As she was putting the groceries in the cart she heard a few clicks and someone jumped on her saying:

- Come on down, let's go.

Startled, Aline obeyed and heard the footsteps of people running, she mentioned to get up, but the man who had jumped on her was still crouched down with his left hand on her ribs and she realized that in his right hand he was carrying a revolver.

Her heart raced, her legs trembled, but she managed to stammer:

- Who are you?

- Stay still, don't get up. I am a policeman. Aline obeyed. A few more shots, people running, screaming. And finally, someone shouted.

- Everything under control.

- The man stood up, looked around and turned to Aline:

- Everything is fine, you can get up now.

- Aline stood up on shaky legs. In front of her stood a tall, dark, brown-haired man with green eyes. He looked to be in his thirties, wore an elegant gray suit and listened with a smile on his face.

- Shortly after, uniformed and handcuffed policemen, two boys stood inside a vehicle.

Two policemen approached saying:

- Good time, Gino. As usual you acted fast - then looking at Aline he continued - you came out suddenly and my colleague didn't have time to stop you. You could have been shot.

- I didn't see anything. How could I know if I was in danger? I was shopping in a supermarket.

Gino intervened:

- The action was very fast and you were distracted. Aline, a little calmer, looked at Gino and smiled slightly:

- Thank you, you saved me.

- The policeman drove away, joining his colleagues, and the car left the scene.

- My name is Gino Marchione.

- Aline D'Angelo.

- Italian name, like mine.

- My grandparents were Italian. I am Brazilian.

- My grandparents are also Italian. They came to America many years ago. Aline looked around for a car with the rest of her shopping that had disappeared.

- I saw where she was going.

- She walked away and came right back bringing a car and lifting the trunk of the car that had come down when he pushed her.

- Thank you once again

- To tell you the truth, I think I'll be leaving here soon. Rest assured that nothing else is going to happen.

- I have done it. The two who tried to rob a market and are in jail. But if you wish we can go somewhere else.

- Thank you, but I'd better go home.

- In that case I'll go with you.

- Don't worry, it's not necessary

- You're nervous. And it doesn't cost me anything to follow to your home.

- I live nearby.

- All the more reason to take her. I want to see her safe at home. Aline agreed and got into the car. The spirit of Marcelo, who accompanied her throughout, was angry.

- Gino's interest in Aline was not lost on him and he noticed her thoughts about Gino. She found him attractive, pleasant. Accompanying her everywhere, he had never noticed her being attracted to either of the two boys she talked to. However, he didn't know what it was. But there was something new in the atmosphere that made her uneasy. That Gino is dangerous. She would do anything to keep him away from Aline. During the ride she watched Gino. He was a beautiful man, his eyes were

Piercing his face was strong, but when he smiled, his physiognomy resembled that of a kitten. Marcelo shifted nervously in his seat. Why was Aline thinking so much about this intruder?

- He arrived home, pulled into the garage and Gino, who had stopped in the middle of the sidewalk, got out of the car. Aline signaled him to enter through the front door, then got out of the car, turned around and Gino was waiting for her in the hallway.

- Do you want me to help you load the groceries? Aline thought about it for a while and then answered:

- Only if you agree to have coffee with me.

- Done

- Marcelo felt like pouncing on him. But he restrained himself. He wanted to know how far they would go.

- The two of them loaded their suitcases and headed for Aline's apartment, who opened the door and invited him in.

- If he had known he would have company, he would have bought something special.

- That coffee is already special.

Aline smiled:

- You saved my life. You deserve more than that.

- She left a bag on the sofa and went to make coffee. Gino watched her with interest.

- She set out the cups, a pot of cream, sugar and some cookies. The delicious smell of coffee filled the room and Aline took the pot out of the kettle and poured it for herself.

- With sugar, cream?

- With two.

- I'll have two too.

- They sat down to savor the coffee

- I can't forget what happened

- I was inside my car, parked a little behind his. I was waiting for the assailants to come out. When they ran and tried to get into the car, I came out with a gun in my fist. They saw me and I felt they were going to shoot, and you were placing your purchases in the car. I pounced on you in time, happily the police showed up and I managed to stop them.

- You are not in uniform.

- No. I belong to the intelligence sector of the police. And have you been in Miami long?

- Just a few months. I was hired by a company here to work.

- Your family came too.

- I didn't come alone.

- Aline thought of Marcelo and a shadow of sadness clouded her face. Gino noticed:

- You became sad all of a sudden, did you leave any love in Brazil?

- No, I was married, but my husband died in a car accident.

- I am so sorry for that. You came here to forget that loss.

- Ever since I was a little girl I dreamed of coming to live in this city.

Marcelo looked at them angrily. She spoke as if she had never loved him. Ungrateful. She forgot the moments of happiness they enjoyed together. She has no courage to say that she ran away from home like a criminal and that her deranged gesture had caused her husband's death.

The two continued chatting, talking about the city, its customs, the differences between Brazil and the United States, comparing them with Europe. Aline felt at ease, as if she had known Gino for a long time. Meanwhile, she had the feeling that this dinner had happened somewhere before. Marcelo was restless, wishing Gino would leave, though he didn't seem to be in a hurry. He steeled himself by saying in his ear.

- You are abusing. Go away now, don't talk anymore. Where do you think you are? I don't want you here. Aline is mine, very much mine.

Gino felt a certain uneasiness and shifted in his chair:

- The conversation is so pleasant that I think I'm abusing. I'm in your way.

- No, I was planning to stay home tonight.

- If you have something to do you can go now.

- Don't worry about it. If I wanted to be alone, you can be sure I'd tell you. Since I'm here. But, as we've already said, customs in Brazil are different from those in the United States. My friends are great, good companions, but they relate in their own way. You, on the other hand, may be of Italian descent, you are very similar to Brazilians We both know each other and it seems to me as if we were great friends a long time ago. 130

- I'm glad to know because I feel the same way too. I have the impression that I know her and that we have already been talking together. Marcelo was pacing back and forth nervously. He had to do something, to get that intruder out of there. He approached Gino, looking at him angrily, and said in his ear.

- Get out of here right now. I don't want you to come back," he continued, noticing Gino's shuddering. Go now. I don't want you to stay. You have to leave now.

- Marcelo touched Gino so angrily that he felt a sharp pain in his stomach.

- What happened," asked Aline, "You've gone pale.

- It was nothing. I felt shivers.

- Aline thought of Marcelo. He was there. Worried, she said:

- It's late, you'd better go.

- You are safe. But, I want your pone

- Aline took her purse and they exchanged cards. Then he said goodbye, kissing her lightly on the face.

- Aline shivered and felt a surge of warmth invade her body. He left and she prepared for sleep.

- Her thoughts were with Gino. She remembered every gesture, every word they had exchanged. She recognized that he was very attractive. Marcelo was very angry. Aline was interested in someone else. She thought he was dead, even though she knew he was "alive", he was her husband and she couldn't do that.

- She went to bed thinking about Gino. And she sat on the bed next to her, worried. How could she do to get Gino out of her way forever.

Chapter XI

It had been a week since she had met Gino and, despite her interest in getting his phone number, he had not called her.

Aline was a little disappointed. After a long time she was attracted to him and was looking forward to his call.

No doubt, he had deceived her. He did not feel the same interest as she did. She decided to forget about him.

Marcelo was satisfied, worried, tried by various means to involve him in work complications until his boss sent him to another city to conduct an investigation.

If it were up to Marcelo, Gino would never return to Aline's apartment. Upon arriving at the company, Aline was met by Raquel, who asked her.

- What happened to your phone. I tried to talk to you last night and couldn't get through. A telephone operator told me you were off the line.

- I noticed that in the last two days it hasn't rung once. I will ask the concierge in my building to check.

- Some friends called me to invite me to dinner and since I didn't answer I ended up going alone.

After checking the phone, Aline thought maybe Gino had tried to call. She felt more encouraged. If so, she could still call.

In the late afternoon, when she got home, Aline went to the doorman and asked for the phone. Aline went to the doorman and asked for the phone.

- I went to check, but there was nothing. Everything was fine.

- My friend tried to talk to me last night and couldn't. I'm sure it works fine. I'm sure it's working fine.

- I had it tested. When it comes in, you'll see it's perfect.

- Aline went into the house, picked up the phone and it worked perfectly, Marcelo who was waiting at home smiled. That phone would never work again. Not while Gino was trying to call.

He had tried several times, even while out of town. Marcelo hoped Gino would give up.

Aline took a bath, was preparing something to eat when the doorbell rang. She went to open it and found Gino and blushed with pleasure.

- I'm sorry I came unannounced, I had been trying to talk to you for a few days. Your phone was out of order. And I was working out of town.

- In fact, my phone wasn't working. You were right to come. I went in. He came in, kissed her gently on the face and said:

- I was anxious to talk to you.

- I waited for you to call me.

- I arrived this afternoon and came immediately. Would you like to have dinner with me?

- I was preparing an appetizer.

- Save it for tomorrow, keep me company and have dinner with me.

- I'll be fine. In the meantime, sit down and I'll tidy up a bit.

- Marcelo looked at the two of them angrily. Aline was in high spirits. And she was grooming herself with care. When Gino returned to the living room, she stood up:

- You look very pretty.

- Thank you.

Aline was beaming with joy. Marcelo didn't understand. Why she was so in love with this stranger. She had only met him once. He never thought Aline was so fickle.

Nervous, he tried to stop them from going out. He approached her, saying nervously.

- You're my wife. You can't go out with him. You're being frivolous, I don't want you to go out.

But his energies didn't even come close to her. Because he failed to convince her Then he approached Gino saying:

- Go away now. Leave her alone. She's engaged and can't go out with you. Like Aline, Gino felt nothing, he continued to feel the pleasure of her company.

- They went out and Marcelo accompanied them. They went to a nice restaurant with live music and dance floor.

- The two had dinner and then went dancing. Seeing them embraced, Marcelo was not satisfied, why couldn't he separate them?

- He sent negative energies on them, wanting them to feel bad, to stop and leave now. But try as he might, he got nothing. The two were still cheerful, happy, feeling at ease together. Aline, in Gino's arms, let herself be enveloped by the romantic music, and it seemed natural to her when he pulled her close to his chest, resting his face against hers. Then time stood still for them. Aline didn't want the night to end. At first she was a little frightened by the force of attraction she felt. But then she gave herself to the pleasure of the moment noticing that Gino also felt the same.

- It was past one in the morning when they left the restaurant. Sitting by the car Aline commented:

- What a lovely place. I love it.

- The place alone

- The company contributed.

- I was afraid she wouldn't say that. She smiled in satisfaction. She continued:

- We have to do it again or what do you think.

- Of course, we have to do it.

- Tomorrow

- She thought a little about the answer

- Today you will say. She laughed.

- Why not?

- Let's go see.

They got home and he walked her to the door.

- Now you won't drink my coffee

- It's already late I'll leave it for another day

He opened the door and held out his hand:

Good night.

He hugged her and kissed her on the lips for a long time. Aline felt her legs trembling and her heart pounding.

Good night," he replied, "dream of me. I will dream of you. She kissed his hand gently as she entered and closed the door, still breathless. She could not remember ever having felt such an emotion.

As she prepared for sleep, she recalled all the moments of that encounter with pleasure and excitement.

In a corner of the room, Marcelo felt unsatisfied. He needed to do something else, but what?

He remembered Victor. Maybe he could help him. He thought about looking for him, but he was afraid he wouldn't find where he lived. He thought of him insistently. Until, to her satisfaction, she saw him enter the room.

- I'm glad you came; I need you to help me.

- I knew that was going to happen. I told her. She's young, she thinks she'll be content to stay alone.

- But I don't want to. You have to help me separate them. I tried and I didn't succeed. Why?

- Maybe because love is too strong.

- That love I don't think I can love him. You've only seen him twice.

- That's what you think. Maybe you know each other from other lives.

- I don't accept that. Aline is mine and I'm not going to leave her for someone else. You say your friends have power, I'm sure they can help me separate them.

- That depends.

- That who can provide some services to the community.

- I'm willing to do whatever it takes.

- But you don't want to give it up. It is impossible Marcelo thought a little later and answered:

- If necessary, if you can assure me that she won't stay with him, I'll make any sacrifice.

- In that case let's talk to Mimo.

- Now.

- It's not late, tomorrow night I'll come for him. It can wait.

- I'm in a hurry.

- I need to talk to Mimo first, see if he can take care of us.

- That'll be fine. I'll be waiting.

- Victor left and Marcelo stayed with Aline, who was sleeping peacefully, looking at her in amazement. He could not accept that she belonged to someone else. He approached her, although he could not touch her lips, he placed them on her with passion. Aline shuddered, felt Marcelo' presence, returned to her body frightened and saw the bed tilted.

Aline's face and wanted to scream, but she did not manage to make a sound. When she managed to open her eyes, she looked around but saw no one. She turned on the lamp light, got up and drank a glass of water. She was trembling, terrified.

Marcelo was still there. She remembered the advice she had been given at the Institute.

- She tried to talk to him, to convince him to leave and seek spiritual help.

- If you can't, pray, ask our guides for help. Aline closed her eyes and prayed for protection from the spirits.

- from the spirits. Marcelo was sad about their relationship. Why he was afraid of her. He wanted to tell her that he was still alive, that he would always protect her. Cora's spirit entered and Marcelo cowered in a corner of the room, wanting to go unnoticed.

- Cora approached Aline, put her hands on her head and beams of bright blue light shot out from them and enveloped her. Aline felt a soft warmth in her body and calmed down.

In the end, she had been told that Marcelo wanted to protect her and that he would never make her year. Then she felt sleepy, but didn't have the courage to go back to bed. She grabbed a pillow and a blanket and went to lie down on the sofa in the living room.

Cora approached Marcelo, who was looking at her regressively.

- How are you Marcelo?

- If you've come to take me away, you can forget it. I'm not leaving Aline.

- I don't want to force her into anything. But I think it would be much better for both of us if you came with me. I can take you to a very good place that would help you balance yourself.

- I will never leave Aline. She belongs to me.

- That's an illusion. No one belongs to anyone. Everyone is is self-owner. You'd save yourself a lot of trouble if you'd come with me now.

- You want to separate me from her.

- No, I want you to be well, to understand what happened and to be able to really help you.

- Don't insist. I don't want to and I won't go.

- Your will be done.

- He walked away, passed by the living room, saw Aline sleeping peacefully and left. Marcelo stood there, pensive, without the courage to go to see Aline in the living room. That woman was powerful. He saw the lights coming from her hands. He remembered Mirela. She, too, emitted lights, though less bright. But they had healed her wounds. His friends were also powerful and were willing to help him stay by Aline's side. That was all he wanted. The next night. Gino called Aline to go out, but she didn't want to go out with him. She felt married, worried about Marcelo' presence in her house. She feared that he was still angry with Gino and would somehow hurt her. However, they continued to talk for a long time. Aline felt more attracted to him and realized that it was reciprocal. Gino was an intelligent and cultured man, whose easy and pleasant conversation delighted Aline. Marcelo watched angrily without being able to intervene. He tried with all his might, but he could not get close to Aline. It was as if there was a barrier around him. And no matter how hard he tried, he could not overcome it. It was eleven o'clock at night when Victor arrived and Marcelo hurried to greet him and ask him questions:

- So, I talk to Mimo. Is he going to help me?

- I don't know. But he'll see us today. Come on, he will.

- I think it's good. Things around here are bad. That meddling woman came back, she wanted to take me, but I wouldn't. After last night I don't know what she did, I couldn't get close to Aline.

- He made a barrier

- That's right. There's no way to end this.

- Your wife is protected by it. It's better not to do anything for the moment. Let's talk to Mimo.

- They set off. An hour later they arrived at the fortress. They entered and were led to the room of Mimo who greeted them like the other time.

- Do you want to talk to me? - he asked

- I need your help.

- In a few words Marcelo told him what was going on. Mimo was silent for a few seconds. Then he answered:

- You know we work in barter.

- Yes, I know that. I am willing to collaborate.

- I don't know if you are really .... In the end you are so attached to your wife that it may not work out.

- If you promise me you'll get that guy out of there. I'll do whatever it takes.

- For that. You'll have to stay here and prove you're telling the truth.

- How's that sound?

- Stay and do the first service, then we'll do our part. At that moment, Marcelo felt that this situation had happened to him before. He saw Mimo in front of him, his body was different, but he knew it was the same. It was quick and then everything went back to the way it was before. But he was a little scared.

- Then he agreed.

- Yes.

- I already have a service for you. You will stay here until it is finished. Victor, in the next room if it's unoccupied. Take him there and let him know the rules. I'll call him tomorrow with instructions.

- They left the room and Victor considered it:

- The boss accepted him. He'll get what he wants.

- Stay calm.

- I've got it. But you have to do everything he tells you. Discipline is rigid here. They returned to the courtyard and Victor took him to his room. He handed him a list of disciplines, schedules. Then he said to him:

- I am tired. I'm going to my room. Tomorrow I'm sure you'll have a busy day.

- When he left, Marcelo looked around. It was a small, dark room, with a single bed, a table and two chairs. There were no decorative objects. From the ceiling, a yellowish light left a sadder atmosphere.

- Marcelo lay on the bed thinking about Aline. About what she was doing. She would have gone out with Gino. It was likely, but soon. They would be separated. He was sure of it.

- He closed his eyes and tried to rest. At that instant Mirela's face appeared before him.

- The nurse

- He thought

- After that time, she looked different, younger, prettier and Marcelo felt like kissing her.

- Since he met Aline, he had never been attracted to any woman. What was wrong with him?

- Mirela approached him and he was swept up in a whirlwind of emotions, embraced her and threw himself into her arms. They were in a luxurious old house and kissed passionately. They went to bed and Marcelo lost track of time. He spent a whole night reliving that passion.

- He woke up and thought it was a dream. Victor opened the bedroom door and said seriously: "What happened, it's past time.

- What happened, it's past time. He did not read the recommendations

- Marcelo jumped up

- I'm sorry, I don't know what happened to me. I had some exquisite dreams, I lost track of time.

- Victor looked at him curiously. He noticed that he looked somewhat different. The features of his face had changed. Was he remembering the past?

He would like to know his own past, but so far he had not been able to. He had returned from the world over sixty years ago and remembered nothing of his past.

- Hurry up. Mimo is waiting for you.

Marcelo got up, dressed quickly and accompanied Victor. As they crossed the courtyard, Marcelo felt an unpleasant sensation and stopped.

- What was that? - Asked Victor.

- I don't feel well. I want to get out of here.

- Why? We are your friends, forget it. We'll help you in any way you want.

- Marcelo remained thoughtful for a few moments and then asked:

- Where are the prisoners?

- Who told you we have prisoners here?

- No one. I see bleachers and people behind them.

- You're seeing too much. I don't think you've woken up here.

- On the contrary, I think I'm waking up now. I think I've been here before and my stay wasn't good.

- You're confusing things. I brought you here the first time you remember.

- I remember. I didn't know it at the time. Now I feel like I know this place. I want to leave. I'm not going to talk to Mimo.

- You're not going to make such an offense to him who is waiting for us. It's better if we go and talk, explain to him what's going on. He'll clear everything up for you.

- I'm scared.

- I guarantee it. Nothing is going to happen. We are going to talk to him. Afterwards, if he wants to leave, let him go. But he can't leave without giving any satisfaction. He may get offended and angry. It would be very cruel of him.

- All right, I'm going but then I'll go.

Victor agreed. They went into Mimo's room, who was still sitting on his cushion, like the other times, smoking and puffing away. When they approached, Marcelo stared at him and immediately shouted.

- I remember you. You locked me in that dark, smelly prison and allowed me to torment myself.

Mimo stared at him and replied calmly.

- I made a deal with Giulio and I kept it. To this day I don't know how he escaped. I imagine someone took him away on the sly. Probably an emissary of the lamb. But it was useless to hide him among the meat. He came back by his own means.

- I came back because I didn't know anything. But now I want to leave. I don't want to ask you anything more.

- It's late because an emissary of mine is already working at Aline's side. To separate her from that man as she asked.

- Marcelo wrung his hands in pain. In his mind, the scenes of his dream mingled with the affection he felt for Aline. He was confused, what was happening to him? He must be going crazy.

- You are not crazy - said Mimo.

- You are confused about what happened in the past, about the present. But now you love Aline and you want to keep her.

- Aline is mine. I want to keep her.

- So why does he want to quit? He is falling in love with someone else. He wants her to marry him. If we don't do anything that's going to happen.

- No. I don't want to. Aline is mine.

- Then - continued Mimo in a soft voice - We can get it for you.

- You can start again.

- No. My engagement with Giulio is over. I have nothing against you. Unless you don't keep the deal we made.

- Marcelo remained thoughtful for a few moments and then answered:

- It's all right if that one like that. I will do as you wish. But I want your word that you will set me free afterwards.

- He has already told you that. However, you need to cooperate, lend us your services.

- All right. What should I do?

- Sit down. I'll explain.

- Marcelo sat down and waited attentively for what I was going to tell him

Chapter XII

Aline looked at herself in the mirror and smiled in satisfaction. She looked beautiful in her blue silk dress, her hair loose and neatly combed, her eyes sparkling with pleasure.

Gino would be looking for her for dinner and she was very cheerful. She seemed to be back in her teens.

The doorbell rang and she went to open the door and saw that it was Gino, he was very elegant. He kissed her on the face saying:

- You look very pretty.

- You look very elegant. Do you want to come in for a while?

- If you are ready, we can go. I want to take you to a very nice place. Let's have dinner, dance and watch the sunrise.

- We can go.

Aline grabbed her purse and they went out. She felt that there was something special about that night. There was something in the air that made her happy, joyful.

Gino looked at her and in her eyes he could notice a new brightness, which made her physiognomy softer, tender.

The night was warm, the sky was clear, cloudless, and the stars were shining around a beautiful full moon.

They went to a place by the sea, with a balcony overlooking the water and the view was wonderful.

The lights of the houses were reflected in the water, the illuminated yachts were passing in the distance, it became a more beautiful landscape.

The enameled balcony, the open windows, under which were vases with flowers, some tables, inside the hall, more tables. An ensemble played behind the dance floor, and soft, semi-dark lighting further embellished the decor. Making the atmosphere dreamy.

Sitting on the balcony. Aline couldn't contain her admiration.

How beautiful.

I think so too.

They sat down, ordered a drink and Gino started talking.

- I don't know what's wrong with me. I'm thirty-five years old. I'm an experienced man. However, since we've known each other I do nothing but think about you. I'd like to tell you many things, but when I'm near you I get excited, I can't say what I'd like to say.

I know what it feels like

- to be attracted to me.

- I'm sorry. And to be honest, it scares me a little bit.

- Why? You don't trust me.

- We've only known each other for a short time. I don't know what you're really like. He took her hand and brought it to his lips affectionately,

- I have the impression that I've known you for a long time. For me it's like a reunion.

- That week at the Institute. Aline heard a lot of talk about past lives and those words gave her the confidence to make him believe it could be true. She also felt she could trust him.

- Maybe we had met in other lives. He looked at her and asked her seriously:

- Do you believe in past lives?

- I have been studying the subject at the Ferguson Institute. I had heard about it.

- I was there last year, taking some courses.

- What a coincidence!

- This topic interested me since my four year old nephew began to say that he used to be called Álvaro and that he had been my grandfather's father, who had that name. At first we thought he was making it up, then he mentioned certain events that had happened with my great-grandfather, some known to my grandfather and never mentioned in the family, we were intrigued.

- So, we went to the Institute.

- I went and discovered much more than I had gone looking for. I found evidence of life after death and that radically changed the way I looked at life. My nephew today at seven years old how he grew up. He no longer mentions the subject. In fact, in the course I took they told me that it could happen. And why did you come to the Institute?

- Now I would not like to mention the subject. I'll tell you all about it later.

- That's all right. I noticed sadness in her eyes. If he doesn't want to, he doesn't need to say it. Let's order for dinner and dance. I want you to feel cheerful and happy. She smiled.

- I am happy.

- They placed the order and went to dance. In his arms she felt protected and a sense of pleasure enveloped her, moved by the romantic music and the beauty of the place.

- It was two in the morning when they left the restaurant. In the car, Gino hugged and kissed her several times. Then, resting her head on his chest Aline. She began to talk and told him all about her.

Life. Her dreams, her wedding. the will to change and why I look for the institute and finish:

Since I was there I feel more protected. I don't dream about him anymore and I don't feel afraid. I continue to study. I want to know more, I need to understand life better. I felt guilty about the accident I was a victim of. But now I know that I was not to blame for anything and that relieves me a lot.

- I think the love I felt for him was not strong enough to make him forget his projects.

- In fact, it started from our marriage. I criticized myself because he showered me with attention, he showed me so much love that I always felt I was lacking because I couldn't give him what he deserved.

- What he felt for me was attachment. For him, you were a crutch he leaned on.

- I had never seen him that way. In fact, he would not decide anything without consulting me first. And when I didn't support him, he would give up.

- You married him and lived seven years without love, but out of gratitude for how he treated you. He manipulated you in such a way that you felt obliged to reciprocate. However, that didn't satisfy you and you couldn't take it anymore.

- In fact, I was at my limit. Every night, when he came into the house, he even felt a certain aversion and criticized me because he didn't deserve it. I was the bad one.

- Gino held her close to his chest and kissed her hair affectionately.

- You did very well to get out of that vicious circle that made you unhappy. Love is not that. It is joy, companionship, friendship, where everyone has the freedom to be as they are.

- Your words make me understand better everything that happened. They take a weight off my heart. No one can love out of obligation. Love is spontaneous, it seems.

Gino kissed her long on the lips and then said with a voice that drove her crazy with emotion

- I am feeling that at this moment we have found love. He is going to illuminate our lives from now on.

- She didn't answer, but as they kissed again, she felt that it was true. That she had finally found love.

- Meanwhile, in São Paulo, Marcio arrived home satisfied and looked for Ivone.

- In the end the aunt gave me the money.

- Your father can't know, otherwise he'll be the devil himself.

- We don't need to tell him. I asked him to keep it a secret.

- But how are we going to pay him?

- Don't worry. She also believes in the insolence they did with everything that belonged to Marcelo. She said we can pay when we can. That very night I'm going to take him to the land.

- Let's see if it works. Your father says it's impossible.

- Don't be negative. They say we have to believe.

- I'm going to try.

- That same night, Marcio returned to the place and delivered the money. He talked to Father José, who agreed to do everything as quickly as possible. Satisfied, he returned home. He did not see that two dark shadows accompanied him, satisfied.

- That's the way to do it - said one smiling

- It's more than ripe. But if it weren't for the fact that I work for the aunt, she wouldn't have given me the money. She's stingy as only she can be.

- Marcio didn't notice anything different. In his mind he saw what he would do with the money when his brother's property returned to his hands. Then his father would see that he was right.

- A few days later, Aríete arrived at the company a few days earlier, she had prepared a demo report for Rodrigo and wanted to present it to him before he started working on the projects, because when he started something he did not like to be interrupted.

- Shortly after, when he arrived, she was already waiting for him and after greeting him I asked him to come into her office.

- Once there, sitting across from each other, she presented him with a report where he could clearly see the positive results of those months of work.

- I knew we were growing, but I didn't expect so much.

- He said satisfied.

- I thought this last project was wonderful. You really have talent.

- Her eyes sparkled and Rodrigo realized how beautiful she was. Her presence in the office had helped to harmonize the atmosphere. The clients admired her and she had a special way of treating them, with class and respect, that gave her company a look of efficiency and capability and inspired confidence.

- He put his hand on her hand saying

- Without you I wouldn't have gotten any of this. Thank you for coming to help me.

- I do it for my sister.

- I know, but by doing this you have helped me. When Marcelo died, I felt aimless. Beyond having lost a childhood friend. I don't understand anything about the administrative part.

- I would understand if I wanted to, I understand that anyone could do it while the projects you do, it would be hard to find someone with that ability.

- Don't repeat that I can believe it.

- My mother would like you to come to our house for dinner on Saturday. She says she misses you. After Marcelo's death, you didn't come home.

- Taken by surprise, Rodrigo looked at her seriously and did not answer soon. Aríete stared at him and asked

- Were you sorry for what Aline did?

- That's not the point. Marcelo's family is not satisfied with what happened. They have come to ask me why you work with me. Then I'd rather not go to his house or yours.

- Do you also believe that Aline is guilty of Marcelo's death?

- Of course, I was surprised. I thought they were living in the lap of luxury. After they got married, I moved away from the couple a bit. I am single, not engaged to anyone and married, their lives were different. A married person needs privacy.

- I understand that.

- However, I reflected afterwards and thought that things must not have been as good as they seemed to me. I preferred not to judge. I wasn't inside her to know how she felt.

- If you'd rather not go to our house. Go ahead, Mom will understand.

- I like Doña Dalva. I don't want her to think that I have anything against her family. But if I go to her house. I wouldn't have to go to Mr. João's house.

- Do as you wish.

- Don't resent me.

- Don't worry. I'm not that touchy. Now, I'm going back to work. After Aríete left the room. Rodrigo ran his hand through his hair thoughtfully. It didn't feel right to turn down the dinner invitation. In the end, it was Aline who acted badly, her family was not to blame. He knew how shocked they were by what had happened.

- He sat down in front of the table where he worked ready to forget the whole thing, but it wasn't easy.

- He concentrated all his attention on the design and began to work. Shortly thereafter, Aríete's assistant nervously entered the room:

- Doctor Rodrigo, run. Mrs. Aríete has fallen down the stairs and can't get up.

- Rodrigo ran out and found her on the floor moaning in pain.

- I think I've broken something. It hurts a lot.

- I'm going to take her to the hospital.

- He turned to the assistant:

- Pick up my folder that's on the chair. Take it to the parking lot. Then he bends down and asks:

- Where does it hurt?

- My right arm and leg.

- Put your arm around my neck and I will take you to the car. She obeyed. Carefully he put his arm around her waist and she moaned a little.

- Have a little patience. You'll be relieved later. Fortunately the parking lot is on the same floor. Neusa, the assistant, was already waiting for her by the car with the requested folder.

- She opens the folder, takes the car key out of the zipper and unlocks the back door. With trembling hands, Neusa obeyed Rodrigo and placed Aríete stretched out on the bench. She then climbed into the car and sped to the hospital, which was not far away.

- Once there, Rodrigo spoke to the traumatologist, who incidentally was an acquaintance of his, to ask him to treat her. They took X-rays and found that her arm was dislocated, but her leg was broken.

- Rodrigo accompanied her in solidarity, holding her hand when the pain was worse.

- Two hours later, with her leg in a cast from ankle to knee and her arm bandaged and suspended, she was discharged. There was no need for hospitalization. Two shadowy figures watched her from afar, exchanging laughter and words with each other.

- This is going to go on for a while.

- We can rest. In a few days we'll come back to figure out what we'll do when she recovers.

- Let's go. This place is guarded, we can't get in and the sooner we leave, the better.

- Rodrigo installed Aríete in the front seat, since he could not climb in the back.

- I'm going to take her home.

- You should have called my mother and she would have taken a cab and come and picked me up.

- Somehow. She would freak out and then I want to take her home, and see if everything's okay.

- But you didn't want to go there.

- Well, I was wrong. You can't be responsible for what happened with Marcelo.

- Thank you for what you do for me.

- I have to take care of my assistant.

- When Rodrigo arrived, he rang the doorbell and Dalva opened it. Seeing them smiling and happy:

- Rodrigo how long

- Good. Mrs. Dalva, Aríete had a fall in the office, broke her leg and dislocated her arm. But she's fine.

- Oh, my God. She's okay? Where is she?

- She's in the car. Her leg is in a cast and I need help getting her out of there. Dalva nervously approached the car.

- Aríete, my daughter, what happened?

- I don't know how it happened. I was coming down the stairs when I realized I was already on the ground.

- On the stairs. Oh, my God, it could have been worse. It could have been worse.

- Rodrigo took me to the hospital, they treated me very well, but now I feel pains in my body.

- Come on, I'll take you inside.

- It's better to take the car to the garden.

- He agreed. Once inside, he opened the door of the car and said:

- Mrs. Dalva, I'll take it, but the lady has to wear a cast on her leg because it is very heavy and can hurt a lot.

- They carefully took her to the room and placed her on her bed. Rodrigo took a package out of the bag and handed it to Dalva.

- These are the remedies she has to take. The prescription is inside. She took an analgesic and if the pains are stronger the lady will give her another one.

- It hurts a lot, my daughter.

- It hurts a little. But the worst is over.

- I'm going to get a coffee with milk. You'll see she hasn't even had lunch.

- Not at all. But I don't want anything, I'm a little sick. Rodrigo hasn't had lunch either, he must be hungry.

- I'll get a sandwich and some salty toast. They help to pass the anger. You like your coffee black or with milk.

Don't worry, Mrs. Dalva. I have to get back to the office. I'll be out soon to get something to eat.

- It's nothing. Sit down, I won't be long.

After she left Aríete said:

- Early tomorrow morning I'm going to call Neusa and ask her to bring me my folder and some documents. I plan to work from here as long as I can't go to the office.

- It is not necessary. You should rest.

- I can't today, but tomorrow, if she can help me, I will organize the most urgent payments and bring them to you for your signature. Some things can't wait.

- If you teach me I could do it. You won't be able to use your right arm.

- Don't worry. Neusa will be able to do whatever it takes. Dalva returned with a tray containing some sandwiches and toast, as well as coffee, and placed it on the table.

Next to the bed was a small table. She served coffee to Rodrigo saying:

- Eat a sandwich. The bread was hot. He took a sandwich. And Dalva extended the plate with toast to Aríete:

- Eat at least one, it will fill your stomach.

- She took one with her left hand and Dalva helped her to sit down by placing two pillows on her back. She slowly ate a piece of toast. She was a little pale and Rodrigo, after snacking and drinking coffee, stood up saying.

- Thank you Mrs. Dalva, it was delicious. Aríete needs to rest. I'm going back to the office.

- He took a card out of his pocket and handed it to her.

- This is my home address and phone number. If you need anything, call me. Don't worry, it can be any time.

- Thank you very much. I don't know how to thank you for what you did for Aríete.

- It's not necessary.

- Try to rest, tomorrow is another day.

- It's true. Thank you for everything.

He went downstairs and Dalva accompanied him to the door:

- Rodrigo, you have to tell me how much the expense was. Mario will send the money to the office tomorrow.

- The expense is on me. Aside from Aríete's commitment to the company, he has provided me with many services beyond what I could have expected. After all, Aline is a partner in the company. You have heard of her.

- I have her despite the sadness of what happened, she is satisfied with the company she works for. Beyond the optimal salary, they have given her a car, an apartment to live in and they treat her very well.

- Good. So, you don't plan to go back to Brazil.

- After all, he realized the dream of his life. She loves living there, she made friends, she only regrets what happened with Marcelo. She never imagined that could happen.

- At least she got what she wanted. Good for her. I repeat Mrs. Dalva if you need anything call me. Tomorrow if I can I'll be back to check on Aríete.

- Come and have dinner with us.

- The lady has enough work taking care of Aríete without worrying. I'll come after dinner.

- Dalva smiled, squeezed his outstretched hand and left. He was in a hurry to go to the office to see how things were going and, if possible, to work a little on his Project.

Chapter XIII

Sitting in front of Mimo, he waits for him to talk.

- Vitor is going to take him to meet Antonio, who will tell him what he is going to do. He is at a post of ours, near the earth's crust, and I promised him that I would send someone to help him. You have the necessary energy to carry out that mission.

- What should I do?

- Do as he tell you. He will give you the details of his task. You must leave by nightfall. For that place it's best to go after dark. Marcelo wanted to ask more, but Victor grabbed his arm:

- Let's go now. The interview ended. Marcelo went out and once in the courtyard he asked:

- What are we going to do until it's time to go?

- I have some things to do. Go to your room.

- Vitor entered through one of the doors, Marcelo remembered the dreams he had had about Mirela and felt like looking for her. He remembered where the nurse worked and went there.

In the hallway there were two people waiting and he sat down ready to talk to her when she appeared.

When he opened the door, she appeared and at the sight of him she was thrilled. Marcelo shuddered and felt like hugging her.

- Wait, we'll talk later.

When he opened the door, she appeared and, seeing him, she was moved. Marcelo shuddered, he felt like hugging her.

- Wait, we'll talk later.

She signaled the other two to come in and closed the door again. Marcelo sat back down.

What emotion came over him when he thought of her? Where did he know her from? Why did he suddenly feel a strong warmth when he thought of her?

- I'm not here by chance," he thought. I have to find out what's wrong with me. I never had another woman, why now this strong attraction? I never had this passion with Aline. Maybe this place is driving me crazy. That's the only thing.

- I better go, I'm getting out of here. I'm not going into that room. But if I go, Mimo will punish me, I promised him I'd serve him in exchange for what I want. I'm going to wait until nightfall to leave with Vitor and forget that woman. It's better to leave now.

- He got up, but at that moment he remembered the dream, the passionate kisses they had given each other, and he didn't have the courage to leave. Struggling with doubts and memories of the past, Marcelo saw the door open again and the two men came out.

Mírela was in front saying:

- Come in. Renato

- Renato? Because he calls me that. My name is Marcelo.

- She didn't answer, she went in and he accompanied her. Mirela saw him and faced him saying

- When we met you were called Renato.

- You're leaving me more confused than I already am. That night that I signed with you We were in an old house and we were making love. You're starting to remember

- It can't be I love Aline. She's the reason I came here Mírela came up to him, hugged him and answered:

- You're here because I called you with my love. Long before that woman you claim to love, we loved each other. And that love is still inside our hearts. It was stronger than everything and continues to overcome time and bring us closer together.

- At that moment Marcelo forgot everything and only saw Mirela's beautiful face, her lips half-open, her chest heaving, her passionate eyes in front of him and he kissed her passionately, pressing her against his chest.

- The emotion took hold of both of them and they exchanged long and passionate kisses. Then, still trembling with emotion Marcelo said:

- I don't know what's happening to me. What magic is this that you have the key to make me lose my mind and forget Aline.

- There is no magic. It's our past coming back, bringing back the emotions of those times. We love each other. I'm the woman in his life. I'm here years ago when I could have been in a better place. But I didn't leave because I knew that here we would see each other for the last time, that you would return to my arms. I've been waiting for you for so long.

- I can't understand all that.

- Come. Sit here beside me. I'm going to tell you everything.

- She settled on the couch and he sat down next to her. He took her hand. Mirela talked about the past. He told her everything.

- As she spoke, her words echoed in his heart, but he didn't want to accept it. Although he had dreamed about her, when he learned there was a prison in the building, he hesitated.

- He thought she was trying to involve him in some kind of witchcraft. To separate him from Aline. This he would not consent to.

The woman he visited would also try to separate him from his wife. If that were true. Because he didn't remember. That reincarnation story could be a hoax.

Without waiting for her to finish, Marcelo grabbed her outstretched hand and stood up.

- You're lying. You want to separate me from Aline, Mirela's face saddened, but she didn't look away and replied:

- You still haven't recovered from the memories of your past life. You have not yet succeeded because you are attached to what has happened to you now.

- She also stood up and brought her face close to his. Without looking away defiantly:

- Tell me that you don't feel like kissing me like before. That the moments of love we lived, still make your feelings vibrate. Her eyes shone with emotion and Marcelo shuddered, embraced her and kissed her lips repeatedly. Then he suddenly let her go, shouting nervously:

- What kind of witchcraft are you using to leave me like this. I love Aline. And she is what I want.

- Mirela looked at her sadly and replied in a calm voice:

- I've been waiting for you for a long time. I can wait as long as it takes. However, lately I have received a very strong call to leave this place. So far I have resisted. But I don't know how long I can do it. I am tired of living here, where evil lurks at every turn. I long to go to a better place, more in keeping with my feelings.

- I don't know what you're talking about. I have no commitment to you. You can go anywhere, I don't care.

- Maybe one day you'll care so much that you'll do nothing but look for me, and maybe it won't be easy to find me.

- I don't believe anything you tell me. I'm leaving today after what I promised Mimo, I won't come back here anymore. I don't feel good in this place either.

Mirle took him by the arm and asked:

Did you commit to work with Mimo?

It was an exchange. He will help me and I will have to render him a service. It's only fair.

- You shouldn't have asked him for anything, why?

- No. I know I have to help a person and I plan to do everything to the letter.

- And if he doesn't make it.

- And if you don't make it.

- Of course, I will. You talk as if Mimo wasn't a good man.

- That's not what I meant. Mimo is the boss of this place and he deserves our respect. But a task can be difficult and if he doesn't do it.

- So, what do you want me to do? Give it all up? I'm not going to do that and I think it's best if you stay out of my life.

- It's just that I'm interested in your future.

- I don't need you, you can take care of me. I'm going to my room. Vitor may be looking for me.

- He left the room and Mirela sighed sadly. How long could we wait for Renato to return to her arms.

- If he got involved in new complications, they might have to be apart much longer than she expected.

- Mirela could no longer bear to live in that place. She wanted to leave, to breathe in a better environment, where friendship, kindness, joy and beauty existed.

At that instant he noticed a light in the corner of the room and saw a pretty middle-aged woman appear.

- Who are you? - she asked frightened.

- My name is Cora. I come from a place like you that wants to live. You could have gone there a long time ago. And not be living in this gloomy place, you have stayed in the good.

- The lady is an emissary of light.

- Mirela replied, kneeling down.

- Cora approached and stood up saying:

- Don't do that. I don't deserve it. Just call me Cora. The place where I live is very beautiful. During the day you can see the sky and at night the stars shine. The houses are surrounded by gardens, covered with fragrant flowers and people are friendly and strive to do good. There is work and leisure, opportunities for progress and joy.

- Mire sighs with joy.

- How wonderful it is to live in a place so full of beauty and friendliness. Here, despite living surrounded by people, I have felt very lonely.

- You are immersed in the past. But it's time to move on. If you look deferentially, progress, grow could effectively help the one you love.

- I'm afraid of losing sight of him. When we parted I spent a long time without seeing you.

- I have come to invite you to follow me. There, in our community, we have more than enough time to locate the people we love, wherever they are, and even, if possible, to intervene on their behalf.

- It's a tempting proposal. But I don't know if I should accept. Just when Renato is here

- He's still attached to what he left on earth. I think you'll be better able to help him by being with us than by staying here.

- Rest assured you won't let him out of your sight.

- If you go with me and do as our elders advise, you won't lose him. Renato needs help. Only a heart like yours, which loves him unconditionally, can help him out of this illusion in which he finds himself.

- He still does not remember our past.

- Because he is attached to a woman he never loved. If you agree, I can take you with me now. In doing so, I am sure it will help you much more than staying here. You need to renew yourself, to feed yourself with energies more in line with your true feelings.

- I would like to go, but not now. Renato is here and I'm afraid… that he will leave and get into trouble. If that happens, there is nothing we can do. He is responsible for his actions and you will have to reap the results of what he does. That's why I've come now. If you come with me, maybe we can stop him from doing the wrong thing.

- He thinks we could.

- At least we could try. What do you hope to accomplish by staying here. What conditions do you have to intervene in what they intend to do?

- None. Mimo has known for some time that I don't support his work. He allows me to live here because I help him by taking care of people and keeping him from having haters. But I am not allowed to go out or visit other places. I am a prisoner.

- So, what are you waiting for? Let's go.

- That's it. The place is guarded. We can't leave without permission. Cora smiled and answered:

- It's very simple. You'll see.

- He wrapped his arm around Mirela's waist and, in a matter of seconds, they were flying off the fortress walls and soaring rapidly.

Mirela was intoxicated, she looked up at the blue sky and felt herself lightly gliding with Cora. In her breast a pleasant thrill filled her with pleasure.

They traveled like this for some time until they began to see the high walls.

- Here we are - said Cora.

They stopped at a door and Cora said the name and he opened it, they entered. Mirela admired it and stopped in front of an immense garden, full of colorful flowers that impregnated the air with a delicate perfume.

Ahead, a beach and some buildings, all very beautiful and harmonious. Cora put her arm around Mirella and said:

- Let's go.

They walked to one of the buildings and went inside.

After leaving Mirela, Marcelo went to the room. ¿He was confused, contradictory emotions were running through him, what was wrong with him, why couldn't he control himself in front of Mirela?

She was very pretty, but in his life he had known women even more beautiful than her and none of them had made him cheat on Aline.

He reminded himself that the night before he had slept badly. He was tired. It would be good to rest. He lay down and tried to sleep.

Exhausted, it didn't take him long to fall asleep, but then he began to dream that he was on a boat playing with two cranes and Mirela was watching him in amusement. He felt that he had already lived that scene. But when where? Surroundings, water and some aged palaces.

He remembered that Mirela had said she had lived in Venice. But he did not believe in reincarnation. However, that place was something like Venice.

Perhaps he had been influenced by Mirela's story. He had to admit that a lot of strange things had happened to him lately. What to believe?

Marcelo was wrestling with questions without finding a satisfactory answer until the moment when Vitor came in looking for him.

- It was about time. We have to go.

Marcelo, half dazed, got up and accompanied him.

- What happened, you're looking...

- I am confused. Mirela told a story that moved me.

- Did you believe her?

- No. But still, what she said won't get out of my head.

- Mimo needs to know what stories she's telling. She's not going to like it.

- She talked about a past life we lived together. But I don't believe in reincarnation.

- Well, you should. We'll all be reincarnated someday.

- It seems impossible to me.

- But it's true.

- Well, I'd like to come back to earth to live with Aline.

- If you're born again, you'll forget the past. I came back years ago and I still don't remember my previous life.

- It sounds crazy to me.

- When I get back, I'll talk to Mimo about Mirela. Now you need to forget all that and concentrate on the job at hand.

- Where are we going?

- To the Earth's crust.

- Then I'll be able to see Aline.

- You'll have to devote yourself to your work. You won't have time for anything else.

- What work I have to do.

- You'll know.

- It was getting dark when they reached Rio de Janeiro and drove to a suburb where they stopped in front of a modest, earthy house. They entered and were soon approached by a dark, strong, thick-lipped man.

- Vitor, I was waiting for you.

- Antonio, this is Marcelo. He came to help you. After the greetings, Vitor said goodbye:

- He's staying with you, but I'm in a hurry to get back.

- What do you want me to do?

- Come with me.

- Marcelo accompanied him to the room where a young woman lay, pale, thin, dejected, so weakened that Marcelo felt sorry for her.

- She looks bad.

- Not as bad as I would like.

- How is she? - asked the frightened man.

- I have come to avenge myself and you have come to help me.

- What did she do?

- Nothing now, but in the previous life we were married and she brought me a child that I thought was mine, it was someone else's. After I died in an accident, I found out everything because she and her lover got married. I never forgave them. I suspect that the accident I was a victim of was caused by them. After returning to the astral realm, I searched for them everywhere without finding them. More than two years ago I discovered that they had reincarnated and remarried.

- Are you sure about what you say?

- Of course, I am sure. I am as old as they were at that time. A friend took me to Mimo and we made a pact. I gave him some services and he promised to help me. In the meantime, I worked on my own. I got him fired from his job and he ended up dying in a car accident. So, I took advantage of the fact that she was depressed and made sure she stayed the way she is.

- She's messed up, I think she's had enough revenge.

- Whose side are you on?

- My own.

- Marcelo hastened to affirm.

- But I think you've accomplished enough.

- Not for me. I want her to come here. Only then will I be able to talk to her face to face. And tell her everything I want. Everything was going well and I thought I'd get what I wanted. But then, I don't know where a meddlesome middle-sized woman came out of and started praying for her. She brought a group of people here who come to pray once a week and I was forced to walk away: I turned to Mimo and now I'm counting on you.

- Marcelo felt uncomfortable. He was in no mood to help. Antonio in his revenge, but if he didn't, he feared Mimo's power.

- What should I do?

- I'm thinking of calling in some friends who specialize in magnetization. I have found out that they will be able to accomplish what I want quickly. But I can't go away from here leaving her alone because those meddling spirits can gain ground and trap everything. I want you to be by her side keeping our work going while I'm away.

- How long will it take?

- I don't know yet, maybe a day or two. But until she comes back you won't be able to get away from her, except when they come to pray. Then it's best to leave before they start. Otherwise you may be dismissed from us.

- How should I do what you want?

- I will show you.

- Antony approached the bed, put his right hand on the woman's forehead and went on to say.

- Traitor! You are to blame for your husband's death. He is in a very bad way, his time has come.

From Antonio's forehead dark, reddish strands came out and penetrated the forehead and the brain of the girl, who trembled, shuddered and ran her hand over her forehead, terrified.

- I am not going to die - She thought.

- I want to live. I can't abandon my son. He needs me. What will become of him if I die too.

- Marcelo struggled to control his rebelliousness. Antonio continued:

- The fault is yours you are a bad woman, you are very sick. You will not be cured. She sobbed inconsolably and Antonio said with satisfaction:

- That's right. Cry and be content. Later I will come for you. You have no cure, your illness is mortal.

Turning to Marcelo he asked:

- Now it's your turn. Let's see how you are doing. Marcelo had no choice but to obey.

- Without knowing why he felt like a prisoner in a cell in the Mimo building and was terrified.

- Antonio waited and Marcelo tried to do everything as he did, struggling not to give in to the scruples he felt.

Antonio felt satisfied and decided:

- I go on like this. Now I'm leaving. I want to settle everything as soon as possible. And he left. Marcelo approached the girl, but he didn't have the courage to send her bad thoughts.

- Inwardly he tried to fight between the desire to help the girl and the fear of confronting Mimo. At that moment he regretted having agreed to work for him.

- He reminded himself that Mirela asked him not to make any pact with Mimo. She was close.

Chapter XIV

A week had passed since Aríete's accident and during that time Rodrigo visited her daily. Instead of sending Neusa to bring him the papers, he himself took them to her every evening at the end of the day.

Two days after the accident, Aríete recovered. His request was for Dalva to turn his room into a desk, setting up a table and a computer that Rodrigo had sent from the company.

Mario and Dalva treated Rodrigo with affection, respect and surprised him with their kindness with which he felt comfortable.

His parents lived in the country and although they had some friends, Rodrigo missed the comfort of home. The affection of Aline's parents and the pleasant conversations with Aríete were pleasurable to him.

At first, when he arrived, he said he had already had dinner, but at Mario's insistence, he had agreed to dine with them the day before and loved the home-cooked food. He was tired of eating in restaurants.

- There's nothing like food from home - said Dalva.

- Do you live alone?

- You have to arrange for someone to cook. It's not good to eat out all the time - advised Dalva.

- I will think about it, Mrs. Dalva.

- After dinner, she went back to Aríete's room, who left the folder ready for her to take and continued sitting on the couch, her leg in a cast on a stool.

He settled into the armchair on the other side of her and said, "Your mother cooks very well.

- Your mother cooks very well. If I keep eating like this I'm going to get fat.

- I don't think so. You don't tend to get fat. He opened his folder, recorded a videotape and handed it to her saying:

- I brought a movie for you. Can you imagine a nimble person like you having to be in the room all the time?

- I'm glad I was able to continue working, even though it took a lot of effort.

- I am pleased to come here and talk to you. Before your accident, I didn't know what it was like to be with family. Being with you is like being with my family.

- You must have friends.

- I have many acquaintances, but few friends. I miss Marcelo very much.

- We miss him too. My mother has even commented that his presence here has comforted her. Yesterday at dinner it was as if Marcelo was still here.

- Rodrigo's eyes were shining with emotion and he lowered them trying to hide it. He didn't want to talk about sad things. Aríete needed to distract himself.

I'm glad I was able to comfort Mrs. Dalva in some way. She is the mother everyone would want to have.

- Marcelo got along very well with us. We are a very close family, we have always lived together peacefully. He used to say that his parents were very different...

- In fact, I lived more with them than with you and I noticed the difference.

- Unfortunately, we are accused of Marcelo's death. To be honest, we didn't know that Aline was planning to leave. It was a terrible drama for us. After the accident, we couldn't communicate with her, because we still didn't know where she was.

- Sometimes I wonder why she did it.

- I understand. That the mistake she made was to marry him when she dreamed of a different life. He loved her very much and ended up convincing her to marry him. I confess that we all helped her to accept this union. My parents did not understand how she could not love a nice and handsome guy who loved her enough to go and try his luck in another country.

- I think she got her hopes up and didn't love him enough.

- I think so too. If she had loved him she would not have been attracted to restart her life elsewhere.

- In any case, it is not easy to judge. Sometimes life calls us to another place because we have a task to accomplish. Who can tell?

- I had thought about it. I have often wondered why Aline had such a will since she was a child. Marcelo's death was an accident. Who can guarantee that it wouldn't have happened to Aline if she were still here.

- It is difficult to answer.

- Life has its secrets. One thing that has me intrigued is what happened with Aline. The night she left, she was asleep on the plane that took her to Miami, when she went to bed she saw Marcelo come in, with blood dripping down his forehead and legs. He approached her saying:

- "I finally found her. Don't leave me again. Say you'll stay by my side forever."

- She screamed in fright, woke up all the passengers and found it hard to calm down. During the following days,

- She felt his presence so much that she ended up going to consult an institute that studies para-normality.

- I don't know anything about that, but I believe that life goes on after death, so Marcelo must have gone there. He was too attached but he called us to ask if he was okay. And when he learned the truth he fainted.

- Rodrigo wanted to know how Aline discovered that Institute, what she had told him and how she was now. Aríete told him everything down to the smallest detail and finished:

- All that left us intrigued. We have never been interested in spiritual matters. But Aline's way of talking made us think. She was always a practical person, not easily fooled. And what she told us must have happened.

- Rodrigo was impressed. He remembered his Aunt Alice, who, when he was a teenager, used to talk to him about life after death and communication with spirits.

- My Aunt Alice used to talk about communication with spirits, but I never understood those things. She was always reading about it. And she claimed that there were many books written by scientists researching and proving that life continues after death.

- That's what Aline says. In high school they study doing experiments.

- It should be interesting. In the end, we're all going to die someday and it would be nice to believe that we're going to survive after that.

- Rodrigo remained serious for a few moments and Aríete asked:

- What happened? You suddenly became serious.

- I was thinking about Marcelo's family. They are full of rage and do not accept his death. If they knew he was alive somewhere else, maybe they would be consoled.

- They would rebel against us. If they were calmer we could talk to them. But as things stand, that is impossible.

- It is true. Another day I met Marcio and he was angrier than his parents, he was very close to his brother.

- It is true. Another day I met Marcio and he was angrier than his parents, he was very close to his brother.

- I tried to talk to him, but he was so aggressive that I gave up. Someday they will understand that we are not to blame for anything. And that Aline no longer loved Marcelo and was sincere, despite everything.

- That night, Rodrigo left Aríete's house thinking about everything they had talked about. He had a very different idea of Aríete

- When he was with the couple, she spoke little while he surrounded her with so much care and attention that it gave the impression that he was such a touchy person that he had to go round and round to please her. From what Aríete had said, Aline was nothing of the sort. The family saw her as a practical, firm and efficient person. If that was her temperament, she would chafe at her husband's exaggeration. He was smothering her and she couldn't take it anymore.

- He was alone because he couldn't stand that women went over everything to please their partner and what was worse, they clung to him as if there was nothing else in the world but him.

- Rodrigo had a horror of being imprisoned, of having to account for everything, even his thoughts. He valued his freedom highly and was therefore reluctant to marry.

- Women swarmed around him like bees around the light, and he would relate to some of them, always making it clear that he had no intention of marrying. Not wanting to deceive any of them, the more he acted yes, the more she was attracted to him.

- At that moment she understood why Aline left her husband like that. But she will get rid of him. Even after he is dead he will follow her. Rodrigo felt a shudder. What horror? Because people like to fall prey to others. More than once he thought it would be much more difficult to marry.

Meanwhile, Marcelo, alone with a sick girl, felt torn between fear of Mimo and not doing the will of what Antonio wants. He looked at the girl, thin and pale, with a troubled face and deep dark circles under her eyes, and felt sorry for her and wanted to help her, but if he did, he would have to pay the price. Beyond not being able to count on her help anymore.

He was sure he would be punished for not obeying. He paid attention and began to listen to her moans.

- My God, help me, I am without strength, I cannot bear this torment any longer. I can't bear this torment any longer, why won't anyone help me, what have I done to be punished?

Tears rolled down her cheeks and she continued to think:

- Maybe it's better to die. Why did God take Gerson away from me? He didn't deserve to die in that accident. When he left, he lost the charm.

- We loved each other so much. What will become of me without him? How can I live a life alone? I wish I had the courage to kill myself. But I'm afraid. If I did, I couldn't go to meet him. Suicide is a sin. Marcelo can't bear it. He too had died in an accident and that death was different from Aline's, who didn't care about his death. She loved her husband and did not deserve to be treated like that.

Without thinking, she put her right hand on his forehead and said, "You can't die:

- You cannot die. Be patient. Death is not the end. Your husband continues to live in another world.

- She did not hear what he said, but thought:

- Where is Gerson, is there life after death?

- Of course, there is life after death. I guarantee it. Have faith. You must fight to be well.

- I have no strength, I'm dying.

- It is a lie. You are subdued by a spirit that wants to take you away. React!

She remembered Geni's words when she came to pray for her.

"What you feel is not yours. You are picking up energies from a disembodied spirit."

- Am I to believe that, can a spirit make me feel that bad?

- It can do that and much more

Marcelo continued. At that moment Marcelo heard voices and some people arrived. One of them opened the door and frightened Marcelo tried to hide. Thinking that Antonio might be among them. But he was not. They were some women and a boy who approached his bed and one of them smoothed the girl's hair and asked her:

- How is Mirian? Is she better?

- No, she is not better.

- She answered in a weak voice, but I was thinking about you Geni.

- And what you were thinking about?

- What you say about the cause of my illness. The presence of a spirit that torments me.

- The boy took her hand saying, think that with God's help everything is possible. I trusted. Let us make our prayer.

- They sat around the bed, held hands and Geni asked for spiritual help.

Marcelo, in a corner, watched and saw that rays of bright blue light shot out from her breasts and enveloped the sick woman, while the multicolored rays formed a circle around her, isolating them.

- Mirian's face relaxed and her physiognomy became diffuse. Marcelo noticed that from above, filigrees of white light descended on the sick woman and little by little she calmed down.

- Marcelo had never seen anything like it. What power those people would have to do it.

When Geni calmed down, they let go of each other's hands and the boy remarked:

- Something different happened today. Mirian was more lucid and reacted better to the treatment.

Another girl intervened.

- She sensed in the atmosphere the presence of a boy who died in a car accident.

Mirian listened to her and cheered up.

- That must be Gerson. I was wondering if there is life after death and he came to warn me.

- I don't think it's him. This is another sign that your husband is not well. However, I am trying to help her.

- Mirian was cheerful and sat on the bed talking. Geni went to the kitchen, made coffee with milk and cut a generous piece of freshly baked bread she bought at the bakery and brought it to Mirian.

- Eat. You need to get stronger.

- Instead of refusing as she always did, she accepted and ate it all with gusto, which made all three of them smile with satisfaction.

- Then Miriam lay down again and felt sleepy.

- You may go. If you have an engagement. But I'm going to stay a little longer. I want to take advantage of your improvement. I'm going to cook some nice soup and leave it for you to eat later.

- The two left and Geni went to the kitchen to check the ingredients for the soup. She found beans and some legumes they had left two days before. Since she didn't get up, they did the shopping and left it in the fridge. Mirian was in an average financial situation. Her husband had left money in their joint bank account outside of a small business that had supported them both. They shopped at the market near the house and she paid for it later. Then she put the beans to cook in the pressure cooker. She returned to the bedroom and sat by the bed.

- Miriam was sleeping peacefully and Geni was smiling contentedly. Marcelo, however, in a corner of the room, was worried.

Antonio could return at any moment and would surely notice an improvement in Miriam and suspect him.

That woman sitting on the bed was powerful. He had seen her when she prayed, a light coming from her chest and descending from above on them. He approached her thinking about what he should do. Maybe tell her what was happening and the danger Miriam was in, tell her to leave and Antonio to come back, take other measures.

- I have to go talk about the sick girl... - she began. Geni felt a chill and sensed his presence.

- Why is she here, what do you want from her?

- Geni concentrated and saw Marcelo sitting next to her. Then she realized it was the boy her partner had mentioned.

- I want to help - he replied.

- She is being pursued by someone who wants revenge for some events that happened in another life.

- Geni heard clearly and asked to continue:

- When they were married, she cheated on him with her current husband. She caused the accident that killed him and he wants to take her too.

- That's what you suspect. But I sense that you have problems too. You are suffering because of what is happening to you.

- My wife left me, I was desperate and ended up dying in a car accident. She doesn't love me. I can't be without her. So, I joined a vigilante group to help me. They agreed, but they wanted a trade, they wanted me to provide some services. And the first thing was this. I should help in revenge, but I don't have the courage. I loved her husband and he didn't deserve that. Now I have to leave before they come back or they will punish me.

- Geni understood everything not so much by the words she was saying, but by the scenes as she spoke.

You did well I can help you.

- I want to stay by my wife's side without that group finding me, you can do it.

- Next to her is the first place they would look for you. But I can hide you in a place where they will never find you. Then, when the case is solved, you can see your wife again.

- Will I have to stay away from her for a long time?

- As long as it takes not to take the risk. You could be arrested and we won't know when we'll be able to release you.

- I have no choice but to accept. You guarantee to help me see my wife again.

- I guarantee it. I have friends who will take care of everything.

- I need to tell you that you must not leave the sick woman alone. When you are not there, the spirit that is harming her takes advantage of it to magnetize her without stopping.

- Thank you for the warning. I will take care of that. I will take care of you now. I will call a friend to put her out of your reach.

- What should I do in return for this favor.

- Take care of yourself. Try to get better. The sooner you do, the sooner you will get what you want. Geni closed his eyes and began to invoke a spiritual friend. In admiration, Marcelo watched as a pink and blue light came back out of his chest and enveloped them.

- Soon after, a young woman of rare beauty, with a joyful smile, entered the room and kissed him on the forehead. Then she held out her hand to Marcelo and said, "Come on, Marcelo":

Marcelo Today you can go to a nice place and your enemies won't be able to find you.

- Marcelo took his hand, put his arm around his waist and they began to fly.

- He was intoxicated. He had never felt such a great emotion. In that instant he forgot everything to live that moment of euphoria and satisfaction.

Chapter XV

- Two months later, Aríete came into the office after a physical therapy session. She was feeling better. At last, her leg no longer hurt and she could walk without pain.

- At the door of the building she met Marcio, who was passing by, and tried to greet her, but he looked at her with a scowl of contempt. Aríete felt a shiver run through her body and an unpleasant sensation enveloped her. She tried not to make light of the encounter and entered the office. Seeing her enter, Rodrigo approached her.

- How's the leg?

- Better: I can walk more.

- Rodrigo's friendship with Aríete and her family had grown closer. While she couldn't go to the office, he went to her house every day and almost always ended up having dinner and staying longer than planned, talking with Aríete or the rest of the family.

- You are not feeling well. Something has happened

- When I arrived I met Marcio who saw me in a way that even made me feel bad.

- Last week I met him and he did the same with me. He didn't respond when I greeted him.

- I can understand that he still holds a grudge against me about Aline, but what can he have against you.

- He has been behaving strangely. One night when I left his house, he was in a corner. Once his father was here complaining about you working with me. He thought I was betraying Marcelo.

He even wanted me to transfer the property that rightfully belonged to Aline. I explained to him that it was not possible. I explained that it wasn't possible. They wanted me to cut off relations with you.

- That's why you didn't want to go to my house.

- I wanted to avoid complications. But life made me learn how wrong I was. Living with your family made me realize the difference between you.

- I'm sorry they think that way.

- Sometimes I get the impression that Marcio isn't spying.

- I don't think so. Why would he?

- I don't know. It's an unpleasant feeling I get every time I think of him. A moment ago, when you mentioned that you were meeting him, I felt a shiver. Aríete was amazed.

- That's what I felt when he looked at me. You'll see that he's not very well.

- Maybe that's what it is

- After she passed by Aríete, Marcio left for home. He had stood in a corner waiting for her to arrive and as he watched her walk by in a good mood he felt some disappointment. In the end he had paid good money and she was fine. Back to work and what was worse, Rodrigo did not leave his house. Could it be that he was in love with her?

- Since Aríete broke his leg, Marcio had started to follow the events, keeping an eye on his house, following Rodrigo's steps. Going there every day and seeing Aríete made him uncomfortable. What good was the accident to him if, instead of pushing her away, it brought him closer to her family?

More than once he went to complain to Father Joseph, but the latter asked him to wait and trust that everything would be as he had wished.

Marcio entered the house in anger. Ivone approached him

- What happened, my son? You seem nervous.

- I am angry. That Father José took our money, but he's not doing things right. Just saw Aríete all happy, walking into Rodrigo's office.

- Maybe he is good

- That's what I'm asking

- You have to go back there. Hold him to what he promised. In the end we paid very well. I still don't know how I'm going to pay his aunt. If only Marcelo' money would come to us.

- That's true. Tonight, I'll ask him again. The waiting is over. This time it will have to be something stronger.

- That night, shortly before the beginning, Marcio was at Father José's house. So he incorporated the medium, Marcio approached:

- Father José, I want to talk to you

- What is happening. I have a lot of people to attend to today. I can't waste time.

- It's about my case. I saw Aríete today and he was very well. She was recovering, she was happy. Sir promised me to get her out of our way and put my brother's money in our hands.

- I did not promise him that. I told him it was difficult and that what I could do was to take care of this girl and get her away. I did that.

- She was cured and went back to work. The worst thing is that in spite of everything, he is my brother's partner and he gets close to her family. Now he does not leave that house. That is not what I asked for.

- I am not to blame if they have protection and will receive spiritual help from the spirits of light. I did my part, they have nothing to claim from me. Now see that I have many people waiting for me.

- The Lord is not going to help me anymore. He is going to let things go on like this.

- Come back another day and we'll talk. I can't today. The medium walked away and Marcio left the place nervously. Now Father José wanted to get out of the way. He couldn't do a good enough job and would have to try again or give the money back.

- He went home and Ivone then saw him and said:

- From the look on his face I think he didn't get anything.

- Father Jose asked me to come back another day. There were too many people to attend and I approached him before the others and told him that, instead of walking away, Rodrigo was now closer to his family.

- And he came with a conversation that he had already done his part, that they have the protection of the spirits of light.

- He clearly wanted to leave.

- That's what I thought. I don't think the spirits of light are going to protect them after what they did to Marcelo. If there is justice, Aline and her family should pay for his death.

- That's what I think. My poor son. You gave so much love to that woman that surely she must be in someone else's arms by now. Marcio hugged his mother saying sadly.

- Leave him, mother. They are going to pay for what they did to us. They did not see the two dark lumps near them and smiled happily.

- They are in our hands," said one.

- This time they will pay for what they have done to us," answered another. Ivone ran her hand over her head saying:

- I'm not liking this story.

- Why is that?

- I don't know. When you were talking I got a bad feeling. Take care of yourself and don't fight.

With that Father José because he might get angry and do some work against us.

Márcio gritted his teeth in anger:

- Let him not dare. If he does anything against us, I'll report him to the police.

- Well, I think you'd better not go back there. I don't like any of it.

- Nonsense, I'm not going to let him take our money without doing what he promised. Let's wait and see what he says at our next meeting and I'll take action accordingly.

- Ivone listened, worried. She felt an unpleasant sense of fear.

- I want to leave things as they are. I don't want him to come back.

- It's easy to talk, but with what money will we pay the aunt.

- We'll find any way we can. I don't want her to get more involved with that father José.

- Ivone was very nervous and Marcio tried to calm her down:

- Are you crazy? I don't want you fighting with him anymore.

- I think I'm going to let him keep our money and I'm not going to do anything. I'm not afraid of him. Now I'm starting to think that Aríete's fall might have been a fluke and he had nothing to do with it. It could be that he is taking advantage of people, fooling everyone and has no power.

- All right, we'll talk about it later.

- Marcio, it's over, stop getting involved with those people.

- All right, stay calm. Even if he said this, he was still willing to confront Father José and demand that he keep his promise or return the money.

- Two days later, Márcio returned to the land to talk to Father José. He waited for his name to be called before approaching him and tried to appear calm. He thought better of it and decided it would be better to try to get what he wanted with skill.

- So, my son

- The master knows what I want. It is necessary to get Aríete out of my brother's company and get the partner to stay on our side. In fact, the way things are going, he, who used to get along well with our family, is now distant, he seems angry with us.

- You want everything to happen quickly, but I need time. People don't do things the way we want them to. You have to be patient, know how to wait.

- Okay, I've been patient, but it's taking too long. The Lord guarantees it will work.

- I told you I got it. Do you have doubts?

- No, but things are getting worse instead of better. Father José took a few puffs on the straw cigarette he was smoking and then said, "You're doubting me.

- You are doubting me. You are offending me. And I don't work for someone who offends me.

- I didn't mean to say that. But things aren't going well,

- Leave it to me. I'll prove I know what I'm talking about. Now you can go. The tone he used did not admit any more conversation and then an assistant took Márcio by the arm, saying: "Come on, I'm done:

- But he hasn't said if he's going to do more work to help me.

- He is going to do it, it is better to go now. Father José does not like to be doubted. Thinking about Father José's words, Márcio decided to leave and headed for the exit. He was near the door when he stopped. Someone was crying inconsolably. Márcio tried to realize where the sound was coming from and noticed that behind the tree next to him, there was a person sobbing desperately. He approached, listened and saw a little girl on the trunk of the tree, with her head resting on her arms, screaming.

Moved, he took a handkerchief out of his bag and held it out to her, lightly touching her arm. Immediately she raised her face and Márcio noticed that she was very young and pretty.

With trembling lips and wet eyes, he took the handkerchief and wiped his tears trying to hold them back.

- If you feel like crying, cry. It is not good to swallow your tears. She broke down again in sobs and Marcio, saddened, waited for her to calm down. Then he took her by the arm:

- Come, let's walk a little. Don't be afraid. I want to help you. She stared at him and looked into his big, beautiful eyes. Without saying anything, she let herself be led by him, who put his arm around her and they slowly walked away.

- Márcio noticed that she had a fit body and walked elegantly. A few steps away there was a square and that's where they headed. When they arrived near a bench, he sat down and pulled her to sit next to him. Gradually she calmed down and he asked her:

- Then she is calmer.

- I am. Thank you. I'm sorry I got out of control.

- There are times in life when people need to let off steam. I've had mine too.

- You must be thinking I'm unbalanced.

- I don't think anything.

Thanks for the handkerchief. Look at this one, it's all wet. I'll have to take it to be washed before I return it.

- Don't worry about that. My name is Marcio and yours is

- Olivia

- Do you live nearby?

- No. I live on the other side of town.

- I saw you in Father José's land.

- Yes, but I don't want to talk about that now.

- Okay, let's talk about other things. I live ten blocks from here. Would you like a coffee or a soda?

- I'd like that, but I must look awful. I don't want anyone else to see me like this.

- You look fine. Your eyes are just a little red.

- I'm going to call a cab home.

- I walked all the way here. If you want to walk a little further home, I'll take the car and I can drive you.

- Don't bother. I think I've tried your patience too much. Marcio got up, took her by the hand and said:

- Let's go. Let's walk. If you don't want me to take you, I'll respect your will. They walked slowly until he stopped:

- I live in that house across the street.

- In that case, I'll walk. I don't want your family to see me going with you.

- Why? I'm a free person.

- Thank you for everything.

- Wait, I'll get the cart.

- He went inside, got the cart and stopped in front of her, opening the door for her to enter. In his head were a series of questions and he wanted to find the answers.

- The crying, the fact that she didn't want to talk about going to that place enveloped him in a certain mystery that attracted him.

- During the drive, she was leading the way, he wanted to talk about quiet topics. He thought he needed to gain her trust so that she would open up. He discovered that she liked to read, go to the movies, that she was nineteen years old and was studying journalism.

- Marcio, on the other hand, had a background in economics, was twenty-two years old and had been working in a company for a few months, but was not satisfied and was looking for a better job.

- He spoke of his brother's death, but refrained from talking about Aline and what he went to do in Father Joseph's land.

- It was a secret he did not wish to share with anyone. But he would like her to talk about what she went to do in the land because he wanted to ask her if she had gotten any results from going there.

- Olivia lived in a beautiful house, with gardens, and Marcio sensed that she must be from a well-to-do family. What would she have to do in that place? He wanted to ask, but didn't. It would be better to wait for her to digest it spontaneously. Olivia, however, did not broach the subject. Outside the car, in front of the house, she held out her hand to him, saying, "Thank you for everything:

- Thank you for everything. You don't know how much good it's done me. Where do I send the handkerchief?

- Don't worry about it. Even though we met at a difficult time for you. I loved meeting you. Ever since my brother died, I've felt very lonely.

- In fact, I'm not good company for anyone.

- That is precisely why I am attracted to you. I suffer a lot from the pain of a loss. Marcelo was my idol, my mirror, my friend. Seeing you cry, I felt that you were suffering as much or more than I was. That, in a way, made me realize that I was being selfish.

Thinking that my suffering was greater than that of others. I think we can be friends and minimize suffering. I think we can be friends and minimize our sadness a little bit.

- She opened her purse and pulled out a card with her name and phone number on it.

- I don't have a card

she lied, as she had never thought of getting one, but I'll write down my phone number.

- He took a piece of paper out of his wallet, wrote his name and phone number on it and handed it to her. Olivia held out her hand, which he shook. She looked at him warmly and, rising, kissed him gently on the cheek.

- Thank you again. If it weren't for you, I might not be here now. Márcio felt a tightness in his chest, not knowing if it was because of the kiss or because of the words she had said. Then she got in and he went back to the car, he looked towards the house, but she had already entered. So he started the car and on the way back he could not forget her face, her sobs, the pain he saw in her eyes and the mystery surrounding her.

- Why was a young woman from a good family, a college student, probably rich and beautiful, crying so much? Perhaps it was a case of unrequited love, a family drama like hers.

- Márcio arrived home and Ivone ran to ask him what his father José had told him.

- He said he was going to keep what he promised us.

- It will be

- I insisted, I hesitated and he got angry. So I thought it best to wait, to trust. You better not doubt it either. He knows everything we say, he even hears our thoughts.

- I don't want him to hear what I think.188

- But he does. That's why it's better not to doubt him, but at least give him time to do what he promised.

- That's right. I don't want to give him a reason to say he didn't succeed because we are different.

You got in, took your father's car and went where?

Someone at the police station was feeling sick and I went to take him home.

You were never like that. What's wrong with him?

I don't know, but she was sick and I wanted to take her home.

- Maybe she was a pretty girl

- Nothing of the sort.

- She lied.

- She was his age.

- He shook his head doubtfully. Márcio entered the bedroom, took off his shoes and stretched out on the bed, thoughtful. Olivia's face wouldn't leave his mind. He would wait a couple of days and call her to see how she was doing and maybe, who knows, ask her out for a chat or dinner.

He hoped she would accept and maybe tell him what was wrong, why she was crying so much.

- She was having trouble sleeping and when she did, dark figures stalked her, she would get scared and wake up. She went to the kitchen, drank a glass of water, lay down again, but sleep would not come.

Chapter XVI

- Rodrigo arrived at the office with a headache. He had not slept well and had woken up tired. Even so, he went to work because he had finished a big project and the owner had arranged to see him in two days. When he saw him come in, Aríete immediately realized that he was not feeling well. After greeting him, he asked

- Did something happen to you? You don't look well.

- Last night I had a terrible nightmare. I didn't sleep well afterwards. If I hadn't had to finish the project, I wouldn't have come.

- Some dreams seem to come true.

- That's the impression I got. I was being chased by two people who wanted to beat me up, and no matter how hard I ran, they always found out where I was. I woke up shaking, in a cold sweat and with goose bumps all over my body. One of them told me that I was going to regret what I was doing. But I don't know what he meant

- Dreams are like that, they have no coherence. But last night I didn't sleep well either. I had trouble falling asleep, I was afraid, I had the impression that my house was under surveillance and that burglars were going to enter at any moment.

Neusa, who was in the room, intervened:

When you started talking, I got goose bumps. There is something that

How? asked Rodrigo.

Bad influence of disturbing spirits. Whenever they're around, we get goose bumps. Look at the chills I get!

That's a belief

replied Rodrigo

- Maybe not. When I broke my leg, my cousin Dora went to a spiritual center to pray for me. They said the fall had been caused by spirits interested in keeping me away from work.

Rodrigo was surprised

Did you believe it?

- At the time, no. But now I'm beginning to think it might be true.

- I don't believe it. You've recovered and if someone had been interested in pushing you away, that wouldn't have happened.

- But since I've been back to work, when I come here I get goose bumps and sometimes a headache. Sometimes I get the feeling that something bad is about to happen. I can't explain it, but I don't feel the same as before.

- If it were me, I would go to the Center for a consultation. Last year my mother was not well, she went there, got treatment and got well.

- I will think about it, Neusa. If she doesn't get better, I'll leave.

- Aríete said.

- When Neusa left the room, Rodrigo returned:

- You're not thinking of leaving, are you? I only said that so as not to contradict her.

- No. I'm thinking of going anyway.

- Do you think you might be suffering from the action of the spirits? In that case, they'd be invading our privacy. I can't believe God would allow such a thing.

- When I was in college, I witnessed such a case with a classmate who was being haunted by a spirit.

- He went to doctors, psychologists and even psychiatrists, but nothing worked. He was only cured when he went to a spiritual center. I have never forgotten that. So it doesn't hurt to go and see what happens. I'm not religious, but I'm not prejudiced either. If it's for the best, I'll go.

- Well, I'm not. Just because I had a nightmare one night and felt bad, that's not the case. Aríete asked Neusa to give him the address of the center.

- It's open every night from half past seven. I can accompany you if you want.

Thanks, but it's not necessary. I still don't know when I'm leaving. Aríete returned to the living room and got down to work. However, Neusa's words were still on his mind.

Late in the afternoon, when he got home, he went to talk to Dalva.

- What did Dora say when I broke my leg?

- That you had been pushed by the spirits. I was very impressed. Why do you ask that?

- Since I've been back at work, I don't feel at ease in the office. I get restless, I feel shivers, I want to leave. And today Rodrigo is not well either. He says he had a nightmare and didn't sleep well. Neusa was nearby, overheard our conversation and got goose bumps.

- The company must have a bad influence. Maybe it needs a blessing. After all, Marcelo died of a disaster, and maybe he had no peace. Maybe his spirit is there. I've heard that many people when they die don't realize they are dead and go back to the places they were used to.

- I don't think so. Marcelo' spirit, if it can be there, is surely close to Aline. Why would he come to the office?

- I don't know. It crossed my mind. We could ask a priest to come and bless it.

- In that case, I prefer to go to the spiritual center that Neusa knows. If they are hurting us, we have to go to the Center.

- In that case, I want to go with you.

- It is not far. We will go tomorrow night for a consultation. Dalva agreed and went to dinner. Soon after, the phone rang and Aríete answered

- Aline, how nice of you to call. How are you doing?

- I'm fine. I want to hear from you.

- We're all fine. We miss you. Dad talks about you every day.

- I miss you too. I'd like to come see you, but I can't travel now. Only to the vacations. But when I think about meeting people there, I don't want to.

- You're still going to that high school

- Rachel and I are taking a course there and we're loving it. Now I am sure that life goes on after death. That the spirit of the departed can communicate with us and even interfere in our lives.

- Are you sure about that?

- I've had some tests done and there's no doubt in a nutshell. Aríete told him what was

- was going on and finished:

- I was thinking of going to the Spiritual Center tomorrow, but I still have doubts.

- I am sure you will feel better. That's what happened to me. I feel very well. I don't feel Marcelo's pain anymore. Dalva was nearby and wanted to talk to her daughter. Aríete said she would go, said goodbye and passed the phone to her mother.

As they talked, Aríete remained pensive. Aline was not an impressionable person, on the contrary. She was extremely practical, objective and uninfluenced. If she believed in the influence of spirits, it must be true.

The next evening, a few minutes before seven-thirty, Aríete and Dalva entered the Center. It was a simple, one-story house, and in the foyer they were met by a young woman who gave them a ticket and directed them to the reception desk.

They sat down in the hallway next to other people and, when their number was called, they entered a simple room with three small tables, two chairs at each, and only one of them had a person waiting.

The two headed that way, someone pulled up another chair for them, and they sat down across from a young man who greeted them with a smile.

They gave their names and addresses and said they wanted to have a spiritual consultation. He looked at Aríete and said

Before the consultation, you must undergo treatment. Naturally, you have come because you are not feeling well lately.

In fact, I am not feeling well, especially in the office where I work. I wonder if something is wrong, because my boss is not feeling well either.

The young man stared at her for a moment and then answered:

The problem is not in the place, but in you. There are people interested in kicking you out. These people have not assimilated a life-changing event. They blame you and are very angry.

- You were attacked, but you recovered because you are innocent and have protection.

I fell and broke my leg.

- You were pushed by the spirits sent to do this.

- Who sent them? - Dalva asked, frightened.

- Angry people with one eye on an inheritance you received.

- How do you know all this? - asked Aríete.

- My spirit guide tells me. He also says they're going to try to prejudge a store. Do you have a store?

- My father does.

- They want you to lose everything, to be left with nothing.

- It can only be the family.

- Dalva said. The boy interrupted:

- If you suspect someone, please do not rebel. People who try to solve their problems by harming others will be penalized by life, which always responds according to the attitude of each one. Let us think about good, let us ask for spiritual help because only good overcomes evil.

I explain to Dalva.

- Do not be alarmed. I have to tell you what my spiritual guide suggested to me, so that you believe in spirituality. But I am going to refer you for treatment and maybe everything will be solved.

- He gave each of you a piece of paper.

- You are going to come twice a week, at the same time you have to bring this paper.

- It's the first time I go to a spiritualist center. How is the treatment?

- It will start today. We donate energies and the good spirits take care of what you need.

- They were led into a room lit only by a blue light and there was soft music in the air. There were people standing and empty chairs where they sat. Aríete felt goose bumps all over her body, she was so scared and wanted to run out of there. He made a sign to get up and a young woman approached him saying: 198

- Calm down. Everything will pass. Try to pray and ask for help from those who love you. Aríete tried to control himself, thinking there was no reason to be afraid. The people were kind, the place was simple, with flowers, nothing to justify her fear.....

- She had not prayed, since she was a child. She thought of Mary, the mother of Jesus, and prayed for help. Little by little, she calmed down. The young woman in front of her laid her hands on her without touching her and Aríete could not hold back the tears that ran down her cheeks. When she stopped crying she felt that she was okay. She was offered some water, which she drank, and they left the room.

Dalva was elated:

How wonderful! I had never felt so light, so good. And the pleasant, rose-scented wind blowing, even though the door was closed?

I didn't feel anything like it. On the contrary, I got goose bumps and wanted to run.

You don't say! How are you now?

It's all over now.

In the hallway, they both found the young man who had been taking care of them and Aríete approached him, telling him what she had felt. He listened quietly and then explained:

The spirit that was disturbing you was afraid and wanted to run away, until it did. You were picking up on its emotions. It is good to know that we can capture the emotions of others, whether they are incarnated or not. The process is so strong that, if we don't know it, we will believe that everything we feel is ours, which is not true.

It's hard to believe, but it makes sense. It may be because he left so suddenly. Because I shed tears without meaning to, would they be his too?

- No. Your spirit was moved by the situation and the tears relieved the tension. You must have felt great after them.

- Actually, I felt relieved.

- See to it that you get the proper treatment and you will feel much better. They thanked him and said goodbye as they walked back home. They could not stop talking about what they had experienced that night.

- When they arrived, they found Mario curious:

- When I got home I didn't see anyone, may I know where you went? - answered Dalva:

- You took too long and we couldn't wait. We went to the Spiritualist Center and had to be there at half past seven. Didn't you see the note I left you?

- I did. But I was curious. You've never been to the Spiritualist Center.

- We'll tell you all about it

- Aríete said.

- In the meantime, I'm going to heat up dinner. I'm starving. Dalva went to the kitchen while Aríete told his father the reasons for going to the Center and everything the young man who had seen them had told them. When he mentioned the store, Mario made a surprised gesture:

- Did he really say that?

- He said.

- Mario ran a hand through his hair and turned away:

- "How can you tell?" "I didn't tell you anything so you wouldn't worry, but this month we've sold almost nothing. The few customers come in and leave without buying anything.

- So, I was right.

- I was right. It's surprising. How could I know?

- I asked him the same question and he told me that his spirit guide had asked him to tell us that.

- Did he say if the store situation was going to improve?

- He said that by chasing away the spirits that were attacking us, everything would go back to normal.

- Mario sighed in relief:

- Good. If it keeps going like this, I won't be able to pay the bills at the end of the month. Come to think of it, I think when you go back there, I'll go with you. I want to see it up close. When I was a kid, my grandfather always told stories about spirits. He believed that good or bad spirits communicated with people. Dalva appeared in the room:

- Let's have dinner. I've heard what you've told me. Then you will tell me about the store and your grandfather.

- I will. I wish he were still alive so we could talk. Now I would pay much more attention to what you told me then. They went into the pantry and the delicious smell of food made them sit down and indulge in the pleasure of a good meal.

Chapter XVII

- Márcio picked up the phone and called Olivia. She answered and, after greeting her, he asked:

- How have you been, better?

- Yes. I'm ashamed of the scene you witnessed.

- I'd like to know what you think of nature. Would you like to have dinner with me tonight?

- It took her a while to answer and she did.

- I was afraid he would refuse, but he answered:

- Fine. You deserve it.

- I'll come to your house at eight o'clock. I'll be at your house at eight. Are you all right?

- I'll be waiting for you.

Ten days had passed since the night he met her and he had often thought of her, of her tormented face, of the tears she had shed and of the pain he had noticed in her tears. He was attracted to her, but at the same time, from the words she had said to him, it could be that she had agreed to have dinner with him just to show her gratitude and there was no other interest.

Even so, he dressed with a whimsical touch that made Ivone notice him:

- How handsome you are! It looks like you're going to a party.

- I'm going to look for dad's car. He doesn't usually go out at night.

- Be careful.

He left very excited. Olivia was a classy girl and her father's car was a little old. He thought it was time to have his own car. He hadn't thought about it before, precisely because his father only used the car for work and never went out at night.

- He thought it was a waste to have another car. But for the first time he realized how old his father's car was.

- He arrived at Olivia's house and rang the doorbell. A maid came to open the door. - Good evening Mr.

- Goodnight Mr. Please tell Olivia that Márcio is here.

- You told him you would come and asked him to come in. He entered and accompanied her to the living room.

Sit down please. It will go down immediately. Do you want a water, a snack or a coffee?

- No, thanks.

He sank into the couch and looked around. The room was luxuriously furnished and very pretty. He felt a little embarrassed to be there. Although he was middle class, he lived in a simple neighborhood and was not used to going to places like that.

Soon after, a delicious aroma filled the air and rose. Olivia was approaching. She looked beautiful in her dark green dress, her bright green eyes and her shapely lips parted in a smile. After greetings he said:

We can go

- They left and once in the car Márcio couldn't get enough of admiring her.

- You're beautiful!

- he commented without being able to contain himself. She sighed and replied:

- Thank you. But sometimes I would like to be poor and ugly. That way I would have a calmer life.

Upon noticing that a shadow of sadness had passed through his eyes, he responded:

- Tonight, we will forget our sorrows and have fun. After all, we are young, we are full of life, we can have fun and dream of good things.

- That's how it is. Let's have fun. Laugh, I need joy.

- Then you have spoken to the right person. I am also tired of suffering and I want to forget the pain. Let's have fun. Where do you want to go?

- Do you know any nice place where we can dance a little? You like dancing?

- I really like to dance. you guide the way

- She accepted. The restaurant was not far away and ten minutes later

- We arrived, left the car in the parking lot and went in. The place was nice, very well decorated with vases and flowers. They take you to a table from which you can contemplate, through a glass window, the beautiful garden that surrounds the building.

What a nice place – commented Márcio.

- I like it here. The music is good and they play everything.

- They placed their order and Márcio realized that the people around him were classy and wondered how much he would have to pay for dinner.

- It was going to be expensive, but he didn't care because the pleasure of being there, with her, was worth any effort.

- They ordered and while they waited Márcio invited her to dance. She accepted. She was enveloped in pleasure, inhaling the delicious perfume that she gave off. The music was romantic and he had never felt so much pleasure at a dance. Olivia was light on her feet and since she danced so well she surrendered herself to the delight of the music. During dinner, Márcio chatted about pleasant things; He wanted her to be happy, although he actually wanted to know the cause of her sadness.

I was afraid that it was a disappointment in love and that I was only going out with him out of gratitude, without any personal interest.

-But she felt that she first had to gain his trust and then talk about his problems.

- It was after one o'clock when they left the restaurant. They were happy and Marcio noticed how pretty she was when he smiled.

-When they arrived in front of her house, he went down the stairs and accompanied her to the door.

- Good night and thank you. It had been a long time since I had had such a pleasant evening.

- I like it too. To dance very well.

- I love to dance. Music is good for our spirit.

- I hope we can repeat it. She hesitated for a moment and then answered:

- Don't know. I'm about to go abroad, when?

Soon. I still don't know the date. It depends on a few things.

- How long will you stay?

- If I could, I would not return to Brazil so soon. Márcio felt a chill when he remembered Aline. Why did women insist on living abroad? Aren't you going to go to university?

- Yes, but if I leave before the holidays I will cancel the registration and continue when I return.

- In that case, we can go out while you are not traveling. Won't you change your mind?

- No, I would have already left. But I depend, as I said, on some things. In any case, we can hang out while he's here.

- she held out her hand to him

- Thanks again and good night.

- Good night

-She responded, squeezing her hand and bringing it to her lips.

-Tonight, has been very special for me.

- I enjoy your company, but I don't want you to fool yourself into thinking about me. I can offer you nothing but friendship.

- I'll call you anyway

- She smiled, opened the door and Marcio got into the car feeling a pang of disappointment. Olivia had been very clear. She had noticed his interest and had tried to contain herself. However, if he managed to make her forget her problems and enjoy her company, perhaps he could aspire to have an emotional relationship with her.

- He felt that she belonged to a different social level, but at the same time he was willing to pay the price of cultivating a relationship that would undoubtedly require him not only to live up to it, but also to try to be elegant, frequenting luxurious places to which he was not used to it, and at the same time trying to improve his life.

- The luxury that he saw in his house, the beautiful objects and a pleasant atmosphere were very good and he would very much like to live in a place like that. If only Marcelo's money had gotten into his hands. He could open his own business. He does not want to be like his father, who more than ten years ago worked in an accounting office and earned barely enough to maintain the standard of living they always had, which did not allow him to travel abroad or buy fashionable clothes. .

- He also, despite being a professional, worked and earned little. Although he didn't need money at home. His salary did not allow for extravagance. If Olivia reciprocated his feelings, he would have to look for another job. Thinking about her, he felt that he had never felt the interest in her for any woman that he felt for her. And everything he would do to stop her from traveling. He fed her thoughts that if she had more time, if she delayed her trip, he might change his mind.

A memory of pleasant moments of that night. She really wanted to repeat it.

When she got home she lay down and began to imagine what it would be like to kiss those beautiful lips, to hold that body that she would feel in her arms. She finally decided that the next day she would go look for another job. In the end, she received an education and should not accept a second-class job. Making plans for the future, Márcio fell asleep.

After saying goodbye to Márcio, Olivia entered her house trying not to make noise. She took off her shoes and was walking slowly when the office door opened and a tall, dark, middle-aged man appeared. His face was contorted, his brow furrowed, his eyes flashed with anger:

What were you doing on the street until that moment?}

-Olivia, she shuddered and glaring at him, she responded.

Leave me alone.

-He took her arm:

- you think you can do that with me. Who do you think I am?

- I do not believe anything. I do not want anything from you. Leave me alone.

- You're not going to get rid of me like that. You are mine and I don't admit that you go out with other men.

- You are crazy.

- I'm completely crazy. So much so that I no longer care what might happen. If you continue to avoid me. I'll show those photos to your mother and tell her you jumped into my arms. That you are a pervert and that I don't even respect your mother's husband.

- You know it's not true. You know everything you did to get those pictures or you should go to the police.

- Go ahead. I'll tell everyone that you're no good, that you've done everything to drive me crazy.

- But I won't because I don't want my mother to know.

- I love you. I can't think of anything else but holding you in my arms.

- The memory of that night never leaves my mind. It's driving me crazy!

- I will never do what you want. That night I was unconscious. But that won't happen again. I'm alert. Let go of me. Do you want Mom to wake up?

- They heard a woman's voice ask:

- She let go of Olivia and said softly:

You have to explain to me exactly who that boy was who brought her home.

- Then she went upstairs and, trying to give herself an air of calm and physiognomy, she met Olga at the top of the stairs and explained:

- I was drinking water and I saw Olivia come in and I was talking to her.

- Olivia went upstairs and her mother, already at the bedroom door, asked her:

- Is everything all right, my daughter?

- Olivia wiped away her tears and replied in a voice she tried to make natural.

- This one is. Good night, Olivia.

- Good night, Olivia.

- She went into her room, closed the door and lay on the bed crying her eyes out. Life at home was unbearable.

Ever since she was fourteen, she noticed that her stepfather looked at her with greedy eyes. That's why she hated him. She ran away from him as much as she could. She didn't want her mother to know.

Her father died when she was seven years old and four years later her mother married Gilberto, a wealthy businessman who inherited a profitable business and a lot of money from her father.

The situation with her stepfather had worsened when her mother was admitted to the hospital for several days due to a kidney problem that culminated in the removal of a kidney.

Olga had been hospitalized for two days when Gilberto invited her to have a snack before going to bed. She took the snack and fell asleep. When she was lying in bed, next to the man who had raped her. Still mute, feeling her body aching, she tried to get up, but he covered her with kisses, calling her my love. And Olivia, horrified, threatened to scream. He told her that if she did, the servants would hear her and tell her mother everything when she got home.

Distraught, Olivia waited for the dizziness to improve and finally managed to go to her room, where she cried in despair.

On the day her mother was due to return home, Olivia woke up and confronted Gilberto. She was determined to tell everything and take the consequences. Then he showed her some pictures he had taken of her while she was unconscious, implying that she was with him of her own free will. Looking at those photos, anyone would think Olivia was her stepfather's mistress. He took those photos in case she went to the police, since she was a minor, it would prove that she had conquered him.

She was very pretty and he couldn't resist that would be his defense. Olivia understood that her mother would not accept her innocence. She loved her husband and was very jealous.

From that day on, her life at home became a martyrdom. Gilberto continued to harass her and took advantage of every moment Olga was absent. Olivia tried to stay out of the house as much as possible, but Gilberto would put pressure on Olga, making her see the danger of her outings.

Interested in getting away from him. Olivia told her mother that she would like to study abroad, that she would get a school in the United States.

Despite not wanting to move away from her daughter, Olga agreed, but then Gilberto intervened and she decided to wait until her daughter was of age.

Distressed, she learned from a classmate that she was going to the land for professional help and would get a very good internship.

Without telling anyone about the problem that was troubling her, she found out the address of the land and went to talk to Father José.

When she told him about her plight, he promised to help her. Encouraged, Olivia waited, but nothing was happening.

That night that she met Marcio, she had gone to the compound to speak again with Father José.

He told her that he had studied the case and advised her to be patient because the situation would be resolved when she turned twenty-one and left home.

Before then, if her mother discovered her, she would accuse her of having judged her stepfather and would never forgive her.

Disgusted, without the courage to continue enduring that martyrdom for more than two years, she could not hold back her tears. So that no one would see her. She hid behind the tree, where Marcio found her.

That night she had arrived home better. The moments spent at Márcio's side, his kindness, the music and the pleasant atmosphere, contributed to make her feel good.

However, an unpleasant dinner with Gilberto, an intervention by her mother and the fear she felt that he would find out everything, made her think that she could not wait another two years, exposing herself to the risk of her mother finding out. She went to her room, lay down on the bed and began to devise a plan to run away from home. She had some money in the bank, which her mother had set aside for when she graduated, but it wasn't enough to go as far away as she wanted.

She needed to scrape together a little more, and to do that, she had to stay a few more days, trying to get as much as she could.

She intended to leave Brazil and go abroad. She could not risk Gilberto finding her. He would be furious that she had run away and would no doubt do everything he could to track her whereabouts and bring her back. When he asked her for suggestions on what she was going to do to study in the United States.

She mentioned an American organization that did student exchanges and might be able to give him a good suggestion.

She had to do it all without anyone at home knowing about it. When everything was arranged, he would leave, however, he would leave a letter for his mother, with a good apology and he would be free.

He did not mind abandoning the luxury in which he lived to earn a living. What he wanted most of all was to be able to live in peace, to rediscover the pleasure of living. She thought of Márcio. Maybe he could help her. He would not tell her the truth. He would only tell her that her stepfather hated her and that her life was hell. He would be willing to help her, he seemed sincere, he was discreet and, most importantly, no one in her circle of friends knew him.

The next day she would call Marcio, showing her interest in cultivating his friendship. She would go out a couple of times with him to get to know him a little better and see to what extent she could trust him.

What mattered to him was to achieve his goal. With his help she could carry out her escape plan.

She was determined. She could not afford to go on living like this. She wanted to change her life, her country, to forget everything, to look for better days where she could be happy and live in peace.

Chapter XVIII

Antonio arrived at Mimo's fortress in search of Marcelo. He was very nervous. As he gave his name, he heard a voice asking him:

- What do you want here?

- You don't recognize me, I'm Antonio, I lived here for a long time. I want to talk to Mimo.

- The door opened, he entered.

- I'll see if he can take care of it.

- It's not urgent. We are friends.

- I follow orders. He wants me to be punished. Antonio agreed and the doorman went in while

- He stood waiting in the courtyard. Shortly after, he returned:

- You can go in, he's waiting for you. I will accompany you.

- No need, I know the way.

A little later he knocked on the door of Mimo's living room. After the greetings, Antonio said nervously:

Where is Marcelo?

He is not with you

No, what a good assistant you sent me. He put everything at risk. Mimo inhaled smoke, let out a puff and said calmly:

First of all, moderate your tone When you speak.

- Call me sir. I did what you asked me to do and I'm not to blame for that boy not behaving well. Antonio tried to swallow his anger and answered:

- Sir it is true that he did not come back here.

- I am. I want to know everything that happened.

- He came, I showed him everything he had to do, 'he did everything right. I thought it was time to speed up the case so that Mirian would be back soon. I left her all the instructions and went to find an acquaintance who had the knowledge to solve everything at once.

- He paused slightly, listening attentively to Mimo who listened with narrowed eyes and noticing that he was attentive, he continued:

- I was away for two days because it was a long trip and I had to wait until the person I was looking for could accompany me. He assured me that it would be easy and that everything would be over that very afternoon he had avenged me. However, when we arrived at her house, there was a light guard at the door, which scared us to death.

- You didn't say I was protected!

- said my companion and, without further ado, left me alone.

- The surrounding light made me shudder because I felt that, even at a certain distance, all my defenses disappeared. I tried to get out of there as fast as I could.

- It was the interference of the light beings, for sure. You'll notice that Marcelo was kicked out - said Mimo.

- I don't think so, when I got home I concentrated and found out what happened. I saw everything. His protégé felt sorry for him and instead of doing what I ordered him to do, he started praying. You can imagine such a thing.

- Mimo opened his eyes and straightened his body, saying irritably:

- That he did it himself.

- He did it without a doubt, look and see

- Mimo concentrated and managed to see what had happened.

- Those spirits always meddle in our affairs. They were responsible. Marcelo knew he had made a mistake and was afraid to come back here. So, they wrapped him up and took him away.

- And now, how am I going to do? You have to help me.

- Everything has limits. I can't get involved with light beings. I know our limits. I don't want to lose everything I've achieved.

- You promised you would help me!

- I delivered. But I didn't count that the other side had an interest in protecting Mirian. If you want my advice, give up for now. Get on with your life, don't try anything.

- I'm not giving up.

- Count me out. Mirian is now protected and you won't be able to do anything against her. You'd better calm your hatred. After all, you hated her a long time ago. No doubt she paid for everything she did. Go take care of your life, try to improve your appearance a bit, it's scary.

- I'm going to ask Mirela to help me.

Mirela disappeared. She disappeared. She got tired of waiting for Renato.

- In that case I don't know what to do.

- Get well. That's all I can tell you, you can go now. With a gesture, Mimo

- said goodbye to Antonio who left disappointed. He imagined that Mimo was strong and could handle anything. But he was deceived. What powerful beings were those capable of intimidating Mimo. He always liked to deal with the bosses, he didn't want to talk to subordinates. He imagined that Mimo was the boss. That was a lie. There were other beings more powerful than him.

He decided to leave, got out and started walking. There was no longer any point in staying there, nor did he feel like going back to the place where he had lived for some years. Where would he go? What was he going to do with his life.

For more than six years he devoted himself exclusively to his revenge. He managed to involve the traitor and provoke the car accident that cost him his life.

When he left his body, Antonio, who was waiting contentedly, threw his betrayal in his face and, although he did not recognize him, he was taken away by a rescue party.

Antonio did not care much because what he wanted most was to return Miriam to the dimension in which she was and to have her at his mercy and make her feel the weight of his mistake.

But now that everything had gone wrong, he felt indecisive, aimless and discouraged. It was then that Cora's spirit approached him. She had turned off the light so as not to frighten him. And she approached him saying: "How are you, Antonio?

How are you, Antonio? he shuddered:

Who are you?

My name is Cora. I was passing by and I noticed you were tired. Very tired, aimless. I come from a very nice place, ideal to recharge your batteries.

That's right. I'm very tired. Life for me has been terrible. If I could at least forget a little, rest...

You can. If you want a ride.

Antonio felt a soft and pleasant energy coming from her that he had not felt for a long time. He sighed sadly:

I want to, but I don't know if I should. Look at me, I'm discomposed, dirty, almost disheveled. I'm ashamed.

Give me your hand.

He obeyed and she continued

And imagine that you are wearing a garment that you had when you lived in the world and that you liked very much, and as if by magic you have found it on.

- Where are we? What beautiful places.

- We are in the recovery zone. Here the treatment uses beauty as a remedy.

- I didn't know that existed.

- Cora smiled

- There are so many things you're going to see. But now, you're going to stay close to here.

- They went downstairs waxing a five-story building, full of windows, surrounded by trees and flowers.

- Antonio was excited, breathing with pleasure the soft scent in the air. They entered through one of the doors and walked down a hallway until they reached a room where a young woman greeted them, hugged Cora and introduced Antonio:

- Nora this friend needs attention. He was aimless and I thought it would be a good place for him to stay for a while. I invited him and he accepted.

- Welcome," said Nora, holding out her hand, which he shook shyly. The place was very clean and tidy and he realized that, although he was wearing better clothes, his appearance was not the best. Embarrassed, he looked down.

- They noticed, but didn't mention it. They talked for a few minutes and finally Nora took Antonio by the arm and said:

- Come with me. Here we cultivate beauty. So before I show you your home and introduce you to your neighbors, I'll take you to a makeover session where you'll receive the care you need to improve your appearance. I get the impression that you haven't been taking care of yourself lately.

- In fact, I haven't taken care of myself in a long time.

- That's our first responsibility.

- Cora said with a smile.

- The beauty treatment here is very good and you will feel so good that you will never neglect yourself again.

- When he's ready, I'll come pick him up so we can go to his new house. They both left and went to Nora's living room. Where Cora told Antonio's story, ending.

- For six consecutive years, he was bent on revenge. Then, there came a time when life gave him a so far, prevented him from continuing, protected the person he was pursuing and withdrew all help from the vigilantes. Then he became aimless, because during that time he had abandoned himself, not allowing himself any joy, cultivating only hatred.

- He felt helpless, realized that a greater force was at work and weakened

- That's right, so I looked it up. I thought I would bring him here to sensitize his spirit, so brutalized by hatred, through beauty.

- His case will take a long time because the more he becomes sensitized, the more he likes beauty, the more he will feel the mistakes he has made within himself.

- The goodness of people ends up making us feel our weaknesses more. The geniuses who live there are convinced that any kind of art sensitizes the soul and they asked themselves: why not use it as therapy with the spirits who still believe in evil as a solution to their problems?

- I know that almost two centuries ago they founded this city and I am a witness to the success of this theory.

- Here the improvement is faster, more objective. But because for many the contrast between what they believed and reality is so great, we have brought in therapists to help them.

- We have brought in therapists to help them when they are overwhelmed by remorse or depression. Some are so ashamed that they want to punish themselves, accuse themselves, hurt themselves or want to leave because they say they don't deserve so many good things.

- It has a refined taste and a better development. He likes it here very much. However, he still finds it hard to forget his wife.

He talks about her all the time, he is obsessed. The attachment he feels for her is terrible.

- Do you know anything about his past with Mirela?

- Yes, I do. But right now he's so obsessed with the memory of Aline that he completely blocks out memories of other lives.

- I realized he had had some flashbacks, but I couldn't reconcile the facts.

- He has been restless lately. It's hard to keep track of him here.

- I'm going to talk to him.

- You do that. Maybe you can calm him down.

- Cora left the room and went to find Marcelo. The day was beautiful and several people were chatting happily in the surrounding garden. But Marcelo was not among them.

- She went to look for him at his chalet. Sitting on the balcony, crestfallen, there he was, alone. Cora approached

- I was close by and went over to give you a hug. He got up and hugged her, saying:

- I'm glad you saw me. I was desperate. I need to go see Aline.

- It's not possible yet.

- You tell me, but I'm beginning to doubt it. Why don't you want me to go see her?

- Why is her house guarded by Mimo's men? If I go there, they'll get me.

- I am on both sides. You say you love her and who loves wants the happiness of the loved one.

- I can make her happy.

- You had your chance, but it's over. It's good to know that people are free, no one belongs to anyone. As much as you want it to be different, that's the truth.

- Marcelo covered his face with his hands and began to cry. Cora did not intervene. When she stopped she hugged him saying:

- I know it's hard for you, but I'm sure you'll overcome that attachment. Now you live in another dimension, here you can find new paths, full of joy and love. Why do you insist on suffering for something that has no return?

- I cannot live without her

- said the sad man. She sat down on the bench on the veranda and pulled him close to her. She put her arm around him and replied

- You are stronger than you think. You can and will be able to take a break from the part of your life where you are separated. Aline will live on in the flesh for a long time. But you can wait for her when she comes back, it will only be a matter of time.

- I'm afraid she'll fall in love with someone else.

- You know that can happen and you're not going to be able to avoid it. Wouldn't you be better off looking to adjust to a life here, make friends, let time pass so you can meet her face to face when she comes?

He wrung his hands nervously.

- I don't know if she's going to love me anymore. She has abandoned me.

- She may have a different path than you. Life always knows what to do.

- Life always knows what to do. If she went on and left you, maybe she stopped loving you No one can force someone to like you. This feeling is spontaneous and natural. If she doesn't love you anymore, it's a waste of time to wait for her, or to want to suffer by her side, which is worse.

I can't stop thinking about her.

- Make an effort. If you let go of that thought, you will surely soon remember other lives and that memory will make you a very happy person.

- Do you think so?

- I am sure of it.

- Sometimes I think I've never had other lives

- Cora smiled and answered

- Dreams, the visions you have from time to time.

- Why don't you try to find out what they want to tell you?

- How do I do that?

- By thinking about the visions, you already have, wanting to know more.

- Are you saying this because you know my past and I'm just a suggestion?

- The symptoms you have make me think that you are ready to remember the past. I even think you just need to pay more attention to your inner world for this to happen.

- What's the point of wanting to know what happened a long time ago if my heart, my thoughts are on Aline, on our current life?

- It's just that a life separated them and she has a just reason for it. To insist now on this rapprochement is a waste of time. You live in separate worlds, there is no way to be together. While she needs to live her experiences in the material world, you are called to renew yourself and move forward in your spiritual life.

- But I don't want to live a spiritual life. I want to be on earth where I have all my interests. My family, my wife. My heart is there, with them.

- I know that. But your heart can remain with them as long as love never dies, but it is not time to be together because each one lives his own process of evolution and has his own needs. For you, it is time to analyze with maturity the experiences lived and try to take advantage of them.

What good is a violent death like mine, without taking advantage of my youth, full of plans for the future.

One day you will understand why you had to go through that. It's good to know that life doesn't make mistakes and does it the right way at the right time.

How can you say that.

Why everything has a reason for being. Nothing happens by chance. Therefore, try to make the most of your time. Instead of continuing to think of Aline with rebelliousness, dissatisfaction, remember the good times you had together in 220 that union of love that you say you feel for her, let her go her own way. And don't make it difficult for me.

You can't live clinging to being a good person. She's just a crutch for you and you don't want to leave her. That's not true.

Of course, love, when it is true, puts the happiness of the loved one first. You don't care about her feelings or whether she was happy with you, you just want to perpetuate your bond with her. That is attachment, not love.

I love her.

Whoever loves liberates, does not subjugate the loved one.

Marcelo could not hold back the tears that ran down his face, contracted by despair.

Cora stroked his head affectionately and waited for him to calm down. Then she told him in a serene voice

While you are thinking about this matter, I would like to invite you to a gathering at the home of some friends of mine. There will be music and much merriment.

- I don't feel like visiting anyone. I am in no condition to be good company.

- You're going with me. What's the point of insisting on your pain? On the contrary. Come with me, I'm sure you'll like it. They are very interesting, intelligent, kind people. The place is nice and very pleasant.

- I don't know...

- It's been a long time since I had a moment of peace and well-being. I'm sure that if you keep calm, it will be easier to find a better solution for your case.

- Maybe that's a good idea.

- I'll pick you up at eight o'clock.

- Okay, I'll come.

- I need a good distraction. I'm usually on time.

- I'll wait for you.

- She left and Marcelo sat pensively by the window. From there he could see the beautiful garden surrounding the building.

- Cora's words were still vivid in his memory. "He who loves liberates, does not subjugate the beloved". As much as it was hard for him to admit it, he wanted to stay by her side anyway. Without wondering if she desired him for the first time, he sensed her gradually distancing herself from him. That was why she had left him.

She had abandoned him. The truth hit him hard and he healed dejectedly. He felt that she did not love him enough.

He thought about how he had known her, remembered the good times in the early days of their marriage, how happy he had been pampering her, indulging her every whim.

Marcelo felt he didn't want to stay by her side if he made her unhappy. That was the reality. He had not been able to make her happy. He felt his chest tighten, his head spinning, unable to think clearly. Cora was right. She needed to pause in her grief, calm her spirit, maybe then she could figure out what she was going to do with her life from here on out.

Chapter XIX

A few days later, Olivia returned home satisfied. She had talked to Marli, her English teacher, who had told her that at that time of year it would not be possible to get what she wanted. However, she was good friends with a former student who lived in Miami:

Give her my phone number and ask her to call me. I think I can find you a place.

Heart pounding, Olivia wrote down the name and number. She had to go to the bank to find out how much she had in the account. But she couldn't do that until the next day. In the meantime, she would take care of organizing her money better. He would try to secure it when he got back. But he needed to have a reserve for the first few years. The next morning, instead of going to college, he waited for the bank to open to check his balance. She did the math on how much she would like to take with her and it wasn't enough. She was sure that in a few days she would get the remaining balance. That night, during dinner, she overheard a conversation between her mother and her husband:

When are you going to give me that money?

Olivia went to her room and called the number Marli had given her to talk to Malu, Marli's former student, and Marli told her she could stay in the building where she lived. The price was reasonable and the location was good. Olivia immediately asked her to book the place, as she would be arriving in two or three days. The next morning, Olivia noticed that the courier had left a package for Gilberto. She noticed that he had put it in a drawer in his desk in the study.

He made his plans. He went out, went to check the ticket, there was a flight for the next afternoon and he bought the ticket and paid by check. He went to the bank, took out the available balance, left the money and check there and went home. I spent the afternoon assessing her clothes and deciding what to wear. I left everything neat and ready to pack.

The whole time her stepfather was home he watched her every step closely and watched as she left a bulky letter for her mother that read:

Here it is. Pay everything and don't get into debt anymore

I will go tomorrow afternoon. Now I have to go to the doctor. Then she put the package in one of the dresser drawers.

The next morning, when Olga left for her stepfather's office, Olivia went to her mother's room and took out the package, opened it and saw that it contained thirty thousand dollars.

She immediately wrote a letter to her mother telling her that she would try her luck abroad. He had borrowed the thirty thousand dollars and would return it as soon as he could.

He left no address and did not say to which country he was going.

Then she grabbed the bags she had ordered the night before, hailed a cab and headed for the airport.

Her flight was leaving in the afternoon, but she didn't want to wait at home for fear of her mother's or stepfather's reaction. She was elated. She kept her ticket and passport. When she boarded the plane, she finally felt she was free from that nightmare. She knew Gilberto would do everything he could to bring her back, but she would not return as long as he was with Olga.

She knew that her mother would be saddened, that she would not understand, that she would accuse her without judging her. However, all that was woman as the truth would hurt her more. When the plane took off. Olivia remembered that she had forgotten to say goodbye to Márcio.

She would go out with him again a few times, if she noticed he was interested in falling in love with her. She liked him. He was a nice guy, nice, but she didn't want to fall in love with anyone because she didn't plan to stay in Brazil. When she reached her destination, she would send him a farewell letter. Her heart was pounding at the thought that she was free to do what she wanted and, above all, to live in peace.

That night, when Marcio called Olivia, a maid told him that she had suddenly left without saying where, he was very sad. Since he had met her, he thought about her all the time. He was in love. He sensed that Olivia did not reciprocate as he would like, but he felt that she liked him, so he harbored the hope that in time she would fall in love with him.

That trip hit him like a bucket of cold water. She would show herself to be his friend, because she wouldn't tell him about her trip. Sure, she would run away from home because of her stepfather's abuse, but why didn't she give him the address? She knew she could trust him.

That thought really irritated him. Why was it all wrong for him? It was the only time he really liked a woman and she went far away.

If only he knew where Olivia had gone, maybe he could think about going there in the future. But for that he would need money. His job wasn't bad, he earned a reasonable salary, but it wasn't enough.

Marcelo gave his parents a generous allowance and Marcio could keep all of his salary, but after Marcelo's death, it was up to him to help with the expenses. If only his parents had kept Marcelo company, he probably wouldn't have needed that money, he could have thought about going with Olivia. He thought of his father José. From the looks of it, he wasn't capable of doing anything. More than once she felt angry that she had given him the money. He had to pay the aunt without having gotten anything.

Father José had promised, and he was going to collect it. He thought about going to the land that very night.

At once I began to work. Marcio was there next to the medium and, as soon as Father José arrived, he approached him.

- Here again, my son.

- Yes, Father José. I came to know if you have any news about my case. The medium was silent. He let out a puff of smoke and then said:

- The girl who left will send a letter. It can wait. Márcio shuddered. He hadn't said anything about Olivia.

- Are you sure? he asked cheerfully.

- One doubt father José, I'm going to stay with her. This girl is very good, but she's not for you. Yes. Forget about her.

- Just because she's rich.

- It's not because of that. It's just that her destiny is different from yours.

- I like her and I want her to come back to me.

I can try. She can try to come back, but she won't stay forever. How did the Lord know about her.

Father Joseph knows everything that happens to his children. I see it here. I am working to have them and know everything.

Thank you, Father Joseph. I will be waiting.

Márcio left the center unsatisfied. He wanted to see Olivia. She was everything he dreamed of in a woman. He didn't believe Father José what he had said. He liked Olivia and in time it could turn into love.

He just needed to go to where she was and take her back to Brazil. The next morning. Olivia arrived in Miami, took a cab and went straight to Malú's house who received her very well.

She was a cheerful, good-humored young woman and her friendly smile endeared her to Olivia.

- Leave your bags here, I'm going to talk to the man who will show you the apartment.

- Upon entering the furnished apartment that Malú had reserved, Olivia liked it very much.

- It has a living room and a small kitchen on one side.

- It also has a garage," Malú explained. Olivia rented the apartment and went to get her bags.

- Sit down and have a cup of coffee with me. I still have half an hour before I go to work.

- Thank you for doing me that favor. It's my first time in this town and I don't know anyone.

- It's a very nice place to live. I love living here.

- I'm going to organize my things and then I'll buy a newspaper and look for a job.

- From your conversation with the gentleman, I have seen that you have very good English. That's why I think it won't be difficult to arrange a recruitment. I work in an advertising company. But I know there are no vacancies here.

- Don't worry. I have time to look.

- The accommodation is modest, I like it here.

You mentioned a building, I was thinking of a building like the ones we have in Brazil. But this one is different. They are individual apartments, more like houses with elegant and beautiful construction. They are also tastefully furnished. I think I will be fine.

- Most of the people who live here are Brazilians or Cubans. You will like them. Although I have no family here, I don't feel lonely. I'll help you with the suitcases.

- The two left with the suitcases and walked through the garden. They saw a girl coming out of one of the apartments.

- Malú smiled at her and said

- Aline wants to introduce you to a new neighbor. She had just arrived from Brazil. Aline approached and Malúi made the introductions. After the greetings Aline said:

- Where do you come from?

- From São Paulo

- My family lives there, in Santana.

- Mine lives in the gardens.

- Now I have to go to work. When I come back, we'll have a better conversation. You are welcome.

- Thank you very much. Thank you, thank you. Good job,

- Malú also said goodbye to go to work, Olivia entered the apartment, opened the windows and began to organize her things.

- She felt free, happy, calm. She was not worried about her mother because she loved Gilberto, she lived more for him, she was sure she would not feel his absence. When time passed, he could visit her and she would never know the real reason that led her to leave home.

During the drive to work. Aline thought of her family and felt homesick. Olivia's presence, recently arrived from her hometown, reminded her of her family. It was very good to live in Miami, she had always wanted to, she had a good job, she earned enough to support herself at a good level, there was Gino for whom she was very interested, but in spite of all the advantages, sometimes she felt away from her place, from her land, from the things of her country. Before, when he compared Brazil with Miami, he only saw the advantages of living in the United States, and the problems in his country. Now, however, when making the comparison, he begins to perceive the spontaneity of the Brazilians, less formal, making friends easily, a people who, in the midst of the bureaucracy of a less developed country, exercised creativity and joy, making smiles and music an escape valve for their frustrations.

Not that he was planning to return to Brazil anytime soon. In fact, he had glimpsed the possibility of a career that would give him professional fulfillment.

If in his youth he wanted to live there forever, he gradually changed his mind. She would stay there for a few years, just long enough to get what she wanted.

Arriving at the office, Aline called Aríete to see how the family was doing.

- All is well

She reported with satisfaction

- I was going to call her myself. Rodrigo can't keep up with the projects and wants to bring in another architect to help him. He has asked me to talk to you to see if you agree.

- I am not aware of the company's business, what do you think?

- We are making progress and beyond hiring an assistant to look for new materials, pricing, etc. He has had to turn down new projects due to lack of time.

- I think if we hire another architect we can grow more. It won't make him a partner in the firm, he will earn half the profit on every project he does.

- Tell him that's fine. Used understands more about that than I do. Whatever you decide, I'll sign downstairs. I called because I miss them.

- We miss them too. Mom never tires of talking about you. She asks you if you're okay, if you're happy.

- Aline hesitated a bit and then asked:

- Do you know anything about Marcelo's family?

- I think everything is the same. We've seen Márcio a few times on the street and he doesn't even say hello to me. I think he hates me for working there.

- You are helping, he should understand.

- What they wanted was for Marcelo's share to stay for them.

- I didn't do anything to inherit that. It's the law. We were married in community property. I thought that with time they would understand what happened.

- I think it's difficult. You shouldn't expect too much from them.

- It's a shame. Tell my mom and dad I'm fine and send them a kiss home one. A kiss for you.

- Another one for you call when you can.

- Aríete hung up the phone and went with Rodrigo to the other room.

- Aline called and gave us carte blanche to hire whoever you want.

I'm going to call Hamilton and arrange a dinner. I am sure he will come to help us. Last week we met by chance, he came to see his family that I live in Sao Paulo, he says he is not satisfied with his job and would like to come back to our city. He was a classmate of mine in college and he is very good at what he does.

- So don't waste any more time and talk to him.

- Aríete went to his office and shortly after Rodrigo went to talk to her:

- Hamilton loved the idea. He will come today to talk.

- In that case, maybe we can accept that project that you were very interested in, but I can't accept.

- Let's see if it can be true.

- An hour later, Hamilton arrived looking for Rodrigo. He was a tall, dark, elegant boy with frizzy hair and bright brown eyes. Despite being thirty-six years old, perhaps because of the sparkle in his eyes, his disheveled hair looked younger.

- Aríete waited on him and introduced himself:

- I'm Hamilton, Rodrigo is expecting me. Aríete invited him and accompanied him to Rodrigo's office.

- When he saw him, he got up to embrace him with pleasure.

- Then he left them in the living room to ask the waitress to make coffee and to see if he wanted anything else.

- When she returned to the living room and accompanied the waitress with the coffee, Rodrigo called out to her:

- I want you to get to know Hamilton better. Aríete is Marcelo's widowed sister who is living in Miami. I already told her about the accident he was a victim of.

- Hello, how are you?

- I'm doing well. Welcome.

- He stared into Aríete's eyes and answered:

- Wow, how did you look at her and see what she looks like?

- Hamilton smiled:

- I'm just observant. By the way, I like to study people, to know how they act.

- Aríete arrived at the right time. While Marcelo was alive, I didn't get too close to his family. After his death, I became a bit of an orphan. I was the one who took care of the administrative side of things, you know how it is, contracts, banks, etc. I have never been good at those things. Aríete came along and offered to help me. I knew she was a very efficient executive. Marcelo always told me so, so I left everything in her hands and I don't regret it. She is ideal. I am very grateful to her.

- She has high standards.

- Much more than I need here. Our company is small, but since she arrived, she takes care of clients, defends my projects, discusses my contracts with a confidence that reassures me. She is also happy with the profit sharing that I receive instead of her sister. I offered her a salary according to our possibilities, but she refused, saying that her sister wanted her to keep her share of the profit.

- You can tell he does it to help his sister.

- And I realized that Aríete's family is very close. When Marcelo was alive, I knew them superficially, but after his death, I tried to distance myself from them because of the disagreement with Marcelo's parents, who blame Aline for the accident. I told them so.

- You were in the middle of their fight,

- I stayed. The situation got worse when Aríete came to work here. They didn't think it was fair that Aline inherited the property, but she was entitled and they couldn't do anything about it. In the situation I was in, I couldn't refuse Aríete's offer, even though it was a very convenient arrangement for me.

- You have done well.

- That's right, but Marcelo's parents and even his brother don't greet us anymore. I'm not happy about that, but there's nothing I can do. They don't want to hear my reasons. I wanted to remain neutral, but I couldn't.

- Why not?

- Aríete fell off the ladder and broke her leg, I had to help her, I took every precaution, and every day I brought her the company papers because she wanted to work at home. Then I discovered what a wonderful family she has.

- Life knows how to show the truth when it is necessary.

- In fact, since I live alone in the city, I ended up finding in them a love that I had lost.

- Ariéte is a very beautiful woman.

- Beautiful and intelligent, and it is rare to find both together. They laughed and Rodrigo began to make a proposal.

- Half an hour later, he called Aríete to write the details of the contract.

- After writing it all down, he smiled and said

- The time has come to celebrate. Let's toast to the success of our venture. Then he called the waitress who came in with a tray of tacos and a bottle of champagne and some appetizers.

- Rodrigo opened, served and lifting the taco said:

- To the progress of us all.

- They clinked tacos and drank contentedly. Hamilton then agreed to start work the next morning.

Chapter XX

- It was eight o'clock, Cora went to look for Marcelo as agreed. She went in and found him crestfallen, pensive, sad. She approached him smiling.

- I came to pick him up, he's not ready yet.

- Excuse me, Cora. But I'm not going.

- Not at all. That victim look you've adopted doesn't suit you. Relax. Come on, get ready. Leave some nice clothes in your closet.

- Cora took him by the arm and Marcelo stood up hesitantly.

- Come on, hurry up. I don't like to be late. Hurry up. She dragged him into the room and in a few moments he was ready. Without giving him time to think, Cora took him by the arm and they left. The night was starry and the scent of the flowers in the garden was delicious.

- How nice

- Cora said, sucking in the air.

- That's nice. Can you feel it?

- Yes, I'm sorry.

- Smile No one can be sad in a place as blessed and beautiful as this. Forget your sorrows, your troubles.

- We are going to a party. Tomorrow you can come back with them if you prefer.

- From the way you say it, it seems I like to live in sadness.

- I don't know if you like it, but you're addicted to looking at everything through sadness.

- If you had gone through what I went through you wouldn't say that. He laughed good-naturedly.

- Get out of the "poor me" where your release valve is, your courage. Why do you turn off the light like that? You're still alive, the accident you were a victim of was just a trip. You are still young, handsome, you have all your faculties, what are you complaining about? What a shame.

He paused in surprise. Her words encouraged his pride and he replied:

- Then relax. Now is the time. We're going to the party and you're going to walk in with me, with a happy face and a desire to forget all about the past and have fun. She was right, he thought. At that moment there was no point in thinking about what had happened. He was tired. He wanted to rest. To forget all the suffering and enjoy a little joy.

- He smiled, offered Cora his arm and said:

- I was always a cheerful boy. You will see how I am able to have fun. They entered the living room decorated with fresh flowers that spread their delicate perfume in the air. Marcelo made a surprised face.

- I have never been here before. It's very nice.

- It is nice. Watch your thoughts when we're in this room. If you allow any negative thoughts. You will be forced to leave here even if you don't want to.

- The room was full. How they manage to control all those people.

There are special energy control devices, this place runs on the positivity of the frequenters.

That's why you brought me here.

Cora laughed and there was a mischievous twinkle in her eye when she answered:

- It wasn't just for that. Let's go for a walk, I'll introduce you to some friends.

At the tables people were chatting happily, an orchestra was playing a Viennese waltz and many couples were milling around in the center of the room. Cora stopped in front of a table and introduced Marcelo. They were pleasant people, the conversation flowed easily. Marcelo turned his attention to the neighboring table. Sitting in the middle of two couples was a girl who looked a lot like Mirela.

Maybe it was her. Maybe not. The nurse Mirela he had met looked older. The younger one was richly dressed and very elegant.

She caught Marcelo's eye and, without looking away, he approached her and asked.

- Is that you, Mirela? She stood up

- Yes, how are you Renato?

- My name is Marcelo, you always call me Renato.

- I still can't get used to the other name.

- You look different. Younger, prettier.

- It's just that now I've recovered my balance a little more. Marcelo looked at Cora and seeing that she was still chatting animatedly with her friends, he asked her:

- Do you want to dance?

- She accepted and after they were dancing around the room Marcelo took her in his arms and felt a great pleasure for that closeness. He felt a thrill come over him and suddenly it was as if they were in a palace ballroom where they were dancing.

He was in the middle of some musicians singing while she was dancing with others and he did not lose sight of her.

Suddenly he realized it was her, who was now in his arms, her face very close to his.

He felt like kissing her and noticed that she was also very excited.

- Let's go for a walk in the garden. We need to talk. Taking her by the hand, he walked into the garden.

- He led her to a flowery meadow next to it and, once there, he embraced her and kissed her on the lips for a long time. Then he felt his chest fill with a joy he could not remember ever having felt before.

- I love you," he said, holding her close to his chest. At that moment he had completely forgotten about Aline.

- I've been waiting for this moment for a long time. Lately I've come to fear that you don't love me anymore.

- I'm still confused. I feel a great love for you, but I can't explain why.

- You don't need to explain anything. It is enough for me to know that you still love me as before.

- I feel as if I have lived through moments of extreme anguish from which I am now freeing myself.

- We lived a great love and life separated us to teach us that we needed to learn. Today, more mature, I recognize that I learned a lot during the time we were apart.

- I feel you are telling the truth. Why can't I remember everything?

- Come, Renato, sit next to me. I'm going to tell you everything in detail again. I'm sure that will help you.

- They sat down on the bench, Mirela took him by the hand and began to talk. She told him everything from the beginning, right down to the revenge that he, with the help of Mimo, imposed on them. As she spoke, Marcelo remembered everything, and little by little her appearance changed. When he stopped, she looked at him, embracing him with emotion:

- Renato! You remembered! He was back to his old self. She wrapped him up and kissed him passionately several times. Then, when the emotion subsided, Mirela said:

- There is one thing I want to tell you. When I came here, I was intrigued by his obsession with Aline. I feared that his love for her had replaced the love he felt for me and that it would have ended between us. I confess that I felt jealous of this woman who was stealing his love from me.

- She paused slightly as she saw that he was listening to her with continued attention:

- I was curious to meet her, I managed to go to see her and as I approached her I was overcome with emotion. I recognized in her the spirit of Giuliana, my daughter with Giulio.

- At that moment Marcelo stood up in fright:

- It can't be! I felt for Giuliana the love of a father.

- I know that's why I did everything for him, like when we were together. I also knew that Marcos was born like his brother Márcio.

- That's why I took care of him as if he were my own son. My God! I didn't know anything.

- It had to be like this.

- They stayed talking, clarifying all the doubts and Marcelo now felt more confident, stronger. Remembering the past, everything made sense, it fit and he naturally changed his way of seeing, of feeling. That dissatisfaction, that need to be close to Aline disappeared completely.

- Let's go find Cora. She was the one who insisted that I come here, I want to thank her.

- I have a lot to thank her for too. That dear friend.

- The two of them, holding hands, walked out of the meadow and into the living room. Seeing them approaching, transformed and radiant, Cora immediately realized what had happened.

- He got up and went to hug them:

- I'm glad to see you too!

- Marcelo returned the hug, saying excitedly.

- Thank you for everything you did for me. I was in hell and now I am in paradise.

- Mirela interjected:

- I told you everything about Giuliana.

- I could never imagine the truth. Cora shook her head smiling and replied:

- That is why I believe that his obsession of wanting to stay by her side, knowing that she preferred to follow another path, was the unconscious desire to revive Mirela through Giuliana.

- I did not know that she was Giuliana reincarnated. In fact, I did not believe in reincarnation.

- You don't remember it, but her spirit knew it because all the events of her past life were there all the time, influencing her decisions.

- She treated you as her husband, just as she had the affection of a father.

- He looked at Mirela

And, Cora continued.

- Aline had a filial love for you. That's why she didn't hesitate to leave you to follow another path. Children tend to do that as adults.

- In fact, said Marcelo

- Everything will become clear. But before I used to confuse my feelings and that made me unhappy. The truth brought me back into balance, I think I'm ready to go my own way. I just hope I can live next to Mirela.

- You are on the same spiritual level. I believe that they had the opportunity to be together as long as they wanted. In any case, it's not for me to decide.

Mirela took Marcelo's hand, saying cheerfully:

- I have many projects I want to carry out, but in all of them you are by my side.

- It would be very cruel to separate me from you now.

- First let's see if we can plan our future together, then I dream of being able to help Márcio, my dear son. He has weaknesses that he needs to overcome to mature. As for Aline, she is more lucid. She knows what she wants and I am sure she will take good care of herself.

- I am also worried about Márcio. He always has difficulties in solving his challenges. While I was by his side, with his older brother, I tried to protect him. I don't know how he will be now that I can no longer be by his side.

- It was good for him to lose the crutch you always offered him.

Cora commented.

- It turns out that João, their father, is very closed and doesn't communicate with his children. But the biggest problem is Ivone, who always sees the bad in everything.

- She distrusts people and thinks everyone is trying to cheat her. That is why she is always very negative and attracts disturbed people, both incarnated and disincarnated.

- It's true, my mother thought that being afraid of everything was to protect herself, to prevent bad things from happening.

- But it is exactly the opposite.

I look at Cora.

- When she fears, she is showing that she believes in evil and that is what attracts evil. Like attracts like.

- She doesn't know about these things. I wish I could help her. In spite of that, she was a devoted mother who cared for me with great affection.

- I know that. That's a plus for her. However, as long as Ivone does not change that belief that there is danger in everything, feeding fear, she will not be able to live in peace or be happy.

- Marcelo felt a wave of sadness, but Mirela intervened:

We can't worry. The important thing is to improve our conditions, ask specialists for advice, learn how to provide effective help and then try to help them. I think that's the way forward. Cora clapped her hands in joy:

- All right, look at her! That's right, count me in. Anything I can do to help; I'll be happy to do. I have a friend who I like very much and he is waiting for me to dance. They played an Argentine tango a while ago and we got to watch the couples dance. Why don't we enjoy the party?

- Mirela put her arm through Marcelo's hair and said cheerfully.

- Let's celebrate our joy by joining in the music.

- Let's go - Marcelo agreed happily.

In a few moments they were in the living room where the couples were dancing to the sound of a bolero and the two began to dance feeling the romanticism of the music that expressed well the love that united them.

The following afternoon, Mirela asked her spiritual advisor to meet with them. At the appointed time, they were both taken to his office. Sergio was a tall, thin, blond, curly-haired, light-eyed man in his thirties, wearing a colorful shirt and gray pants. Marcelo's first impression was that he was too young to be a counselor, however, as they got closer, when their gazes met, he felt such a thrill that he forgot his first impression.

Sérgio's emerald green eyes emitted a vivid energy that penetrated his interlocutors like a devastating lightning bolt.

Marcelo was sure that just looking at him had penetrated his whole being and he felt a little embarrassed.

- Sit down," he asked.

- he asked.

They obeyed and Mirela introduced

- This is Renato. You know my whole story.

- Make yourself at home, Renato. What can I do for you?

- Mirela stated her desire to live together and the desire to progress, to study and, when possible, to help loved ones who remained in the flesh. She listened in silence and then asked Marcelo:

- How do you plan to do it?

- I would like to be by their side, inspiring them with good thoughts. I know we all have a better side and that's what I want to make them feel.

- Marcelo says.

- I would do the same with Marcio and I could transmit regenerating energies to him.

- Mirela added

- At this moment it would not be good for you to be next to him in the cortex. The astral there is very charged, there is a lot of violence, hatred, riots, wars and you still don't know how to be immune to those energies.

- I would very much like to help you.

- Marcelo commented somewhat disappointed.

-- You don't need to go there to do what you want to do. You can do that from a distance. Help only works when the donor is well.

- How so?

- Mirela asked.

- You need some time together to revive your relationship.

- We loved each other a long time ago

- Marcelo recalled.

- But you were estranged, living other experiences. During that time, you have changed. You have to evaluate if you really want to stay together.

- That's what I'm most looking forward to now. I hope for many years to come. My love remains the same - I look at Mirela.

- I feel the same way too.

- It's great. But living together is always an eye-opener. So I'm going to find you a place to live and a job that you'll have to do as cooperation according to the rules of our city. But.

At the same time, I will direct you to a magnetization course, where you will learn to help the people you want, even at a distance.

He got up and Marcelo returned:

- Thank you for the help.

- Sergio called an assistant and asked her to guide them both to the indicated course.

- My name is Angela. They wanted to accompany me.

- They obeyed and signed up for the course receiving instructions to start the next day. Then Angela said smiling:

- Sergio instructed me to take you to the house where you should live. Mirela exchanged a look of satisfaction with Marcelo and, hand in hand, they followed Angela, walking through the flowery gardens until they reached a street where there were some small but funny little things surrounded by gardens. Although they were all on the second floor, one was different from the other.

Excitedly they entered and at first sight they loved the place. Mirela was happy as she had not felt in a long time and Marcelo seemed to be dreaming.

- Today you can change if you wish.

- Angela clarifies.

- That's what we will do.

- Marcelo answered with satisfaction. They left, went to organize their belongings and an hour later, they returned to the new residence.

- As soon as they found themselves alone. Marcelo hugged Mirela and smilingly said to her

- Pinch me to feel that this is true. It seems that I am dreaming and that I am going to wake up and suddenly live that nightmare that was my life in recent times.

~ 230 ~

- It is not necessary, Renato. This is a real life, and we are together again. And this time forever.

- Yes, we are together and I will never leave you again. I could never have imagined that life would go on afterwards.

That I left my body dead in that accident. But that's the truth of life! If only people knew that when they were still in the world! They would do everything differently. Someday it will happen. For now, we have to be patient and wait.

Mirela opened the window, Marcelo hugged her and they stood looking at the flowery garden outside.

- Can I ask you something? - said Marcelo.

- Speak.

- I prefer you to call me Marcelo. I like that name better.

- All right, Marcelo. The name doesn't matter, what I want is to stay with you. He kissed her on the lips with love and they embraced and kept looking at the flowers outside with their eyes shining with tenderness.

Chapter XXI

Aline got up and got ready for another day of work. She was ready when the doorbell rang and she went to answer the door.

- Come in, Olivia. I'm ready. Have you ever had coffee?

- I don't want to be late anymore.

- It had been six months since Olivia had arrived in Miami and since then she had become friends with Aline and Rachel. So much so that Rachel had gotten her a job at the same company where they both worked.

- As Aline was always in the company of Gino, and the romance between them continued to grow stronger and stronger, Rachel found in Olivia the companion for the walks she used to take with Aline. From time to time, Aline and Gino would schedule a walk as a couple, but they liked to travel on weekends to other cities, which was difficult for Rachel, because of John, who always liked to play sports and she would accompany him.

With a friendship that bound them together, Olivia had told her friends the reason she had run away from her mother's house.

- A fortnight after her arrival in Miami, Olivia had called her mother, who was very angry with her for leaving without telling her.

- I always listened to what you had to tell me. You didn't have to go off like that and leave me so distraught. You are ungrateful. I never thought she would do that to me.

- I know mother, but if I decided to live here you wouldn't leave me.

- Gilberto is inconsolable. I never thought I'd love you so much. He was despondent, almost sick. It was hard for him to be content. He wanted to go to the police, find her and bring her back. If he were her real father, he wouldn't be so worried.

- I can imagine how he felt. That's why I didn't say anything. I had wanted to be independent for a long time.

- Are you with someone, a boy?

- No, Mother. I came here to work, to learn to take care of myself.

- At the university? Gilberto went there, he knows you canceled your registration. He wants you to come back

- Don't think that. Tomorrow I'm going to start working in a company and I plan to continue studying here. I'm calling to tell you I'm fine.

- Where are you?

- I'll tell you, but I don't want you to give my address to Gilberto.

- Because he's the one who's most worried.

- That's why. He's going to want to come looking for me. I don't want to go and if he insists, we'll end up fighting. I'm doing very well. I live in a nice place, I have everything I need, I have a Brazilian neighbor, my age, and an American friend who arranged a job for me. I don't need anything.

- Don't you miss your home?

- I miss you, not the rest.

- I'm going to write down your address.

- Look, I'm in Miami, I'm just going to give you my phone number. If I find out Gilberto is coming for me, I'm not going to tell you, I'm going to change cities. So, I beg you, don't let him interfere in my life.

- He has never interfered in your life. You are being very ungrateful. But I don't want to be the cause of any trouble.

- Olivia handed him the phone and hung up. After that, from time to time her mother would call and they would talk.

- During the drive to work, they exchanged ideas about work. Olivia was satisfied with her job. Although she had started in a simple administrative assistant role, the salary was sufficient for her expenses and there was great potential for advancement.

- Enthusiastic and mentored by Rachel, she was always striving to learn more.

- They arrived at the scheduled time and each took her place and began to work. By the end of the afternoon. Olivia was called by her area manager and told that she had been promoted to secretary to one of the executives. After greetings, she was ushered into her new boss's office and discovered that her salary had been doubled and that she had benefits related to her duties.

- He could have a company-financed car and monthly bonuses; by the end of the afternoon. When he met with his friends, as usual, he told them the news.

- This can't go on like this.

- We have to celebrate.

- I agreed.

- Rachel agreed.

- Let's go to the reception bar and get together. I'll call John and bring Beth and I'll meet you there.

- I'll call Gino and I'll meet you here.

- Olivia was radiant. For the first time she felt the pleasure of victory. She had achieved a promotion thanks to her own effort and skill. It was a modest victory, but she knew she had the conditions to conquer more.

- The conviction of her own ability made her look to the future with pleasure and hope for better days.

- It was after ten o'clock when Olivia arrived home from the celebrations. She had been introduced to some of Rachel's friends she didn't know; she was cheerful and happy.

- She remembered to call her mother to tell her the news. From the schedule, he knew she would answer.

- A housekeeper answered and soon after Olga was on the phone. Oliva told her about her promotion and how happy she was to be moving up.

- Olga replied a little sadly.

- You're happy to be promoted to a simple secretary, why don't you go back home? You don't need that to live. Here you have everything you want.

- You've never needed to work to support yourself and you can't know the pleasure of being independent, self-sufficient. I'm sorry to have to tell you just that.

- I'm not belittling your progress. But when I think that being a rich girl, who could be enjoying a life of luxury, you are working for strangers, living in a small apartment and on a mock salary that seems insignificant to me, I feel sad.

- But I am happy. And that's priceless.

- You mean you were unhappy here?

- I didn't mean that. But I like to be useful, to prove my ability, to know that I can support myself. You can't imagine how good it is to work, to have dignity, to spend money you've earned on your own merit. It's an achievement.

- You are happy and that comforts me. But you know that when you get tired of all this, your place is here, as it always will be. Come back whenever you want and you will be welcomed with open arms.

- Thank you very much, mother. You are welcome.

- Olivia said goodbye to her mother and hung up the phone. Gilberto who overheard part of the conversation said:

- But I am happy. And that's priceless.

- You mean you were unhappy here?

- I didn't mean that. But I like to be useful, to prove my ability, to know that I can support myself. You can't imagine how good it is to work, to have dignity, to spend money you've earned on your own merit. It's an achievement.

- You are happy and that comforts me. But you know that when you get tired of all this, your place is here, as it always will be. Come back whenever you want and you will be welcomed with open arms.

- Thank you very much, mother. You are welcome.

- Olivia said goodbye to her mother and hung up the phone. Gilberto who overheard part of the conversation said:

- That was Olivia. She doesn't want to go back.

- Era she says she is happy, she was promoted in her job. Imagine, she works as a secretary.

- I don't think that girl is right in the head. I think we should go there to talk. Try to make her understand that she should go home.

- No, not that. When she comes back, it will have to be of her own free will. We have our dignity too. In the end, she was the one who left because she almost gave me to understand that she was not happy with us. One day she will remember and feel that her place is here, with the people who love her most in the world. You and me.

- And if she doesn't want to come back.

- I don't think so. He's playing at being independent. One day she'll get tired and come home, you'll see.

- He didn't answer, but he felt sad and worried. He could no longer bear to miss Olive. Her presence gave light to that house. Without her everything was faded. But he dared not say anything.

- Hamilton had been working with Rodrigo for six months and everything was going very well. The two were still friends as when they had been classmates in college, and they worked together with gusto and enthusiasm. Since Hamilton arrived Aríete felt attracted to him and every day this attraction, which she did her best to hide, grew more and more.

- Hamilton had been dating for two years, when he wanted to get married, he discovered that his girlfriend was in love with a former lover. They broke off the engagement and he, disillusioned, did not want to fall in love with anyone, he was afraid of suffering again. That's why his relationship with women was superficial, weekend companionship, casual encounters without any commitment. He noticed in Aríete's eyes a greater sparkle, and a new interest, but, although he found her attractive, he didn't want to mix things up because he kept his job, he was satisfied and didn't want anything to stand in his way. That afternoon, Aríete walked into the room where they were both working and approached them smiling:

- I have great news. That great project you did together has just been approved.

They both shouted almost at the same time:

- How wonderful!

- Great

Aríete gave an air of mystery:

- And there's more…

- What else? - Rodrigo asked.

- They want to hire them for construction. Doctor Méndez. He called personally and wants to schedule a meeting with you to discuss the matter. He stated that our project portrayed what they wanted and went beyond what they think we are capable of doing as is. They don't want to change anything.

- Rodrigo looked at Hamilton hesitantly:

- I don't know... We usually accompany in the execution, but we never take on a construction of that level. I don't know if we have the conditions for it. Aríete intervened.

- Why not? It will provide work, we will have to hire people, but I am sure we will be able to do it too. Our company is growing.

- It is tempting.

- I know that a construction company is very profitable. Let's schedule that meeting to hear what they have to tell us and mainly, if it's going to be worth the effort.

- I've been monitoring the execution of our projects, doing profit calculations, and I'm sure they're paying off.

- Do you believe it?

- Rodrigo asked in amazement.

- Yes, I did. I needed to discuss our pricing with customers, and that information makes our conversation easier.

- Now I know why Rodrigo left that matter to you.

- I don't know.... Look Rodrigo - it's a lot of responsibility.

- We will hire an engineer and skilled labor. You can't economize on a project like this without losing quality. That's precisely why Dr. Mendez wants to hire us.

- I don't think we won't lose anything by going to that meeting," Hamilton suggested.

- He's confident. Set up a meeting for two weeks from now. In the meantime, you will do the research, the calculations, so that we can secure the proposal he wants to make to us.

- I'm inviting you to dinner tonight. We have to celebrate.

- Unfortunately, I have an engagement tonight. But if you leave it for tomorrow I'll go with you.

- He answered me. Aríete.

- Hamilton looked at her in surprise. He had not expected that answer.

- In that case, it's for tomorrow," Rodrigo decided.

- It is for tomorrow - Hamilton agreed - but then I want it to be a big gala. I'm going to take them to a wonderful place. Aríete left the office satisfied. She had no commitment, but she said it to see Hamilton's reaction. She was always being courted, but she was never really interested in anyone.

- If she wanted to, she could go out with someone every night, but when she did to distract herself, some people hovered around her incessantly, and lately she had decided to accept an invitation only if she was really interested. The next night, Hamilton arranged to pick her up at her house at eight o'clock and they went to meet Rodrigo at the agreed place.

Aríete was elegantly dressed, wearing a long moss green dress that molded her body, leaving her shoulders bare and a V-shaped neckline that, besides showing off her perfect cleavage, was very elegant

She perfumes herself and looks at herself in the mirror, satisfied. Her slightly wavy brown hair, loose on her shoulders, her brown eyes, her plump and shaped mouth enhanced her beauty and her class. Seeing her fall, Dalva did not hold back.

- Aríete, how beautiful you look

- Hamilton is taking us somewhere to celebrate.

- You should get out more. It's been a long time since I've seen you so well groomed. The doorbell rang and Aríete said:

- It must be him. Good evening, mother.

- Have fun, my child.

- He opened the door and seeing Hamilton's admiration left him in a good mood and ready to make the most of these moments.

- Good night, Hamilton '

- Good night

- He continued to look at her without saying anything, noticing her stupor, she asked:

- Shall we go?

- He seemed to wake up and answered

- Sure, sorry

- She smiled and he opened the car door and for her to get in. Aríete's eyes sparkled with pleasure as he noticed her embarrassment.

- You are punctual

- He commented smiling.

- I don't like to keep anyone waiting.

- It's a quality I admire.

- And what else do you admire in people?

- Intelligence, good humor, discretion, cheerfulness. Is Rodrigo coming with me?

- No, we agreed to meet here. He started the car and they left.

- You look different today.

- she said and gave him a curious look.

- You said it would be a gala celebration and you're trying to live up to it.

- If I had said that I would be dressed in a tuxedo.

- That navy blue suit is very elegant.

- I'm glad you think so.

They went chatting about various matters up to the restaurant where they were going to have dinner.

The place was very nice and elegant. The room had tables in a semicircle in the middle of the dance floor and the musicians in front. The designs were artistic and tasteful and the popular music, very good. Hamilton introduced himself and the receptionist and led them to the table he had reserved. After seating Aríete, he sat down.

The waiter approached and asked Aríete:

- Would you like something to drink?

- She asked for an appetizer and so did he.

- Rodrigo is still the same

- He smiled and commented

- Since his college days he was never on time.

- I have already discovered this. But her qualities far outweigh this flaw. Hamilton looked at her and thought: "Maybe Rodrigo was already interested in her. After all, he had been with such an attractive woman for so long. He asked her:

- You like him a lot, don't you?

- Yes, at first I didn't know him well. But over time, especially when I fell down the stairs and hit myself, he got close to my parents and we all learned to like him very much.

- You broke your leg, didn't you?

- I dislocated my arm. It was a difficult moment. Rodrigo also had a hard time. He had headaches, bad moods.

- They must have picked up negative energies

- Do you believe that?

- Yes, I have studied this subject and I know they exist.

- Because when I fell down the stairs, my cousin Dora went to pray for me and in a spiritual center she frequents they always told her that my fall had been a negative energy.

It was not by chance. That a spirit nudged me and that it would be good to do a treatment.

- And you went?

- Yes, and I had a very interesting experience, so much so that it changed my thinking.

- I knew it would be good for you and that it would surely shorten your cure.

- In fact, my doctor told me that I was cured faster than other people with the same problem. I got a lot of help. Look, Rodrigo is coming. Rodrigo came over, greeted them and said:

- Today you have become more beautiful than you already are,

- Thank you. You are more elegant than you already are. They laughed joyfully and Rodrigo ordered an appetizer saying:

- That already counts as a celebration.

- The conversation flowed easily, but Hamilton was not unaware of the male gaze that Aríete was attracting. This made him a little uncomfortable. He turned to her and asked

- Would you like to dance?

- Aríete: Yes.

- You don't mind being alone?

- she asked Rodrigo.

- I don't mind.

- He was more interested in a table where there were two pretty girls with whom he exchanged smiles at the entrance.

- The ensemble played a samba song and Hamilton wrapped Aríete around him and they began to dance. She noticed that he danced well, gliding with lightness and pleasure. She wanted to dance with you, but at the same time she didn't want Rodrigo to feel uncomfortable.

- Why would I be uncomfortable?

- I don't know. You've been working together for a long time and I still don't know what kind of friendship unites you. There has been another feeling between you.

- Do you want to know if we fell in love?

- And always as direct as you are now.

- I'm like that. I don't like half words that can confuse us.

- You haven't answered my question.

- Rodrigo and I are just friends, we never had anything like that. Why do you ask?

- Curiosity. You are very attractive, he is an intelligent man, he is always successful with women.

- In fact, Rodrigo, besides being a beautiful and intelligent man, has many qualities. I think he has the conditions to make a woman happy.

- You mean that went through your head?

- No because there has to be more than that, there has to be attraction. We've never felt that way about each other.

- You say that with such certainty, how can you know?

- She laughed and her eyes sparkled with mischief as she answered:

- A woman feels it when it happens, even if there's no reciprocation.

- You dance very well.

- Years ago I used to dance a lot. But in the last few years I've stopped dancing for over a year.

- She stopped the music and started a bolero. They both looked over to the table where Rodrigo was and looked at him.

- He was seen chatting animatedly with two girls at another table.

- It seems that he has already organized himself very well," said Aríete - said Aríete.

- In that case, we can go on dancing.

- He put his arms around her again, this time putting his face against hers, and they continued dancing.

Hamilton felt her closeness enveloping him, making him forget everything, noticing that she was also giving herself with pleasure to the dance. She came a little closer and they continued to dance, forgetting the world in their wake. Enveloped by the emotions that welled up and let them flow.

Gilberto came home and looked for Olga insistently. He went and found her in the bedroom, saying euphorically:

- I know where Olivia is.

- How come?

- She's in Miami. I have the address of the company.

- How did you get it?

- I found Silvina, Dr. Niro's daughter, and she stopped by to tell me that she was back in Miami and that she found Olivia by chance when she was leaving work. She passed me her address. I think we can book our trip to look for her.

- Look for her. But she doesn't want to come back.

- It doesn't make sense. We'll go and convince her to come.

- But I'm not going. She lives far away from us, she prefers the company of strangers to ours, because we should take the trouble to go and look for her and ask her to come back.

- Because she a naive girl, she needs our protection and should see with her parents.

- But I do not think so. When she was, she lived unsatisfied, sad in the corners, discouraged. That's enough. She will come back when she has the will. If she is well away from us, we can also live well without her. He was not satisfied.

- You are wrong. By now Olivia must be sorry. She just doesn't have the courage to ask us to come back.

- What are you thinking? Why is he so keen to get her back?

That seems strange to me.

He decided to dissemble.

- There's nothing strange. I just want to protect our daughter. But if you don't want me to, I won't insist.

- I'm fine. She needs a lesson.

- Disgusted, Gilberto went to the library, locked the door, opened a secret drawer, took out some photographs and stared at them.

- He had to find a way to bring her back.

- That obsession kept him awake, and many times, while Olga was snoring peacefully, he got up and went to look at the photographs, thinking of Olivia with despair. During the day, when Olivia was served a dish she liked, didn't eat well, or when someone mentioned her, or even when she saw the portraits in the room Olga had left in her usual place, she would fall into a state of depression. Suddenly, she began to think: what if she had found someone else in Miami? She was too beautiful to be alone.

- Surely she didn't want to go back because of that. Imagining that she could be in someone else's arms, exchanging caresses, loving him, kissing him, giving herself to him as she had never done before, she felt a rush of hatred invade her chest. 260

- And, suddenly, that hatred grew, became unbearable, then his vision darkened, a tremor shook his body, he fell right there and the photos scattered on the floor around him.

- An hour later, Olga went to look for him in the library, but the door was locked from the inside. Why had Gilberto put the key in the door?

- She knocked on the door, first softly and then loudly, but got no answer. Frightened, she called the servant saying:

- Gilberto locked himself in the library more than an hour ago. I'm knocking and he won't open. Something must have happened. Maybe he went out, locked the door and left the key.

- I saw him go in, but I didn't see him come out. I think we'd better try

- open that door. He might be having a bad time.

- You have a duplicate key. Go and get it, hurry.

- He went and came right back, tried to put the key in the door, but it wouldn't fit.

- The other key is on the other side. I can't open it.

- In that case let's force the door. We have to get in any way we can. He called the driver and they both forced the door without getting it open. The driver said:

- I'll get a screwdriver and try to open the door. Shortly afterwards he returned with the screwdriver.

- Olga stood in front of the door and when she saw Gilberto lying on the floor, she shouted in desperation:

- Run, Gilson, go call the doctor

- Then she approached him, trying to see if he was breathing. It was then that she saw some photos under the desk, others scattered on the floor. At first she didn't understand what was going on-what were Olivia's pictures doing there?

While the servant went to call the doctor, the chauffeur was listening to Gilberto's chest, trying to hear if his heart was beating. Olga, frightened, picked up one of the photos and what she saw shocked her. It was Olivia, naked in Gilberto's arms.

She almost fainted, but the rage, the surprise, made her react. She forgot the state of her husband and put the photos together, looking at them one by one and her face went from pallor to an intense blush and she looked at Gilberto's body lying on the floor, she threw herself on him screaming:

- What did you do to me? Answer me, answer me, why aren't you saying anything?

- She began to shake him, wanting him to answer, but he remained mute. The chauffeur, frightened, showed him to the maid who had approached:

- Please help me. Mrs. Olga is beside herself

- Has Doctor Gilberto died? - asked the frightened maid.

- I can't hear his heart, but he is breathing very weakly. Go tell Gilson to call an ambulance. The doctor won't help. HE needs to go to the hospital. Run.

- Olga continued to shake Gilberto demanding that he respond. The driver leaned over her saying:

- Doña Olga, restrain yourself. Doctor Gilberto is very ill. He may die. Please don't do that with him.

- She looked at him as if she didn't understand and he continued:

- Come on try to calm down. We need to help him. Dr. Gilberto is in very bad shape.

- Still holding the photos, she looked at her husband's motionless body, then at the driver, this time she understood him and asked:

- Is he dead?

- He is still breathing, but his breathing is different, I've seen people with that way of breathing and I can assure you it's not good. I asked Gilson to call the ambulance. Olga got up with difficulty. She felt immense pain in her chest and in her head there were many questions.

Gilberto could not die before answering all of them. Gnashing his teeth in anger he said:

- Olga, despite feeling her legs trembling, went to the room, dressed quickly, put the photos inside an envelope and then in the bag, went downstairs exactly when the ambulance was entering the garden of the house. The crew came in with a doctor and Gilson took them to the library. The doctor immediately put his finger on Gilberto's neck, then with a stethoscope examined his chest, eyes and eyelids and asked:

- Bring emergency material.

- The two bakers left and returned shortly with some apparatus and an oxygen tube. The medium immediately turned on the oxygen and placed it in his nostrils. He gave him an injection into the vein and returned:

- As it is, we can't move him. Let's help him to react. Olga listened and did not respond. What she didn't want was for him not to die before answering the questions burning in her brain. She was not satisfied with the fact that Gilberto had had an affair with Olivia. She could never imagine such a thing. That was why she walked sadly, sighing at the corners. That was why she couldn't get over his departure and wanted to bring her back at all costs.

- Damn traitor! The traitor with her own daughter, And Olivia, because she lent herself to such vileness He would never forgive them.

- Lost in thought, Olga did not realize how much time had passed until the doctor finally said:

- He reacted. Let's move him very carefully. While the bakers were carefully moving Gilberto to the ambulance, the doctor approached Olga:

- The lady is with us. We need someone from the family to admit him.

- I'll go. How is he?

- He suffered a heart attack. He reacted a little. But for the moment I can't say anything. During the trip to the hospital, inside the ambulance, while the doctor, seated next to the patient, accompanied him attentively to the case, Olga watched sitting next to him.

- Where she stood near Gilberto's feet, she looked at her husband's face from time to time, reflecting on the terrible discovery she had made.

-- At the hospital, he was taken to the ICU. The doctor asked her to leave. When she refused, he argued:

- It's better for the patient. But the lady could come from time to time to see him. I guarantee he will get everything he needs and we will do everything we can to make him well.

- He doesn't come to. He is in a very bad way.

- He is in a provoked coma. So he has a better chance of recovering. We're going to run some tests and then we can make a prognosis.

- Olga went out, but stayed in the next hallway, where there were some armchairs and a sofa.

- She couldn't forget the photos. She wanted him to come to his senses and ask for explanations. At the same time, she wanted to ask Olivia to come back to confront him about his betrayal.

She was called to the secretary's office to arrange for hospitalization and then returned to the couch near the ICU.

The doctor, seeing her there, approached her:

- How is she?

- She is not getting worse, on the contrary, she has a slight improvement. The lady is very depressed. Why don't you call someone else?

A relative to accompany her and go home to rest.

- We have no one else. My only daughter lives outside. I am not leaving here, I want to be by her side when she wakes up.

- This may take a while. In that case it would be better to go to her house, leave the phone number and we'll let you know if she wakes up.

- No, doctor. I want to be here near him

- The lady can't sit up all night. She won't be able to stand it. When she wakes up, she will have to stay for some time for treatment.

- In that case I will ask for a room. So that I can rest and come to see you from time to time.

- That's all right.

- He left and Olga got a room on the same floor and lay down on the bed wanting to rest.

- She knew she wouldn't get to sleep, at least relax a little. Her body ached and her head throbbed.

- There were times when her breathing seemed to slow down and she took deep breaths for relief.

- The hours passed and she knew that for the moment she could do nothing but wait.

- In Miami, Aline went to talk to Olivia. Gino was away on business and would not be arriving that night. He had been working for a little over a year and missed his family.

- Aríete had called to say that business was booming and that the estate she had inherited from her husband was growing.

- Hamilton's presence contributed to this, and Aríete spoke of him with such enthusiasm that Aline realized that her sister was in love. At first she denied it, but eventually confessed:

- You're right. I am in love with him. But although he throws me meaningful glances, it doesn't go any further. I don't think he's interested.

- Something tells me that someday he'll realize what a wonderful woman you are.

- Aríete laughed happily and replied.

- You say that because you are my sister and you love me.

- Aline wished she could have a face-to-face conversation with Aríete, like in the old days. He was the person who understood her the most.

- She rang the doorbell and Olivia answered

- It's good to see you. Come in, Aline.

- Gino is out today and I'm homesick. I've come to console myself with you.

- There are times when I feel it too, even though I've suffered a lot with my family.

- My vacation starts next week and I'm thinking of going to Brazil to visit my family.

- And Gino

- If you can, maybe I'll go. But I'm sure I'll go alone.

- He won't mind.

- Happily, Gino is very different from my ex-husband. He respects my individuality and allows me to be myself, and I do the same with him because that's how I think. That's why we get along so well.

- I was impressed. After all, he is Italian and they are very jealous.

Gino is not, sometimes I notice he notices when someone looks at me with admiration, but he controls it and pretends not to see it. He trusts me, he knows I like him. And with that, I like him more every day. He doesn't like routines, like me, and is always creating new things. Being with him is always a pleasure, Olivia laughed and commented.

- And with that he conquered her.

- It's true

- How long do you plan to stay in Brazil?

- I have a month, I don't know if I will stay all that time. It will depend on a few things.

- I know I will miss Gino.

- No. That I will meet in Brazil. Although more than a year has passed, as far as I know Marcelo's family still reproaches me for leaving him. When my parents, as for my parents, I know they will reproach me when I arrive, but they love me, they miss me and this will pass soon. You must have a wonderful family. I wish mine was like that.

- Actually, my family is great, but I think even if it wasn't, I would love them just the same. You don't love your stepfather for what he did to you, but your mother, despite everything, I know you do.

- I love the time when my father was around, everything was different. After he died and she fell in love with Gilberto, she seems to have lost track of reality. So she did what he wants, she completely lost her individuality, she shut down. And he abuses her, plays needy, and then she melts and ends up doing his every command, satisfying his every him.

- Many women do that and end up putting out their own light, and in the end even their partners get tired of it. That's what happened with Marcelo. He became my shadow and the love was over.

- The phone rang and Olivia answered.

- Olivia!

- Mom!

- I'm calling to tell you that Gilberto had a heart attack and is unconscious in the ICU.

- That's why you're in that different voice.

- I thought you'd like to know that he's in bad shape and the doctors don't know if he's going to make it.

- I'm so sorry, Mother,

- You feel the same way. Well, it doesn't seem that way. If you really cared about him like I do, you wouldn't have done what you did.

- Mother, I came here because I couldn't stand living next to Gilberto. I never got along with him. You were happy next to him. You didn't need me. I thought it was better to take care of me. And go my own way.

- He never settled for that. I didn't know why. But now I do. I saw the pictures and I want to tell you that you can stay there for the rest of your life. After what you did I never want to see you again. I can't forgive your betrayal of 'him let alone yours she's my daughter at least you should have respected me. Olivia turned pale and couldn't hold back her tears.

- Mother you have to listen to me. It's not my fault. She gave me a sleeping pill and when I woke up I was in her bed.

- Now you want to play innocent because she's in no condition to talk, but I don't believe you. You were holding her, naked, and you want me to believe it.

- Mother, for God's sake, I'm telling you the truth. She took those pictures of me so she could blackmail me. He doped me and raped me when I was fourteen. After that I never had anything more to do with him. My life was to run away from him, who was always chasing me.

- That's a lie. If it were true, you would have told me.

- He took those pictures while I was sleeping and blackmailed me with them all the time. He told me that if I told, I would show him those pictures and he would say that it was me who had done it. I couldn't take that pressure anymore and decided to get out of there. I ran away because he wouldn't let me leave the house.

- I can't believe that the man I loved so much was so depraved. You say that to make me believe in his innocence.

- No mother, I swear to you by the most sacred thing that I am telling you the whole truth.

- I do not believe you. You have betrayed me and I will never forgive you. That's what I wanted to tell you.

- Olga hung up the phone and Olivia kept trying:

- Mother, please don't say that.

- But she had already hung up and Olivia hung up the phone crying desperately. Aline hugged her affectionately saying:

- Calm down Olivia. She is affected, but she will reflect, think things over and repent.

- She says she will never forgive me. I was a victim of that scoundrel. But once again she believed him. She refuses to believe he could have done that. She says he wouldn't be capable, but he was.

- Aline took a glass of water and gave it to him:

- Drink, calm down.

- She took the glass with trembling hands and took a few sips. Then she continued sobbing letting flow through the tears all the anguish, all the fears, all the rebellion she kept in her heart.

- Aline stayed there, hugging her, sending her vibrations of affection and affection, waiting for the storm to pass.

- Then, sitting side by side. Taking Aline's hand, Olivia began to talk, recalling in detail all the tragedy that was her adolescence.

- Aline already knew the story, but she let her talk because she sensed that she needed to get out all the rebellious energies stored in her heart.

Olga woke up with a start. She looked back and thought of Gilberto. She went to her room, took a shower, got dressed to rest for a while and, overcome with fatigue, fell asleep.

She got up in a hurry and went to the ICU in search of news. A nurse saw her looking through the glass, signaled her to wait a moment and went to attend to her.

- How is he?

- At that moment he opened his eyes and closed them again. The doctor came and examined him and said he was better. Now he sleeps and his sleep is more natural.

- I want to go in to see him.

- You can wait a little while.

- Olga came in, sat on the side of the bed and looked intently at her husband's face. He was sleeping, but despite the oxygen, his breathing didn't seem normal to her.

- A nurse was still attentive, which made Olga think that the improvement had not been so great.

Suddenly, she opened her eyes and Olga stood up and brought her face close to her.

- Olga... I stammer in a weak voice:

- Where am I?

- In the hospital. You fainted in the library and we brought you here. He closed his eyes and remained silent for a few minutes. Then he opened them again, looking at her in terror.

- He remembered that he was looking at the pictures when he felt sick. Olga must have seen them.

- Their gazes met again and, from her expression, he was sure she had found them.

- He began to feel short of breath and the nurse intervened:

- You'd better let the gentleman out. He can't be nervous. He needs to rest.

- He's not well and I'm not going out.

- In that case I'm going to call the doctor. Your presence will hurt her and that may harm her.

- He went out to call the doctor. And Gilberto said in a whisper:

- I'm sorry, Olga tells Olivia that I forgave myself for everything I did to her. It's not her fault that I drugged her.

- He took a deep breath and continued.

- Don't blame me, Olga. I fell in love with her from day one, I fought against it, but I couldn't take it. I suffered so much all this time. Tears streamed down Olga's face; she couldn't find words to answer. The doctor rushed in and said the lady has to go.

Gilberto intervened:

- No doctor. She has to stay. I don't have much time. I feel like I'm at the end. Say you forgive me, Olga, for God's sake.

- Olga felt a dazed head and a great pain that she didn't know if it was from the fear that he would die or from discovering that he had never loved her as she thought he had.

- Suddenly he raised his head, his shoulders, his body shuddered and then he fell backwards onto the bed.

While the doctor tried to revive him, a nurse took Olga by the arm and led her outside. Still in shock, she continued to sit on the couch, unable to react, letting tears soak her face. Half an hour later, the doctor approached her saying:

We have done everything, but it was difficult to save him. I am very sorry. Seeing her condition, they took her to the room, gave her an injection and then had the nurse call her residence, asking someone to go take care of the legal formalities because Olga could not do it.

Driver Gilson came immediately; they took him to the room and Olga was awake despite the painkiller.

They took all the necessary precautions and informed a cousin of Gilberto's who agreed to help them in any way necessary.

It was this cousin's wife who accompanied Olga home, assuring her that her husband would do everything necessary for the burial. After the funeral, exhausted and without strength, Olga was finally able to sleep.

Whether it was because of the amount of painkillers she had taken or because of the depression that followed the events, Olga slept for more than sixteen hours straight, worrying the maid who from time to time went up to her room to check if she was all right.

When she woke up, she did not feel like getting up, she stayed in bed, thinking about everything that had happened.

The maid insisted that she be fed and Cousin Juliet called Olivia. She did not understand why she had not been told of her stepfather's death. Olga justified herself:

It was all so quick. I didn't want to worry her. I thought she was going to recover.

If you want, I can do it myself.

- No. I want to.

Juliet was so insistent that she feed herself that Olga ate a little more to get rid of her. Then she said she wanted to stay alone to rest some more and left.

- She had never been very friendly with Juliet's cousins. Now, after everything that had happened, their presence reminded her even more of what he had done to her. So she made up her mind: she got up, pretended to be strong, got ready and went downstairs for dinner.

- On seeing her enter the room, Alberto, Julieta's husband, said with satisfaction:

- I'm glad you reacted.

- We were worried.

- Julieta added

- You can't give in.

- That's what I thought. That's why, despite the pain, I'm here. Dinner was served and Olga tried to be natural and then when they went to sit in the living room she looked at them:

- I don't know how to thank them for what they did for us. My daughter is abroad and I have no other relatives.

- We didn't do more than necessary. We have always wanted to get close to you. But no opportunity has arisen. I'm sorry it had to be this way," said Alberto.

- I think you have your commitments too, children, business, etc. I don't want to take up any more of your time. Despite the sadness, I am willing not to let myself get discouraged. Life goes on and there is no stopping it.

- Surely. We have not done more than necessary. We have always wanted to get closer to you. But no opportunity has arisen. I'm sorry it's like this now," said Alberto.

- It's not necessary. You can't abandon your family. I'm fine. Then I have the servants, who have been with me for years and are very dedicated. I don't need anything. You can leave in peace.

- In that case we're leaving - said Alberto.

After a few minutes, they said goodbye and Olga breathed a sigh of relief. She thought about calling Olivia, but she felt exhausted and left it for the next day. She did not call her earlier because she knew Olivia would not want to attend Gilberto's funeral. Her last words confirmed everything she had told him on the phone.

Thinking more calmly, he imagined how much Olivia must have suffered with everything he did to her, unable to say anything.

For the first time he thought, IF Olivia had told him the truth, he would have believed her.

Surely she wouldn't have. She was blind. Deceived by a scoundrel who took advantage of her blindness to rape her teenage daughter.

A wave of remorse hit her. The guilt was hers for not having been more careful and for having perceived that his interest was not at all paternal. At fourteen, Olivia was a child. That was a crime. She deserved to be in jail. She realized she didn't mourn his death. What would their lives be like if he were still alive?

Would he have the courage to do so? A thousand contradictory thoughts ran through his head without finding an answer.

The next morning, she called Olivia.

- Olivia, we need to talk.

- I know, mother. You hung up on me, you didn't believe me.

- Yes, I didn't believe you, but things happened that made me believe. I know you're telling the truth.

- Olivia got emotional:

- Mother, you don't know what a weight you take off my heart.

- I assure you, my daughter. I ask you to forgive me. I have not been a good mother.

- Don't say that. I adore you.

- I adore her too. I need to tell you that Gilberto suffered a heart attack and went to the hospital, but he did not resist and I saw him pass away.

- I'm so sorry.

- It was better this way. After I found out what he did with you, our life together would be impossible. Life worked out for us. I am calling to ask you to come home. To give me a chance to be for you a companion, a friend, a mother that I was not. Please, daughter. Come back. It's just the two of us in the world. Let's stay together.

Tears streamed down Olivia's face and she emotionally responded:

- It's okay mother. I'm going to get everything organized and go back to the house. I really miss her so much.

- That's good, daughter. Let me know so I can pick her up at the airport. They said goodbye and Olivia breathed a sigh of relief. She felt free, at ease with life. For the first time she felt the pleasure of being young, beautiful and able to look forward to the future.

- His mother knew everything and believed in his innocence. She seemed to have woken up from a nightmare.

- He was going to ask permission at work, check the plane tickets and return as soon as possible to go to Brazil.

- Late in the afternoon he found Aline in the parking lot. He went home with her every day because he had not yet wanted to buy a car. When Aline saw her, she immediately realized how happy she was.

- Did something happen? You look radiant!

- It has happened. My mother called me and I'm going to quit my job and go back to Brazil as soon as possible.

- Why? Gilberto had a heart attack.

- Gilberto had a heart attack, he died. But first he told the whole truth to my mother. She asked me for forgiveness and wants me to come home.

- Very good. I have already spoken to the personnel department, informed them of my stepfather's death and that I need to go back to Brazil. I think I will come to an agreement and they will let me go immediately. I am going to report on the tickets today.

- I will be on vacation on Monday and have booked mine for Sunday. We can travel together.

- What about Gino?

- He can't travel, he'll stay, but he'll look after my house while I'm away.

- Olivia smiled:

- It looks like you've found an ideal partner.

- It's true every day that goes by I'm surer it's true. I like being with him. His presence does not burden me, on the contrary, it motivates me to progress, to realize my projects. That's why I feel so much pleasure next to him, because I can say what I feel and listen to what he has to say.

- I would like to find a love like that someday. Aline looked into her eyes and answered

- I have it because I don't mind paying the price.

- I know what you mean. You were not happy; you knew what you wanted. you turned the situation around and gave it all up. Of course, you paid the price and got a better life.

- That's right. Let's go to the travel agency to book your ticket for Sunday. We'll go together. You think there'll be time.

- I think so. The company has understood and I think they'll let me go soon.

- In the event of a death in the family, they are usually very understanding. They went to the travel agency and managed to book a ticket on the same flight as Aline, albeit in separate seats, with the promise that they would give it to her a change of seat so they could stay together during the flight. Then, both excited, they planned everything. Olivia wanted to buy gifts for her mother and her servants, her old friends. Aline pointed out some stores where she could buy gifts for the family. They were cheerful and happy.

- The next morning, when Olivia arrived at the company, she learned that it would be her last day of work. When she left in the afternoon, she said goodbye to her coworkers, and it was Rachel who felt her departure the most.

- The two had become close friends.

- John is going to miss you - Rachel commented with moist eyes.

- Just him?

- No, many colleagues here, me and my friends who learned to love her.

- You can be sure that I will miss you very much. Especially you, and John. But I also hope to see you again and that you will visit us in Brazil. Our house will be at your disposal and we will be happy to receive you.

- I don't know Brazil and I would like to come.

- I would really like to.

- Let's not say goodbye. I plan to go to the farewell party at the airport.

- I will be waiting for you.

- In the three days until Sunday. Olivia went shopping. She had to buy two more suitcases to fit everything in. When she traveled to Miami, she had used two small suitcases so as not to attract her mother's attention.

- All ready, they drove to the airport accompanied by Gino and there they met Rachel with her son and some friends.

Both Aline and Olivia were excited. Aline because she was going to see her family again, and she had to remember Marcelo's death, maybe even confront his family. Olivia because she wanted to meet her mother. To know the details of her stepfather's death and naturally to talk about the past.

They managed to exchange seats during the trip and the two of them talked about what they expected to find in Brazil, how it would be painful to relive sad events of the past.

In spite of that, they were returning happy, because they had both succeeded. Olivia was coming back more mature, more confident once she had managed to live alone in an unknown country, work, make friends and return because she wanted to.

On the other hand. Aline realized her teenage dreams, conquered her space and a stronger and truer love than she had found in her marriage. With her heart pounding. The two got off the plane in São Paulo, went through customs and finally left each one pushing the trolley with the suitcases.

Aríete was waiting and when he saw Aline he ran to hug her effusively. Immediately Olivia saw Olga who was anxiously waiting for her and threw herself into her arms excitedly. After the first moments it was an hour of introductions.

Mom, this is my friend Aline, who lived next door to my apartment in Miami. She was very supportive.

- Olga hugged her with a smile and Aline introduced Aríete to the two of them:

- This is my sister Aríete, who has been my right arm all my life. After hugging, they left and Olga gave her card to Aline, saying:

- I would like to receive them at my home.

- Olivia has my mother's home phone number. I would like to introduce her to you.

To my family. I'm on vacation and will be back in Miami in three weeks.

- We'll be seeing a lot of each other in the next few days," Olivia promised. They said goodbye and once in Aríete's car, Aline asked:

- How are things at home?

- At home, fine. Our parents are very excited about your arrival. It seems to have reminded them of the past. They don't talk about anything else.

- That's what I was afraid of. I even wondered if it wouldn't be better to stop coming on vacation next year. But the nostalgia was strong and that made me decide.

- So, I did. Good. Rodrigo is anxiously awaiting your arrival. He only didn't come to the airport because he thought it would be better for you to be more comfortable with our family?

- He was always very delicate.

- I love working with him. He is delicate, attentive, a little closed, but very correct and hardworking. The company is growing and doing very well. I think we have improved his estate.

- That reminds me of Marcelo's family. They have reached an agreement for me to inherit the property.

- I don't think so. They still don't understand it and Rodrigo, who had a good relationship with them, was also left out. They were offended because he had accepted me to work.

- How did Rodrigo react?

- It bothered me a little at first, but then he didn't accept his attitude as a definite step away from us. He came home a lot when I broke my leg and we got to know each other better. Since then he has come to appreciate us and today we are all very close friends.

- I am happy to meet Marcelo's family again, it will be awkward because I know what they think of me. I am comforted to know that Rodrigo is on our side.

We are partners and I tried to talk to him, discuss personal issues and it would be much easier.

- Hamilton is also anxious to meet you. I talk about you so much that he is curious.

- I want to meet you too. I know you have good taste and I imagine he must be very interesting.

- Aríete sighed and replied

- There are times when I feel that I am not indifferent to him. But he seems to be afraid of something. Every time he realizes he's getting close; he cuts off immediately.

- He must have had a love disappointment. I never talk to him about it.

- I know they were engaged to be married, but suddenly it all ended. He doesn't like to talk about it.

- Well, I think that's why he's afraid of you, that's why when he's attracted to you, he runs away.

- That may be. But that's why he's the one who will have to solve it. I can't do anything about it. It's an intimate question.

- Aline smiled mischievously and said:

- Maybe I can give a little push.

- What are you going to do? Careful. I have my pride and I'd rather die than let him know how much I love him.

- Trust me. I think a woman needs to have dignity and not run after the man she loves. But nothing prevents her from using some artifices to accelerate the conquest.

- They both laughed and Aríete answered

- I missed you. In a few moments you made me laugh a lot.

- Great, that's the way to talk.

- They arrived home, both Dalva and Mario were waiting impatiently. He didn't go to the store, he left it in the hands of the employees. Something he rarely did to wait for his daughter.

They both hugged her with tears in their eyes. And a lot of love. Aline came back more beautifully dressed,

Mario nodded and Aline realized that the most dreaded moment had arrived and she had no choice but to face it. 282

- Two days later, the phone rang at Olivia's house and she answered:

- Aline is fine.

- Yes. I was going to call her yesterday, but I didn't have time. I had to go to the company to see how things were and take care of what they wanted. But today I want you and your mother to come to my house for dinner. In addition to my parents and Aríete, there will be Rodrigo, who was Marcelo's partner, and the other architect who works with him.

- What time is dinner?

- Eight o'clock. But if you come earlier it's better so we can talk a lot.

- Thanks for the invitation. We'll be there.

- He hung up the phone and said to Olga, who was approaching:

- Aline invited us to dinner today. I accepted.

- She's a nice, pretty girl. Besides, she's your friend. She did well.

- She's more than a friend. She helped me get a job in the company where she works, she always supported me. When I was down, she always cheered me up.

- That's more than a reason not to like her.

- Aline invited us to dinner today. I accepted.

- She's a nice, pretty girl. Besides, she's your friend. She did well.

- She's more than a friend. She helped me get a job in the company where she works, she always supported me. When I was down, she always cheered me up.

- That's more than a reason not to like her.

- Olga, despite the sadness of what had happened, sought to react and redeem herself before her daughter for feeling guilty for not having protected her enough. The shock of discovering Gilberto's behavior, which not only betrayed her trust, but also harmed her daughter, had destroyed in one blow the love she felt for him, leaving in its place not only disappointment, but also a feeling of repulsion that made her accept his death as a lesser evil. She kept asking herself: if he had survived, what would her life have been like?

- Surely they would have been separated. Death had spared her from having to decide, and now she was anxious to make up for the fault she thought she had committed in noting her husband's unhealthy interest in Olivia for a year by striving to make her daughter's life happier.

- Olivia had spent her entire adolescence tormented by Gilberto's wickedness and wanted to make it up to him somehow, doing everything she could to make him happy. It was five to eight when the two rang the phone at Aline's house. The maid opened and ushered them into the living room, where Rodrigo and Hamilton, as well as the family, were already seated.

- Aline got up and walked over to embrace them warmly and then introduced everyone. The conversation flowed pleasantly, about life in Miami, which the boys were also familiar with.

- Rodrigo, ever since he was introduced to Olivia, could not take his eyes off her. While Olga accompanied Dalva who wanted to show him a collection of antique porcelain pieces she inherited from her maternal grandmother and Mario accompanied them, the young people stayed in the living room chatting.

- The maid poured them a glass of white wine and placed some appetizers on the table. Hamilton approached Aríete and Aline said with a smile:

- You don't look alike physically, but spiritually you have a lot of affinity.

- How do you know that? - Aline asked.

- He knows it.

- Aríete looked at him.

- Hamilton had a very keen sixth sense.

- I'm a good observer.

- Because you don't assume his sensitivity.

- Aline said.

- Are you an atheist?

- No. I believe in a higher force, but I'm not religious.

- To be a spiritualist is not to be religious - Aline replied. We are all spirits. I accept that as a natural thing - Aríete intervened:

- Since I started studying the sixth sense, I discovered that Hamilton has it very well developed. There are times when he says things that we are thinking or that have already happened to us. Just now he felt that we have an affinity. He laughed and responded:

- I have studied a life and I know that paranormal phenomena exist. I have been with mediums and had the opportunity to witness convincing phenomena. I am not incredulous as you seem to believe. On the contrary, I look at these events as natural occurrences. I know that we are spirits who survived the death of the body, that we can even communicate with those who remain, depending on the circumstances.

He paused slightly and continued:

- But I don't like religions. They contain half-truths; they were devised by men who interpreted spiritual revelations and put a little of their own beliefs and ideas into that interpretation.

- On that I agree. Never accept certain moralistic, out of touch with reality ideas that some religions preach as absolute truth - Aline said.

- Then she thinks like me. We have studied life as it works, how we should choose our paths to live better by valuing our qualities, trying to improve our weak points.

- I didn't know you thought like that. Why didn't you ever tell me? - Aríete asked admiringly.

- Because we never talked about it.

- I would like to talk about it more. I'm beginning to study spirituality, but sometimes I don't go deeper for fear of falling into illusion.

- You have a good practical sense,

- he replied earnestly.

- That's why I like to listen to the facts of life, openly, without preconceived ideas. That way I protect myself not only from fanaticism, but also from illusion.

- I like it.

I look at Aline.

- She has spoken to our professors at the Ferguson Institute. They are researchers and are looking for evidence to prove every day.

- The conversation continued animated among the three of us. In the meantime. Rodrigo sat down on the couch next to Olivia and asked:

- Are you going back to Miami too?

- No, I'm going to stay. I have missed her a lot and besides my mother has lost her husband, she is alone and I want to be by her side.

- It might not be for long.

- Olivia looked at him in surprise.

- Just like that.

- A girl like you must be engaged by now, you'll soon find someone and your mother will lose your company.

- Not a chance. I have no intention of getting married. I want to live my life in peace.

- You think so badly of marriage

- Yes, I do. I had a very stormy and unhappy adolescence. Now I am free, I want to live, to take advantage of my freedom. I'm not going to tie myself down in any way. Rodrigo was amazed. Most of the girls he knew were eager to join someone, getting married, traveling, living together. I had never met anyone who was against the idea. Was she sincere?

Olivia was being sincere. For her marriage meant suffering, illusion, betrayal. It reminded her of a bitter experience she had had with her mother's marriage.

Rodrigo looked at her:

- I think like you. I cherish my freedom. So far I have escaped from a serious relationship and I plan to keep it that way.

- Olivia looked at him and smiled. Rodrigo was a fine, handsome, educated man. He should be very besieged by women.

- What happened? - she asked him.

- I'm thinking it must not be easy to escape from women, you're what they call a catch.

- He laughed and nodded. Aline walked over and looked:

- I am going to stay here for three weeks. I want to go out, visit the city again, have fun and I would like you, who must be up to date with your social and night life, to suggest what to do and where to go.

- That's what we'll do," Rodrigo replied. We'll take her to all the trendy places and she'll have so much fun that maybe we'll convince her to stay here forever.

- No, we won't.

- Aline protested.

- I appreciate that, but I need to go back to Miami. As nice as it is here, I intend to stay here for more than a little while.

- In that case.

I look at Hamilton

- It only remains for us to accompany her everywhere to show her the advantages of living here.

- I accept the challenge, if Olivia and Aríete accept. They both accepted and Aríete raised the wine glass saying:

- May these days serve to seal our friendship. They all toasted and soon after Dalva invited him into the living room where dinner was already served. At midnight, when Olga and Olivia said goodbye, Rodrigo and Hamilton felt they had to leave as well.

- After promising to find a place to go the next night the two said their goodbyes and once in the parking lot before getting into the car they started talking about dinner.

- Aríete's sister is very pretty.

- Hamilton said.

- I think Olivia is more interesting.

- Good thing I noticed her interest

- Beyond being pretty, she told me she wants to be free and has no intention of getting married.

- That's strange.

- She's the only one I've seen so far. Yeah. She was being sincere...

- It's hard to tell. Women like to manipulate.

- She claimed she had an unhappy adolescence. Why is that?

- Aríete would talk about anything. Sounds like her stepfather was abusive.

- That's why he talks so badly about marriage. She surprised me with Aline. When she was married to Marcelo, she spoke little, seemed introverted, but tonight she seemed completely different to me.

- As far as I know, her husband treated her super well. He even went overboard doing all the favors for her.

- Marcelo spoiled her too much.

- But that didn't let her relax. Now that he's gone, she can be who she is without anyone holding her back.

- I'm beginning to understand why she left him. I couldn't stand living next to someone who surrounded me with so much affection. It suffocates me.

For that and other reasons I am also reluctant to get married.

- For me, even though I don't want commitment or marriage, someday I want to get married, to start a family like my parents did. But only when I find the right woman.

- Hamilton remained silent and Rodrigo asked:

- What are you thinking about?

- What you said. That if I found the right woman I would have the courage to marry.

- This single life is also exhausting.

- There are times when I feel it. But I still prioritize my freedom. I can ask you a question.

- Ask it.

- Aríete is an attractive woman. You never felt any interest in her?

- No, for me Aríete is just a good friend and an excellent companion. Why do you ask?

- No reason. She's an exuberant woman, wherever she goes she attracts attention. And I wonder. Why is she alone until now. She must be over thirty.

- Thirty-two although she looks younger. Beyond that, she is very elegant and classy. I also notice how she attracts the attention of our clients. However, she is always very discreet and I never notice any interest on her part. Unless it's for you. Sometimes, when you are leaning over the desk, I notice a look of affection she throws you.

- I never realized...

- She lied.

And that she disguises it when you look at her. It never crossed your mind that she might be interested in you.

But when I sense danger, I run from it like the devil from the cross. They laughed happily. Then they said goodbye and each went to his car. At the end of the following afternoon. Rodrigo asked Aríete to agree like the other days what they would do in the evening.

They could go to a string orchestra concert at the town hall or to a party at the Portugal club, where there would be a dinner and invitations that Rodrigo would get with a friend.

They preferred to go to the party at the Portugal club and loved it. After that, they moved on to dating.

Almost every night they would go out for pizza, or to see a show by a famous artist, or to dinner at Olga's or Aline's house. From the first night they went out together. Rodrigo didn't do ceremonies, he stayed all the time by Oliva's side, he danced with her and Hamilton as a good gentleman, danced with the other two.

But it was with Aríete with whom he felt excited. The perfume that came from her left him stunned; he held her close to his chest without realizing it. There were moments when he found it hard to control the urge to kiss her and closed his eyes, trying not to stare at her beautiful mouth. Aríete felt that he was attracted to her and did not understand why he resisted so much. What was he afraid of?

Alone with Aline, he opened his heart to what was coming.

- Be patient. She is struggling. You can see the effort she is making to contain herself. There will come a time when he can't hold back anymore.

- It will.

- You'll see.

- It's a week before you leave. If you hold on until then, I don't think we'll be together as long as we are now and everything will go back to the way it was.

- After what we observed those days, nothing will be like before. It can wait.

- You talk a lot, but I don't have the same optimism. Aline laughed heartily:

- You look like a teenager in love. It's about time you did something.

- You can't criticize me. I've never seen you do with Marcelo what you do with Gino.

You don't even mind spending so much money on the phone.

- That's true. I admit that with Gino it's different. I've never felt for any man what I feel for him.

- It is a dazzle, a living emotion, an euphoria. When we are together, time flies. Sometimes I think that, because he is so passionate, I get carried away by his energy.

- It's not that. It's that now you've found a real love. You always thought you had never loved Marcelo.

- Maybe I haven't.

- I've already fallen in love twice. Once when I was a teenager and once a little later. But I never felt for either of them what I feel for Hamilton. It's an affection, a feeling that does me good.

- Tomorrow night we agreed to go out dancing. I know what to do.

- You know what?

- Leave it to me.

- The next night, when Hamilton came to pick them up. Aline wasn't ready. Red-nosed and teary-eyed, she appeared in the room where Aríete and Hamilton were waiting for her.

- What happened?

- he asked.

- I have a cold... headache, pain, chills, I think I have a fever. I won't be able to go with you today.

- In that case we won't go.

- Aríete said.

- Not at all. Rodrigo must have already gone to pick up Olivia. You guys are ready, I feel guilty if you stay home because of me. I'm taking a lot of medicine, tomorrow I'll be better and I'll be able to go out with you. Aríete hesitated, but Aline insisted. Hamilton did too and she agreed and they went out.

- In the car Hamilton looked at Aríete trying to hide his admiration. She was wearing a dark red dress. A wide neckline revealing her beautiful chest, her slightly wavy shoulder length hair was the perfect frame for her figure.

- Expressive face, where her large brown eyes and fleshy mouth stood out.

- Moreover, from her came a delicious perfume that Hamilton breathed with pleasure.

- Aríete noticed that 'he was uneasy about her presence, and looking at him she suddenly asked him.

- Why do you control what you feel so much?

- Why?

- She repeated the question and this time he understood:

- 'Because I don't let myself be easily swayed by emotions. A man needs to be in control of himself.

Aríete moved closer to his face, saying softly:

- Well, I don't. When I feel a pleasant emotion, I let it flow, why don't you do the same?

- She looked at him with parted lips, eyes that showed her affection and he could not control himself.

- He placed his lips on hers in a long kiss that overflowed what they both felt. With their hearts beating wildly. They continued kissing with more and more euphoria and pleasure.

- When they calmed down a little. Hamilton said in a voice somewhat hoarse with emotion.

- What are you doing with me? I've always known how to control myself.

- Don't you like the experience? - she asked defiantly.

- In response, he kissed her again repeatedly. Afterwards, they remained in each other's arms in silence, each immersed in his own thoughts. Aríete broke the silence.

- Why did you resist so much?

- He sighed and answered.

- I suspected that with you I was running the risk of getting deeply involved.

- It was the same for me.

I got out of a painful relationship in which I suffered a terrible disillusionment. I didn't want to go through the same thing again.

- Aríete touched his face affectionately:

- Who's to say the same thing will happen now?

- I was betrayed by a person I trusted so much that I wanted to marry. She was going to marry me. She was in love with someone else. It was terrible.

- But it's a very different situation. I am in love with you.

- He kissed her again several times and then asked:

- Do you still want to go to Rodrigo and Olivia's meeting? Aríete smiled and answered:

- No, I prefer to stay here with you. I have a feeling Rodrigo will thank us for it.

- Me too. And Olivia?

- So will Olivia.

- Behind the bedroom window. Aline looked out and, seeing that the car was still stopped in front of the house, smiled with satisfaction.

Chapter XXII

Rodrigo went to pick up Olivia to meet his friends as they had agreed. When she appeared, he held his breath. She was wearing a bottle green silk dress that made her eyes greener and brought out the golden brown of her hair.

He found it difficult to contain his admiration. During the ride, they talked about banal matters and finally Olivia said:

- Aline is unwell and will not go to meet us tonight. But Aríete and Hamilton will go.

- What's wrong with her?

- A cold. I hope she'll be better tomorrow. We agreed to go out. She wants to buy some gifts to take to her friends.

- You know she's in love.

- She is and she seems very much in love. Aríete told me that she never felt for her husband the way she feels for Gino.

- I don't think she ever loved her husband, otherwise she wouldn't have left him.

- She was upset to know that he enjoyed someone else's company.

- If it were in other times, maybe, but not now. When Marcelo met her he was interested.

- So much so that his life revolved around her. He was so insistent that he managed to marry her, but she was not happy at his side.

- Why?

- Marcelo was very clingy. He stayed by her side even during the day, called her, controlled everything she did. This made her uncomfortable and ended up killing her interest and she wanted to free herself from this fixation.

You're not being nice to your friend at all.

- I was exaggerating and that doesn't work with anyone. When you love, you can't smother the loved one. Nor absorb even her thoughts without her having the freedom to choose what she wants. She got tired and left him.

- Now I understand. Aline always comments that she appreciates Gino because he does not interfere with her tastes, nor does he impede her freedom. She highlights that as a great quality he has and says that's why she feels happier by his side every day.

- I wouldn't like to live next to a woman who sticks to me either, who is always around me without giving me the freedom to be myself.

- I know what that is like. I was very watched and controlled by my stepfather and I ended up running away from home. Nobody puts up with that kind of thing.

- Maybe that's why you say you don't want to get married. But in all honesty I must say that not all men are like that. I, for example, respect people's individuality. The day I want to have a serious relationship with someone. I will allow her to be the way she is and I want her to do the same with me. Without that a relationship doesn't hold up.

- You are single and apparently you don't want to get married.

- That's where you're kidding yourself. Someday, if I find the woman I want, I plan to get married and have children. A family can be the best thing in the world. 296

- Olivia remembered the times when her father was still alive and missed him.

- It depends on the family," she said. While my father was alive we were very happy. We had moments of joy and pleasure. But when he left and my mother remarried my torment began.

- My family lives in the interior and I feel that I miss them very much. But they don't want to come here.

- They arrived at the restaurant, went downstairs, went inside and looked around. Aríete and Hamilton had not arrived.

- This time we got here earlier; I'm going to charge them - Rodrigo commented.

- The waiter came over, asked for a table and they settled in. The place was classy, there were fresh flowers on the tables and good music. They ordered an appetizer and decided to wait for their friends to order dinner. The band was playing blues and Rodrigo asked Olivia to dance. Feeling her closeness, he became excited. He had never been so attracted to a woman. Olivia noticed his interest, but pretended not to notice. Time passed and Hamilton and Aríete did not arrive. While they waited they had appetizers and got excited about the music. Everyone was dancing," Rodrigo finally suggested.

- Let's order dinner. I don't think they will come.

- It's for the best. I feel a little in the air - They sat down, he ordered and then a samba started to play and Olivia took Rodrigo by the hand:

- Let's dance, you can't miss it. Excited, they danced until the end. Olivia was happy. She had forgotten her sorrows and for her there was only this moment of joy.

- As they danced her eyes shone radiantly and her lips parted in a smile. Rodrigo did not hold back, he pressed her against his chest and brushed his lips against her hair.

She did not pull away and when they began to play a bolero, they continued to dance cheek to cheek, feeling the pleasure of closeness and a sweet feeling in their hearts.

It was natural for Rodrigo to kiss her lips and she reciprocated. Rodrigo felt his love grow at the possibility of being reciprocated and said softly into her ear:

- I love you Olivia. You are the woman I want to be my companion for life.

She pulled back a little, staring at him as if wanting to read his eyes if it was true.

- Let's sit down.

- She said separating from him and heading to the table.

- Rodrigo accompanied her and pulled up a chair for her to sit down. Then he sat down.

- At that moment, the waiter brought dinner and set up a side table, taking her plate to serve himself.

- They stood in silence, waiting for him to leave. Rodrigo looked at her trying to figure out why she had reacted that way.

- He was shocked by the emotion the kiss had caused him.

- Olivia, what happened, are you uncomfortable?

- I don't want to talk about it now.

- Very well, let's eat

- Rodrigo liked to be direct, he felt uncomfortable, it was hard to expect her to talk about it. But he tried to calm his emotions. He wasn't used to getting so out of control.

They ate in silence; they didn't want dessert and Rodrigo had a coffee.

- Let's go now

- Olivia asked.

- Okay.

After paying the bill they headed to the car. Once there. Sitting next to each other, Rodrigo didn't hold back, he grabbed her hand and told her:

- Olivia I want to know how you feel about me. I am very excited. I feel something very strong and deep for you and I'm afraid it's not reciprocated. I need to know. I can't go on with this doubt that torments me.

- Olivia raised her face and her eyes were full of tears.

- You're crying. What happened to you?

- I'm so sorry.

- Is that it, that you don't love me.

- No. I'm confused, sad, I don't know what to do.

- Olivia, I love you. I want you to be happy. If you don't return my affection, I won't hold it against you. No one can force a heart. Tell the truth. The tone in which he said it, the affection he saw in her eyes, made her cry even more.

- Speak, Olivia, tell what is tormenting your heart. She did not resist. I told her everything that happened to her in her adolescence and ended:

- Rodrigo I cannot love him. I carry with me a great resentment and I would not be a good woman for you.

- She took off her handkerchief and dried his eyes, then answered:

- For me only one thing matters: don't you feel anything for me?

- I loved you from the first day. But I reacted. I didn't want to suffer and I tried in every way to tear that feeling out of my heart, but I didn't succeed.

- That's all I wanted to know. Nothing else matters to me.

- It matters like this. The wounds of the past still hurt inside me.

- Rodrigo kissed her eyes, her face, her mouth and finally answered:

- I'm sure you want that.

- I love her. You are the woman in my life. They exchanged long kisses, then embraced, he started the car and drove her home.

- Olivia entered the house excited, in her heart was a joy she hadn't felt in a long time. When she shared with him her regrets about the past, she found love for an answer, understanding, relief and comfort. She felt an opportunity for happiness opening up before her that she dared not hope for. The house was dark and Olivia went to the bedroom, went to bed, but did not sleep soon. She remembered the kisses they had given each other, relived all the moments of that magical night when everything conspired to make them understand each other until, overcome by exhaustion, she finally fell asleep.

- The next morning, she woke up well disposed. Her face flushed, her smile calm. At the coffee table, Olga, seeing her, noticed the change and commented:

- You look radiant! It's been a long time since I've seen you like this, you look beautiful!

- Unable to contain herself, Olivia told the whole story with such warmth that Olga finally commented:

- That you were in love, I could tell, but I was afraid you wouldn't reciprocate.

- Why?

- I consider Rodrigo an excellent boy, and I would like to have him as my son-in-law. But because you were never interested in anyone. Always reluctant to date, I feared you would reject him. But I was fooled.

- I was, I liked him from day one, but the past haunted me. I was afraid that when I told him the truth, he wouldn't want me. That's why I tried not to get my hopes up.

- You were a victim. Anyone with common sense would understand

- He was a wonderful, loving friend.

- Olga stood up, kissed her daughter's face affectionately.

- You deserve it, my daughter.

- After coffee, Olivia called Aline to check on her. The fact that Aríete had not come to the meeting made her think that he might have taken a turn for the worse. Aline replied with satisfaction:

- I've never been sick.

- How so, you were not sick?

- I never was. I just wanted to lend a hand to Aríete and Hamilton.

- In a few words she told him what a good result they had obtained. Olivia listened to everything and when she finished she said:

- So, it was those. You wanted to help Aríete and you inadvertently helped me too.

- Rodrigo and I went to the restaurant, we waited for Aríete and Hamilton to have dinner, while we had appetizers, we danced non-stop, we were happy and then, we kissed. It was a magical night; we are in love.

- How beautiful. I knew Rodrigo was in love and I felt it was reciprocal. You look good together, you understand each other, there is a great affinity between the two of you. That will work.

- I told him about my past and received a lot of affection. I am happy.

- I'm glad to hear that. Now I'm on my way to the office. I have to bring some assigned documents. Would you like to come with me?

- I wouldn't want to intrude. It's your place of business.

- I'm sure you don't. You come over here. We'll go together to pick them up for lunch. It will be a happy surprise, you'll see.

- All right, I'll be there in half an hour. I'll be there in half an hour.

- The two said goodbye and Olivia went to the bedroom to touch up her makeup. She took the car, picked up Aline and they went to the office.

- Just then she heard a voice call out:

- Olivia and you?

- They looked around and Márcio was standing in front of them. It was then that he noticed Aline, lost his temper, paled. Olivia smiled back:

- Marcio?

- He looked at them dumbfounded, not knowing what to say. Aline noticed him and tried to break the ice.

- How is Marcio?

- Still surprised, he stammered:

- Well. I didn't know you were back. Your mother didn't tell me. He was embarrassed and tried to pretend he hadn't seen Aline. He didn't understand how they could be together.

- Aline thought he meant Dalva and asked:

- You are talking to my mother.

- I don't mean you. I mean Mrs. Olga.

- But it was good to have met.

- Aline said, looking him straight in the eye.

- I wanted to talk to you and your parents.

- What for? We have nothing to say to each other. What you have done is unforgivable. My brother died because of you. It's better if you don't talk to my parents, they won't see you.

- Olivia intervened

- You have to give Aline a chance to explain. You can't judge the facts without listening to her.

- You seem to be on her side, who knows what story she was told. The truth is that she killed my brother.

- Her eyes flashed with spite and Aline felt an unpleasant shiver run through her body.

- I'm coming in, Olivia. I'll wait for you inside

- I'll go with you, Mire Marcio, you're being unfair. It was an accident. I have to go now. We'll talk some other time. I feel like getting back to the subject. He followed Aline into the building and

Márcio watched her disappear, feeling the hatred in his heart reawaken. He had to find out why they were together. What had happened?

Surely they were going to the company from which he considered himself expelled. He had to find out everything. He walked away from the place where no one would see him and decided to wait.

Half an hour later he saw Aline next to Aríete who was walking hand in hand with Hamilton. Further back Olivia on Rodrigo's arm.

He felt his hatred rising. He did not want to be seen. He entered the next pharmacy and hid behind a pillar. He watched as the group walked through the pharmacy door, Rodrigo and Olivia exchanging loving glances. He noticed her kissing his hair revealing a certain intimacy that made him feel more bitter. Rodrigo was turning out to be worse than Aline herself. That was why they understood each other well. Beyond joining the family of assassins, he was still stealing Olivia's love.

Why Rodrigo had to win at everything while he was a loser. He could not be satisfied. He wanted to know more. He began to follow them from a distance and increasingly sensed a romance between Olivia and Rodrigo.

He couldn't go on like this. Since Olivia had left, he would occasionally walk past her house hoping to see her again. 303

When he was away, he would occasionally call Olivia's house. Asking about her. When he heard of Gilberto's death, he went to the funeral hoping she would be there.

When would she have arrived? How long had she been in a relationship with Rodrigo?

He would have left her several messages, asking her to call him when she arrived, but she did not.

The culprit was Rodrigo, who stood between the two. They entered a restaurant and Márcio continued to watch them discretely. They were chatting, laughing happily, forgetting about

Marcelo's death, about his parents' suffering as if nothing had ever happened.

It was disgusting. Oliva leaned over Rodrigo, her eyes shining with love, and showered Aline with compliments.

Marcio felt his mouth sour and his stomach burned. He could not allow this to continue. His brother was dead, he could not defend himself, but he was there, seeing it all, and he would have to find a way to make them pay for that evil.

They finished eating, went outside and walked slowly to the office building. They went inside and Márcio kept waiting outside. No matter how much time passed, he could not get out of there. He had to know what was going on. While Olivia went to interact with Aline and Rodrigo. Half an hour later, laughing and talking, Olivia and Aline left the building and walked to the parking lot. They got the car and left. Only after that. Marcio went home. Watching him go inside was disgusting. Oliva leaned over Rodrigo, her eyes sparkling with love, and showered Aline with compliments.

- You took so long to come for lunch. I was worried. Did something happen? You look...

- If it happened, the killer is back.

- That's not news.

- We meet on the street. You remember Olivia, the girl you met on Father Joseph's land.

- The one you wanted to move in with.

- That's the one. She came back, she was with Aline and what's worse. Hanging on Rodrigo's arm who was all melty and nice.

- I knew the story that Rodrigo liked us and only accepted Aríete into the company because he represented his sister was a big lie. He wanted to be on both sides. We were right to cut ties with him. He already knew Olivia before she traveled.

- No, he didn't.

- How come they were together then.

- That's what I'd like to know too. In addition to giving Marcelo's assets to Aline, Rodrigo now stole the only girl he wanted to date. Ever since he left, I've been anxiously awaiting his return. How did he have time to get in front of me?

- Maybe they're not in love.

- I saw how they treated each other. She seemed very interested in him.

- She saw him.

- We passed each other on the street. I didn't realize Aline was with her. I called Olivia and they stopped. That's when I saw Aline. I lost contact.

- What about her?

- I would love to meet her face to face and tell her everything I want to tell her.

- It wasn't what I thought. What she says won't bring Marcelo back or ease the pain we feel. So it's better that she doesn't show up.

- You need to cool your head, go find Olivia, have a conversation with her. You may be fooling yourself, that you're, she has nothing with Rodrigo and is waiting for you to propose.

- I don't think so. She never looked at me the way she looked at him. But, even so. I'm not giving up. I'll go find her. After all, we're friends. Olivia has always treated me well. There's no reason to keep me distant. She asked me to find her.

- Now you're talking. If you want to win that girl, you have to fight. You're a good boy, full of trained and well-used qualities. You lose nothing with that traitor Rodrigo.

- I'll do that. Now I want to have a quick lunch because I'm on time to get back to the office.

- Ivone immediately hurried to serve lunch to her son, who was eating and could not forget the dinners he had witnessed moments before. That evening, meeting with Aríete and his parents,

Aline discussed the encounter she had had with Marcio and finished:

- Despite having told him that her parents did not want to see her, she felt like trying to have a conversation with them.

- What for? - Dalva asked. They don't want to hear it. Anything you want to say won't do any good.

- It's a waste of time.

- Mário commented.

- Still, I'd like to try. I'd feel better if they understood why I left.

- You say Márcio's attitude was aggressive, proof that they are still angry with all of us.

Aríete commented:

- Beyond wasting your time, you're going to make them hate you more. Aline kept silent. Márcio was always very close to Marcelo and affectionate with her. That afternoon, when they met. She noticed

- She immediately noticed his sad expression, his spiteful look, very different from the docile, soft-spoken boy she had known.

- It was evident how much he had suffered with his brother's death and how much he tormented himself believing it was her fault.

- Despite his rabid attitude, she felt sorry for him. The unexpected tragedy caused him to lose his peace.

- And sink into bitterness, hatred, and that could have disastrous consequences. In analyzing the facts. Marcio instead of seeking to know the truth entered into the trial, blaming her for his brother's death, and that was not true. At first, she also felt guilty and spoke to Dr. Morris, her spiritual advisor at the Ferguson Institute. To which he responded.

- You are not to blame for anything. It was your husband who provoked the events that victimized you. First by lashing out at you, which provoked what I consider a healthy reaction of letting go. It was his right.

- But he didn't understand.

- She got carried away. His desperation in running after you to keep you from boarding denoted the fear he felt of losing your support. So much so that he intended to stay by your side after he was dead.

- But the accident happened because I let him

- No, Aline. The accident happened because he was so scared that he ended up causing the accident. Hold on to your heart. You are not to blame for anything. He did it all by himself.

- On second thought, Aline accepted it and from then on, analyzing Marcelo's attitudes during their courtship and marriage, she realized that, in reality, the failure of their marriage was due to him because of his attachment.

- The more she thought about it, the more she realized how much her husband's behavior bothered her. She was a free person, full of ideas, but, although he seemed kind, she only accepted ideas that would keep her close to him. She wanted to talk to Márcio, to Marcelo's parents, but how could she make them see the truth?

- It would be better to wait for time to pass and one day she could find them better.

- It was five days before Aline returned to Miami, she would buy gifts for her friends and some special ones for Gino.

She had told her parents that she was seeing someone, but had not told them she was serious so as not to worry them: they were not yet ready to see her in another marriage.

But to Aríete she confessed that she was very much in love with Gino and that she planned to spend the rest of her life with him.

The next day Marcio met Olivia and her friends, called her and she answered cheerfully. After the greetings she returned.

- I'd like to talk to you.

- That's great. Come have tea with us this afternoon.

- What time?

- Any time you like, I'll be waiting for you.

- He hung up and got ready. He had bought a new car and that made him feel better. He didn't go to work after lunch and before four o'clock he was ringing Olivia's doorbell.

- She greeted him cordially and led him inside, where Olga greeted him politely, escorted them into the living room and, after talking for a few minutes, left them alone.

- Sitting down next to the other sofa, Marcio commented:

- Excuse me, I was perplexed yesterday when I saw Aline. I never imagined that they knew each other.

- We met in Miami. I went there to live next to her apartment and we became friends. We traveled to Brazil together. She goes back to Miami in a few days.

- Are you staying or not?

- Yes. I left because I didn't get along with my stepfather. You know. But he's not here anymore. I came back because I didn't want to leave my mother alone. I missed her so much.

- While you were away, I stopped by from time to time to catch the news. I missed you very much.

- I needed to leave and I did very well. I learned to live on my own, worked to support myself. It was a very positive experience.

- Marcio was silent for a few seconds, hesitated a bit and then asked:

- Have you known Rodrigo for a long time?

- Since I came back to Brazil. Aline introduced me to him.

- He was my brother's partner.

- Yes, I know. He told me.

- Maybe he didn't tell you that after Marcelo's death, my family and I broke up with him.

\- No, he didn't tell me anything.

\- I thought he told the story his way.

\- He would never do that. Other people's lives are none of our business.

\- He acted badly towards us. He was like Marcelo's brother, after his death, he sided with our enemies. He got close to Aríete, frequents Aline's parents' house, and all sorts since they were never interested in helping us recover my brother's inheritance.

\- Olivia did not hold back:

\- Let's change the subject. I don't like to speak ill of Rodrigo, who is not here to defend himself.

\- You defend him. I noticed you were very connected.

\- We are dating.

\- Marcio turned pale and asked.

\- You said you didn't want to get married, now you've changed your mind.

\- Márcio, I appreciate you; you helped me at a time when I was suffering a lot, you were my friend, but that doesn't give you the right to investigate my life and give your opinion about my decisions.

\- Márcio bit his lips and restrained the impulse he felt to shout out his anger, his disappointment.

\- Excuse me. I was anxiously awaiting his return, imagining that when he came back we could resume our friendship.

\- Nothing prevents us from remaining friends.

\- But I expected much more.

\- I am very sorry. I can only offer you my friendship

\- It's Rodrigo's fault. If he hadn't crossed my path, you would accept my love.

\- He's being unfair. He even knows we knew each other.

- Yet you defend him. I don't understand. Olivia put her hand on his, saying affectionately.

- I like you, Marcio, but love is a feeling that arises spontaneously and cannot be forced. What I feel for you is gratitude, friendship. That's all. It's nobody's fault. It's just something that happens.

- Márcio lowered his head, trying to hide his anger. How could she be so ungrateful. He spent sleepless nights imagining the reunion when she returned. Idealizing love dinners, where they both gave themselves with passion. He took it for granted. He couldn't accept that she was cheating on him all that time. But at the same time, he thought it would be better not to argue. He answered in a voice that tried to be calm:

- I'm sorry you don't love me. I feel something true and sincere for you. But, as you say, love can't be forced. Olivia was relieved, held out her hand and said:

- Friends.

- Friends. - he replied, squeezing her outstretched hand. Then she changed the subject, asked him about life in Miami, the experiences she had had and told him that she had been promoted at her job and had bought a new car.

Olga called them to tea. And the conversation became generalized. It was after six o'clock when Márcio left Olivia's house.

- He was bitter, sad, disappointed. He could not accept the situation without doing anything. He needed to get Rodrigo out of his way. But how?

- He had spent the money, he was still paying off his aunt's loan and both Aríete and Rodrigo were fine, nothing had happened to them. Apparently Father Jose had no strength at all. He needed to organize a stronger place, one that really worked, but where?

- At that moment, two lumps enveloped him, he did not see them, but he felt shivers.

One of them said in his ear.

- Don't worry. We are going to help you find a safe place - said another -. We know a place that works.

- I'm sure I'm going to find it - thought Márcio.

- He really is, let's help him.

The two dark lumps laughed in satisfaction. They had long been waiting for that opportunity to wrap it up and get it. Now Márcio himself would favor that opportunity. He came home thinking about the matter. Ivone, seeing him, realized that he was not well.

- What was wrong with him? You look bored.

- Yes, I am. He went to visit Olivia and was disappointed. She and Rodrigo are dating.

- They are.

- I told her of my intentions and she gently replied that what she feels for me is just friendship. I can't accept that. I love her too much.

- And what do you plan to do?

- I don't know... I'm thinking of going to Father Joseph's land, but...

- That doesn't work for us. We spent money for nothing, it didn't do any good.

- That's it. But I don't know anywhere else to go.

- Well, I do. Malvina told me that her *comadre* found out that her husband was betraying her. She went to that place, did the job, the other one had a bad time, she even changed cities and the husband came home with his tail between his legs, all sorry. A place like this is what we need.

- I knew I would find it. I asked for the address. I'll call as soon as possible. An hour later, Ivone handed him a piece of paper that read:

- That's the address. She is a very powerful woman who has a group that works with Ella. She says the price is not expensive.

- Márcio took the paper and read what it said:

- I am going there today. What time does the center open?

- It is not a center. It does not have a fixed time. You call and coordinate the time. Márcio went straight to the phone, called a person wanted to know what he had indicated, he said and then the frame and then made an appointment for half an hour later.

- The two dark lumps celebrated with satisfaction. Márcio was nervous, washed his face to calm down, combed his hair and looked for Ivone.

- Mother, I'm coming,

- Careful my son. If she wants to charge too much, her father won't want to give us the money and we won't be able to pay.

- You did not say it was cheap.

- Malvina said, but you never know. No more debts

- No problem, I know what I'm doing.

- Once in the car, he consulted the newspaper, looked for the guidebook and after locating it, he headed that way.

- Twenty minutes later he was in front of the house, which despite being old was well kept.

- He rang the doorbell and was answered by a dark-haired girl:

- I want to talk to Doña Rosa. My name is Marcio. She is waiting for me.

- You may come in.

- He went inside. He was led to a room where she knocked softly on the door before opening it.

- The room was dark, there was no air, a smell of herbs mixed with a strong perfume. On the walls, pictures of different graphics, a console with images of saints, a rosary hanging from a wooden cross, many-colored candle and a table background lined with a red cloth, illuminated only by a red lamp. Behind the table waited a middle-aged woman, dressed in a mantle embroidered with rhinestones, wearing a green velvet turban on her head, with an oval face and large, dark, piercing eyes.

- Impressed by the atmosphere, Márcio hesitated:

- Come in - she asked him, pointing to a chair in front of the table. Her voice was deep and he obeyed. She continued.

- You don't need to tell me anything. I know everything. She put a deck of cards on his forehead and asked him, "Cut with your left hand.

- Cut with your left hand.

- She obeyed. With her hands full of rings, she mixed and took out the cards, making the bracelets on her wrists jingle. Then he looked Márcio in the eyes and said:

- You come here for a woman.

- It is true.

- You love her, but she likes someone else.

- That's true. That other one is always in my way.

- They want to get married.

- Not that - she protested

- They are going to get married; their destiny is marked. It would be better if they desist from doing what they want.

- I can't! He was a companion of my brother who died and a friend of the family. Now, he became our enemy, he doesn't go to our house anymore. And finally, he stole the woman I love.

Rosa shuddered and her hand dropped a deck of cards she kept. She closed her eyes, sighed deeply, her face was transformed and her voice was deeper when she said:

- Márcio, I've wanted to talk to you for a long time. It's me, Marcelo. At last, we can talk.

- Márcio paled, began to fear and stammered:

- It can't be. How does he know your name?

- He doesn't. It is I Marcelo who speaks to you. Don't be afraid. Listen to what I'm going to tell you.

Márcio shuddered, but at the same time, in his throat came a scream that he couldn't contain.

- You have felt my absence, I know. But believe me: I also miss you and our parents very much. I know you still don't accept my death. But I think I had to go through everything I went through. I had to die the way I died.

- Aline was guilty - Márcio said.

- No, Aline is not to blame for anything. He is deluded. She needs to go her way and I need to go mine. The only one responsible for what happened to me was me. I was wrong and I learned my lesson. Now I have learned a lot and I know that it was me who didn't know how to treat Aline. I suffocated. I couldn't take it.

- You couldn't. You were always so good to her. You did everything to please her. She was ungrateful.

- No, Márcio. Aline was sure. I didn't give her peace or freedom to do what she came to do. I blocked her way.

- You loved her.

- What I felt for her was not love, it was attachment. Attachment does no one any good. She freed herself and with that I also freed myself.

- You mean she helped you?

- She sought her path and with that I found mine. That is the truth. That's why I'm here, talking to you.

- I was lost without you.

- I take that guilt too. I always solved your problems and I didn't teach you how to do it alone. When I left, you were lost. That's why I'm here. I mean, you're a brave person.

- I don't think so.

- It's true. You are looking at the facts in the wrong way. That is why you have had thoughts of revenge, of resentment and that can lead you to many sufferings. I have come here to warn you, to tell you the truth and to ask you not to judge anyone. You are a boy of good feelings and you cannot let yourself be wrapped up by those bad thoughts.

- Márcio couldn't stand it any longer, the sobs came out loud and he cried all his pain. Rosa got up and began to run her hand over Márcio's head with affection. When he finally stopped crying, she passed her hand over his forehead saying with a smile.

- So, dear, are you ready for another one?

Márcio did not contain his emotion. That was a gesture Marcelo always made, saying the same phrase every time he had a problem they talked about.

Márcio felt that he himself was there, a true miracle, speaking to him again.

Without holding back, Márcio stood up and embraced Rosa saying

- It's you, Marcelo. I know it's you.

- It's me. Now I need to ask you a favor.

- Do it. I'll do anything you tell me.

- I want you to put aside that grudge and go talk to Aline. Tell her that I am well and that I found my true happiness. That I want her to always be very happy. And that someday we will talk again. Because life goes on after death.

- Do you want me to tell her?

- I want and I also want you to tell everything we talked about to our parents. I would very much like you to look for Rodrigo and Aline's family to clear up this misunderstanding.

- I don't know if they will accept.

- If they will. Tell them everything I told you.

- But Rodrigo stole the woman I love.

- She is in his destiny, not yours. Be patient and wait because a destined woman will appear and make you very happy. Accept reality and take better care of yourself and be at peace. Don't want to change the facts of life. By doing so, you could be hindering the happiness that life has in store for you and plunging you into pain. Promise yourself that you will.

- I accept. I will do everything you ask of me.

- That is my dear Márcio who will always remain in my heart. I knew that even though you can't see me, I will always be by your side to inspire you with good things that will make you happier. Tell our parents that I am still alive and loving them as always. I have to go now. Goodbye.

- Rosa shuddered and would have fallen if Marcio hadn't wouldn't have held her. She ran her hand over her forehead looking around and then dropped into the chair in fright.

- What happened here?

- I don't remember.

- I didn't lose consciousness. While I was at the Lady's side

- Lady I received the spirit of my brother Marcelo, who spoke with me. Thank you very much. I never thought this could happen.

- My God, it happened again! I lost my senses a long time ago. Excuse me, let's continue.

- No, madam. Thank you very much. I've already received much more than I came for. I will be eternally grateful to the lady for this evening. God bless you.

- He got up and asked her how much he owed her, to which she replied.

- I cannot charge you anything. You may go at ease.

- I can't charge you anything. You can leave peacefully.

- He left relieved, elated, wanting to return home soon to tell his parents what had happened.

- The two dark lumps outside wanted to approach him, but failed.

- One commented.

- What happened to Rosa? Because she had those guards at the door. I had never seen anything like that, beyond the fact that they didn't let us in, they threw us in the garbage anyway.

- And now they prevented us from continuing with him. She noticed that he was with a light on his chest.

- I saw it. It's better to leave now. This time we got nothing. With him I don't want to deal anymore nor I let's go.

Marcio got into the car euphoric. He was in a hurry to get home and tell his parents the news. He felt a joy in his chest that he had never felt after Marcelo's death.

When he entered the house he found his parents talking in the living room. Ivone got up. She immediately realized that she was different.

How nice to find them together. I have some news - Let's talk in the kitchen - Ivone said - I've made a cake I want you to taste.

- See you later mother. The message I have is for both of you.

- A message from whom - asked João, looking up from the newspaper.

- From Marcelo.

- What are you doing, are you crazy? He's dead.

- No, father. I talked to him.

- How come? -a sked Ivone.

- What's that like? - Ivone asked.

- I am going to tell them what I feel, mother.

- She obeyed, Marcio also sat down and began to talk, first about his rebellion and the reasons that led him to look for Rosa.

- At that moment the spirits of Marcelo and Mirela entered and placed themselves next to Marcio who excitedly began to relate what he had spoken with his brother.

- Marcelo stayed by his parents' side. While Mirela remained next to Márcio. The two of them made the light vibrate so that those people could perceive the truth. As Márcio spoke, his parents became emotional and tears rolled down their eyes. They felt a very strong longing for their beloved son as they listened to his message, it was as if he was there again to give them back the peace they had lost since his tragic death.

Márcio finished:

Marcelo gave me proof that it was he who spoke through that woman. He pronounced his name and Aline's name; he made a joke with me that he used to make when we were children. Then I felt that he was there. It was him! I knew it was him!

The three embraced excitedly and both Marcelo and Mirela joined them. They remained like that for some time. Then João said seriously

- We have to do what he asked us to do. We were wrong and we have to apologize to Rodrigo and Aline.

- I don't know how to do it. He may not receive us - Ivone commented.

- I don't think so. When we met. Aline said she wanted to talk to us, she didn't seem angry - Márcio clarified.

- We need to see Aline before she returns to the United States - João commented.

- Tomorrow I will go to her house to talk to her and tell her what happened - said Márcio.

- Do it, my son. Let's see how she reacts. For some time, they continued talking.

- And both João and Ivone never tired of asking Márcio to repeat Marcelo's words.

- The next morning, Aline woke up early thinking about the strange dream she had had in which Marcelo appeared, with a different face from the one he had, but she knew it was him. He was holding hands with a beautiful woman, they had talked, but Aline didn't remember what about. It could have been a fantasy. But that encounter seemed so real to her that all day long she could not forget it.

- Late in the afternoon. The phone rang and she answered.

- Aline. Yes

- This is Marcio. Something has happened and I need to talk to you. I can stop by your house now.

- Yes, of course you can.

- Thank you very much. I'll be there in a few minutes. I'll be there in a few minutes.

- Aline hung up the phone in admiration. What could have happened to make him change so much. The day before he had been so angry and now he was so nice. Dalva entered the room and asked:

- What are you doing near the phone with that scary face? Who called?

- Marcio, he's coming to talk to me. Yesterday he seemed very angry. He says something happened.

- Whatever it was must be something good for him to change.

- Let's wait.

- When the doorbell rang, Aline went to open the door. She noticed that Márcio was shy. She pretended not to notice and smiled:

- Come in, Márcio.

- She led him into the living room, pointed to a sofa and sat down next to him.

- Márcio took a breath to gather his courage and began.

- I suffered a lot with the death of my brother. I remained a rebel. He was my partner, my friend.

- I remember how they loved each other.

- But my parents also suffered a lot. They still haven't recovered from that loss.

- I know. We all suffered. My family also felt his death.

- However, we were left with anger, we blamed you. We were left with a lot of anger, even from your family, but yesterday an event happened that changed all that.

- Speak, Marcio, what happened?

- He was moved, took a deep breath and continued:

- You have to know the truth. I was very angry about Rodrigo because I found out that he and Oliva were dating. I had long been in love with her, anxiously awaiting her return. I was not satisfied with her love, especially since Rodrigo had stolen Oliva from me. So, I decided to go to a woman who is dedicated to separating them.

She fell silent and Aline noticed that it was hard for her to continue.

- Go on.

- It's not easy for me to make a confession like this. But I'm willing to tell you the truth.

- I'm not here to judge you. Speak without fear.

- Thank you. Last night I was given an address and went to find this woman.

- He then went on to relate the encounter with Marcelo' spirit. Aline listened attentively and could not hold back her tears. He left out no detail and finished.

I did what you asked me to do, I told my parents, we did not perceive the injustice we were doing to all of you. I am here to ask you to forgive us. You are not to blame for anything.

- Aline got up and hugged him warmly, giving him a kiss on the forehead:

- Bless Marcelo for telling the truth. I was very saddened by your attitude. Since I arrived I was thinking of looking for you to talk about my feelings. My love for Marcelo is over. But he didn't want to understand. I couldn't continue a pretended relationship that I didn't feel, even though I have great respect for Marcel and that's why I left him.

I thought he would suffer at first, but then he would find another woman who would love him as he deserved.

Love cannot be forced. I love Olivia, I was willing to fight to conquer her, even if it was for my resources, but Marcelo made me understand that they were destined for each other and that I needed to forget.

He is right. The two were attracted to each other from the day they met. It was something very strong. Even if they got what they wanted, they would not be happy with her.

Life knows what it does. Your destiny is another.

- I understood that. But it's good to know you're not angry with us. For the wrong we did you.

- No. In four days, I'll leave. But first I plan to visit your parents, hug them.

- You'll be very welcome.

- I'll call you to let you know.

- Marcelo got up to say goodbye, but stopped because Dalva entered the room carrying a tray. His eyes were wet and it was evident that he had cried. She put the tray on the table and, turning to Márcio, said:

- She won't leave until you've had a cup of tea and eaten a piece of that cake you liked so much. When I made it yesterday, I thought a lot about you.

- Thank you, Mrs. Dalva. I accept it.

- Dalvia served, Aline wanted a cup of tea and they talked about other matters. The atmosphere became quiet and pleasant.

- When Márcio left. Aline commented:

- Mom, I told you what I was learning about spirituality and life after death. You listened to me, but you had your doubts. After what happened today, I think they disappeared.

- I was in the next bedroom and heard everything they were talking about. I was shaking. I never thought that Marcelo's spirit would come back to defend us. I thought that if he were alive in another world he would be angry with all of us.

- If he were alive in another world he would be angry with all of us. But no. He not only defended us; he justified his motives.

- One sentence of his left me relieved. "What I felt for her was not love, it was attachment. She freed herself and with that I also freed myself." She discovered what I had always felt, but didn't know how to explain it.

- I'm glad that's the way it is. For you to come back to the house for good

- Now everything is all right.

- No mother. I like my life in Miami, I want to live there a little longer. But rest assured that someday I will come back to stay.

- We will be waiting for her with open arms. I can't wait for her daddy to arrive to tell him what happened. He will be happy.

- I know he will be. Now I'm going to the company to talk to Aríete and Rodrigo. They'll like it too.

- Aline went to get organized. She left and was soon arriving at the company. Seeing her enter, Aríete smiled.

- It's good that she's coming soon. Then we can have lunch together. I'm starting to miss her. It's only a few days before she comes back, I want to take advantage of her company every minute I can.

- You can also go to Miami from time to time.

- I'm thinking about it.

- I'm very busy around here right now. I don't want to leave Hamilton alone.

- Of course, not when I leave, he will come with me.

- It's really very serious relationship.

- Yesterday Hamilton asked me to marry him and I accepted.

- Congratulations. I'm sure you will be happy. I have great news to tell you. A miracle has happened.

- What happened.

- Let's go get Rodrigo.

- They entered the office where Rodrigo and Hamilton were working and after greetings Aline talked about an unexpected visit from Márcio and everything he told her. She finished:

- I told you that Marcelo's spirit after he died settled in me and I began to linger, I dreamed of him, I felt his presence. That is why I looked for the Ferguson Institute, I was sure it was the same one. He did a spiritual treatment that was indicated to me and I got better. I am sure that Marcelo received help, he understood that he could not continue to be near me and he left. The words he said to Márcio enlightened me, brought me relief and peace. Rodrigo had listened to everything with great emotion. As Aline spoke, he felt goose bumps all over his body, he seemed to see his friend's face in front of him, which made him say when Aline was silent:

- Aríete spoke to me about spirituality and life after death, but I have never really looked into those subjects. Marcelo's words touched me deeply and I felt the impulse to understand what he meant. As if to say: Wake up. Life continues after death and the spirit is eternal.

- That changes the way of looking at life. Knowing that people who have already died are still living somewhere else and that one day we will see them again is comforting and gives a lot of peace.

Hamilton exclaimed.

- It's true. If you want, you can come with me to the Spiritual Center I frequent with Mom. Dad wants to go there too. You can study there, learn about paranormal phenomena. It's a nice place that renews our energies and elevates our thoughts. Since I started going there, I feel much better.

- The same thing happened to me - said Aline.

- At the Ferguson Institute they study a lot, they do a lot of research, they recommend books by scientists about mediumistic phenomena.

- Those are the books I would like to read - Rodrigo answered.

- I already read some of them, I was very interested in going deeper, but I came to Sao Paulo and I didn't have the opportunity. I also want to go with you.

Hamilton added.

- When you arrive in Miami. I will send you some books and pamphlets used in the Institute's courses. She will love them.

- I will invite Olivia to go - Rodrigo said.

- I will tell her something new - Aríete encouraged.

- Olivia and I are getting married

- looked at Aline:

- I want to see who is the bravest and book the wedding first.

- We're getting married before you.

- Hamilton provoked.

- I'll be the first.

Rodrigo said with conviction.

- Olivia knows - joked Aline.

- She knows and approves and gave me the yes.

- The conversation flowed easily and happily. Aline thought of Gino and felt nostalgic. She consoled herself by remembering that in a few days he would be in her arms. Those days of absence made her realize that the two of them were very close. She had never felt for her husband the love she felt for Gino. Next to him she felt free and safe, it was a delicious feeling of pleasure she had never enjoyed before. His temperament was good with her, no strings attached, only respect and affection.

- After eating with them, Aline left for home. Dalva waited contentedly. As soon as he saw her, he told her:

- You can't imagine how your father was when he found out everything. He came in crying. Of course, he hides it and I pretend I don't notice. I didn't think he'd be so excited.

- We all are. It's very good to clear up that misunderstanding. In the afternoon I intend to go to his house.

- Would you like me to accompany you?

- That's not necessary. I wish to talk, to clarify all the facts better. Dalva was silent for a few moments and then said:

- I am thinking of having a dinner on the eve of your trip, to bring us all together and seal our friendship.

- What a good idea, Mother. We'll call Olivia and Hamilton, too.

- Wouldn't it be better just the family? Aline burst out laughing.

- Hamilton asked Aríete in marriage. Soon he will be family. Dalva put her hand to her lips, trying to hold back an exclamation of surprise:

- Is it true? Aríete is getting married? How come he didn't tell me anything?

- It's true. Things are happening so fast. Rodrigo also proposed to Olivia.

- You don't say. I noticed the looks he was giving her. In that case, they should both come too. Mrs. Olga. Our family is growing. I feel that she is alone.

- Aline hugged her mother and replied

- It won't be for long. Gino is waiting for me in Miami and I am not going to let him escape.

Dalva looked at her seriously and asked:

- Are you sure you will be happy with him?

- I got it mother. Don't worry about it. Our relationship is very different from the one I had with Marcelo. He understands me, he doesn't suffocate me. He is a man of beautiful body and soul. I love him as I never loved Marcelo. We are very happy together.

- If you marry him. You'll never live in Brazil again.

- Don't say that. I'll stay there for a while. But not for the rest of my life.

- But what if Gino doesn't want to come.

- Gino is a man of the world. He travels a lot. He doesn't know Brazil. But he wants to know a lot. I'm sure he won't put any obstacles.

- In that case, everything is fine. But my dream is for you to come back and live here again.

- I know, mother. You and dad can go there and spend some time. Miami is a nice city. I'm sure you'll like it.

- Your father won't leave that store.

- I will send tickets and he will have to come.

- Dalva smiled happily. The bad time had passed and she felt she could trust the future.

- It was seven o'clock when Aline rang the bell at Márcio's house. The maid opened it, Aline asked to speak to Mrs. Ivone.

- Shortly after, Ivone appeared and seeing her, she was at a loss as to what to do.

- How is Mrs. Ivone?

- Ivone regained some coolness and answered:

- 'Well come in, Aline. You called and Márcio said he would come but I didn't believe him. Aline came in and then Márcio appeared saying kindly:

- I'm glad you came, Aline.

- Is Mr. João at home?

- He's reading the paper. Let's go over there.

- Márcio invited her.

- Ivone was still not in the mood. She had spoken so badly about her daughter-in-law that she was afraid he wouldn't come to talk about it. But Aline was there to seal the peace. Once in the living room, Márcio called:

- Father, Aline came to visit.

- João closed the newspaper and stood up a little tense. Aline held out her hand:

- How are you Mr. João?

- Fine and you.

- Aline noticed that he, like his wife, was inhibited.

- Sit down, Aline - invited Márcio, indicating an armchair.

- They all sat down and Aline looked them in the eyes and said.

- I have wanted to talk to you for a long time. Marcelo's death hit us all. I know it must have hurt you even more. When I heard what had happened, I was in shock. I was very shocked, I suffered a lot, I thought of you. I analyzed the facts and wondered if I was to blame for what had happened. A deep sigh came from Ivone's chest as she struggled to hold back tears.

- We thought so too - said Márcio.

- But after analyzing the facts, I considered that it had been an accident and that victimizing him had been a fatality and I was not to blame for it. My only mistake was agreeing to marry Marcelo. We were very different from each other. While I wanted to travel, to work abroad, to see other places. Marcelo did the opposite. He wanted to stay and come back with me to take care of me.

- It was very good and you shouldn't complain - Ivone protests.

- I'm not complaining. On the contrary. Marcelo was a good boy, affectionate but very attentive, he never let me make any decisions, he solved everything. I left feeling unsatisfied, unable to say anything.

- But he let you work.

Ivone came back.

- That's true. And for a while that helped me. But then I began to feel an emptiness in my heart and then I discovered that we could never be happy together. That wasn't the life I wanted to lead. I wanted to do things on my own. He never allowed me to. Until the moment I found out that the love I felt for him was over.

Why then didn't you be honest and tell him that? - Ivone asked.

- He would never have accepted it. He was too clingy. He would call home or work many times a day. I had the feeling that I was being watched. I left feeling unhappy. I thought it wasn't fair to continue home if I didn't love my husband as he deserved. Then I was offered a job in Miami and I decided to accept.

- Why did you run away like that?

- Ivone said as tears streamed down her face.

- If I did not love my husband as he deserved. Then I was offered a job in Miami and I decided to accept.

- Why did you run away like that?

- Ivone said as tears streamed down her face.

- Marcelo would never let me go. He would do anything to keep me. So, I thought about running away, leaving a letter. But I never imagined I could run like that and suffer such an accident. If I had at least suspected that possibility, I would have done something different. I knew he would suffer, but I believed that in time he would recover and find another woman who truly loved him.

- She paused briefly and seeing that everyone remained silent, she continued:

- However, I will be leaving in four days. I wanted to look for you since I arrived, my parents and Aríete told me that you were angry and that it would be useless. You can't imagine the joy we all felt when Márcio went to look for me, talking about Marcelo's message. Asking us to be friends again.

- Ivone could not hold back her tears and Aline hugged her, telling her with affection.

- Even on the other side of life, Marcelo thought of us. He understood my gesture and went further, saying that by seeking my freedom I was freeing him. He is a noble and kind spirit who left because it was his time.

- He was such a good boy, so beautiful.

- Ivone replied through tears.

- That says a lot. But, Mrs. Ivone, he is still alive on the other side of life. He is the same loving son that Madame had. We will all die someday.

- When his time comes. I'm sure he'll be waiting to greet you and give you the same loving embrace as always.

- Is it too good to be true?

Márcio came closer:

- It's true mother. He is alive. Life continues after the death of the body. We had that proof - João intervened:

- Marcelo is still alive. One night, before Márcio received the message from him, I dreamed about him. I was very overwhelmed, depressed, very nostalgic. But I didn't say anything to anyone because I didn't want to make them sad. I found him sitting on a bench in a wonderful garden. then he saw me, got up and gave me such a nice hug. it was so real! So real that I could smell his scent, like when he was alive. I could not stand it I cried then he told me:

- Father I am still alive. Don't cry for me anymore. Here I found my happiness. Let's forget the pain and cultivate joy.

- I remembered immediately, hearing his last words. I could still smell his scent. That's why when Márcio gave me the message I was sure it was true.

- Why didn't you tell me João?

- Why make her even sadder.

- Ivone stopped crying and Marcio gave her a handkerchief which she took, wiping her face. Seeing her calmer, Aline said:

- What Marcelo asked Mr. João, we must strive to do. The spirits see us, even if we can't see them. Have you realized how much he must suffer seeing the state we are all in?

- Ivone looked and asked:

- Do you think he sees our suffering?

- Of course, he does. He must be very worried, especially about you, whom he loves so much.

- He was a golden boy.

- That's right, Mrs. Ivone.

- It saddens me that you have made him suffer.

- The pain of loss is natural. But now Madame already knows that he is still alive in another place which is.

- Happy and what's better he still loves us all. That's why he says it's time to cultivate joy and let go of sadness and get on with life.

- I wonder if he's around.

- He might be

- Aline replied

- In that case, let's not cry anymore. I don't want him to be sad. I'll make coffee and bring a piece of cake for all of us to celebrate this moment. João hugged her with shining eyes.

- He enjoyed looking at her. From now on we will remember it with fondness and longing, not sadness.

- Aline accompanied Ivone to the kitchen while she prepared the coffee. Aline cut a few pieces of cake and placed them on the serving plates. When she was married to Marcelo, she always used to help Ivone organize the trays and decorate the plates.

- Seeing her do that naturally, Ivone felt a soft warmth envelop her heart:

- It seems a lie that you are here, with me!

- I am happy. I always enjoy you so much. They went to the living room to serve coffee; they asked her about her life in Miami.

- About her life in Miami, she talked about her house, the company and finished:

- I'm fine, now I'll be better after our meeting. My mom is having a farewell dinner at our house. And we would be very happy if you would come. Ivone looked at her husband and at Márcio, who answered:

- We will go with the greatest pleasure.

- Aline said goodbye and Márcio offered to drive her home. Aline accepted. Once in the car she commented:

- Rodrigo and Olivia will be at that dinner. They are sweethearts.

- I can imagine. Don't worry, I won't be sad or nervous. I know I wasn't for me. Marcelo says that a suitable woman will appear in my life, with whom I will be happy.

- It's good that he understood that. If Marcelo had done that. He wouldn't have married me. But surely we had to go through that experience, to learn to value our freedom.

- Why? Didn't you value it before?

- No. Marcelo became attached to me in the wrong way and I let myself be wrapped up in the love he claimed to feel, in the qualities he possessed as a good boy, and I let myself be imprisoned. Marriage for us was a prison. While he only had eyes for me, I wanted to be myself, to be able to do things on my own and with him it was impossible. Love only works when it is intelligent, even if you live together, you can still be yourself. Our union was doomed to failure from the beginning.

- In that case, I think that if I married Olivia the same thing would happen. From the beginning I was fascinated by her beauty, but also by the class and refined environment in which she lived. But I sense that we are different and that a relationship with her would never happen.

- Be patient and wait for life to bring you the person who will make you happy.

- Arriving at Aline's house, they said goodbye with the promise that they would all go to Aline's farewell dinner.

Chapter XXIII

Marcio looked at himself in the mirror meticulously. He would wear his best clothes, he would sport a clean-shaven beard, the hair, the discreet, pleasant perfume, but at the same time he noticed that his face was downcast.

He would accompany his parents to dinner at Aline's house, since he found out about Olivia's engagement he could not evade a feeling of loss and discouragement.

He thought about not going to the dinner where he would have to endure the happiness of the bride and groom, witness the affection they gave each other, but otherwise he would go. Aline might have thought he still harbored a grudge. She wanted to fulfill what she had promised Marcelo. In her heart there was no longer the old rebelliousness that had tormented her so much. The meetings with Aline's family had the gift of restoring his serenity, and resuming that friendship was good for him, for he appreciated them.

His father knocked on the bedroom door:

- Let's go, Márcio. It's about time. We don't want to delay.

I am ready. I'm coming.

- Throwing one last glance at the mirror, he tried to soften the expression on his face and walked out.

- They arrived at Aline's house and were greeted by her, who embraced them:

- What a joy to see you! Please come in.

- Ivone came forward, embraced Aline, then Dalva approached, the two embraced and could not hold back their tears.

- The two men were waiting behind, moved. Mario, seeing them, approached with his hand outstretched. They shook hands and he said:

- Come with me. Perhaps you would like to talk. Aline accompanied them into the living room,

- Márcio noticed that Olivia was not there and sighed in relief. He thought she had noticed his sadness in the hallway, after controlling her emotions a little. Dalva returned:

- Today is a happy day for me. I am very glad that you accepted my invitation.

- Being here brings back sad memories.

- The same thing happens to me. It is difficult to forget a person as dear to me as Marcelo.

- He loved everyone very much, but he had a special affection for you.

- And I for him. But today is not a day of sadness. In the end he wanted us to be happy. So, let's let bygones be bygones and celebrate our friendship. I think if he sees us, he'll be happier.

- He is right. Today is a joyful day.

- The two entered the room and Aríete got up to hug her, introducing Hamilton.

The doorbell rang and the maid went to open the door. Olivia entered in the company of Rodrigo and another girl.

- After hugging Dalva, Rodrigo introduced the young woman:

- My sister arrived today from the interior and I took the liberty of bringing her here unannounced.

- You have done very well. You are welcome.

- Thank you very much. Thank you, thank you.

- Come on, I'll introduce you to the others. What's her name?

- Márcia.

- Aline approached and after hugging Olivia and Rodrigo, Dalva introduced her:

- My daughter. Aline. Márcia, Rodrigo's sister.

- How do you do? You look so much alike, only she's much prettier.

- I think so too,

- Rodrigo joked with satisfaction. Dalva introduced the young woman to the others and she captivated them with her charm. Her lively eyes, her easy smile, her contagious joy enlivened the atmosphere a little tense from past memories. Trying to pretend he wasn't sad about Olivia's courtship, Marcio stayed by Marcia's side, laughing and joining in the banter, becoming witty, which provoked a comment from Aline:

- Márcio did not know that side. He surprised me.

I'm inspired today, he joked.

Dinner was served, they returned to the living room. Aline commented:

Today after a long time I feel completely happy. That's why I want to thank everyone for coming. When I am far away, I will remember these moments with great joy. For many reasons, this is a special dinner. Everyone applauded and Aline continued:

I also feel like thanking God for giving us this opportunity to rescue our bonds of friendship that I hope will be strong and eternal. They could not see, but Marcelo and Mírela were there, together, excitedly watching the dinner. Mírela approached Aline, put a hand on her forehead and continued:

After Marcelo's unexpected departure, we all left, but I had the joy of discovering

That when he dies he does not exist and that he continues living in another dimension of the universe. The body that died in that accident was only a coat from which his spirit detached itself when it was no longer useful to him. And the proof came when he himself, annoyed by our tears, tried to tell us that he was still alive and that our sufferings made him unhappy.

Aline paused slightly and, observing that everyone was listening to her with emotion and attention, she continued.

- He sent me to tell me that he is well and asked me to cultivate joy, trusting life in our future. So tonight is very special. It is magical because right now I feel that he is here, next to us, embracing us happily. Let us also wish him the best in his new life. And to him I say: I thank you for everything you have done for me. I will never forget you. Thank you, God, for so many gifts.

He kept silent, Mirela pulled away a little. Marcelo approached her and kissed her gently on the forehead.

Aline felt a shiver run through her body and had the impression of seeing a face near her, she moved closer and smiled. He was there.

The atmosphere became calmer, people were cheerful, conversation flowed easily. Marcelo looked at Mirela and said

- She finally saw me.

- Márcio doesn't know yet.

- Marcelo's eyes sparkled with mischief and he answered

- Then he approached Marcio, who was talking to Márcia, whispering in his ear:

- She is the woman of his life, look how beautiful she is! Don't waste time, you'll be very happy!

- Marcio did not hear what he was saying, but he felt his attraction for Márcia increase. She was beautiful and very intelligent. Qualities he always dreamed of finding in a woman. She had tempting lips and he found it hard to control the urge to kiss her. Mirela smiled. And looked at Marcelo.

- Don't you think you're being hasty?

- No, the sooner I forget Olivia's illusion, the better. I'm just giving her a little push. Didn't you see how she turned out?

- Mirela hugged him, saying cheerfully:

- Now we can go. Everyone in peace.

Yes, and we can be on our way. Marcelo put his arm around both their waists and flew away. The night was clear and the sky was starry. Gliding over the city, embracing, both contemplated the beauty of the universe on their return, honoring life and God's grace.

End.

Zibia Gasparetto's Greatest success stories

With more than 20 million titles sold, the author has contributed to the strengthening of spiritualist literature in the publishing market and to the popularization of spirituality. Learn more of the author's successes.

Romances Dictated by the Spirit Lucius

The Life Force

The Truth of each one

Life knows what it does

She trusted in life

Between Love and War

Esmeralda

Thorns of Time

Eternal Bonds

Nothing is by Chance

Nobody is Nobody's

God's Advocate

Tomorrow Belongs to God

Love Won

Unexpected Encounter

On the Edge of Destiny

The Sly One

The Morro of Illusions

Where is Teresa?

Through the Doors of the Heart

When Life chooses

When the Hour Comes

When it is necessary to return

Opening for Life

Not afraid to live

Only love can do it

We Are All Innocent

Everything has its price

It was all worth it

A real love

Overcoming the past

Other success stories by André Luiz Ruiz and Lucius

The Love Never Forgets You Trilogy

The Strength of Kindness

Under the Hands of Mercy

Saying Goodbye to Earth

At the End of the Last Hour

Sculpting Your Destiny

There are Flowers on the Stones

The Crags are made of Sand

Books of Eliana Machado Coelho and Schellida

Hearts without Destiny

The Shine of Truth

The Right to be Happy

The Return

In the Silence of Passions

Strength to Begin Again

The Certainty of Victory

The Conquest of Peace

Lessons Life Offers

Stronger than Ever

No Rules for Loving

A Diary in Time

A Reason to Live

Eliana Machado Coelho and Schellida, Romances that captivate, teach, move and
can change your life!

Romances of Arandi Gomes Texeira and The Count J.W. Rochester

Lancaster County

The Power of Love

The Trial

Cleopatra's Bracelet

The Reincarnation of a Queen

You Are Gods

Books of Marcelo Cezar and Marco Aurelio

Love is for the Strong

The Last Chance

Nothing is as it Seems

Forever With Me

Only God Knows

You Make Tomorrow

A Breath of Tenderness

Books of Vera Kryzhanovskaia and JW Rochester

The Revenge of the Jew

The Nun of the Marriages

The Sorcerer's Daughter

The Flower of the Swamp

The Divine Wrath

The Legend of the Castle of Montignoso

The Death of the Planet

The Night of Saint Bartholomew

The Revenge of the Jew

Blessed are the poor in spirit

Cobra Capella

Dolores

Trilogy of the Kingdom of Shadows

From Heaven to Earth

Episodes from the Life of Tiberius

Infernal Spell

Herculanum

On the Frontier

Naema, the Witch

In the Castle of Scotland (Trilogy 2)

New Era

The Elixir of Long Life

The Pharaoh Mernephtah

The Lawgivers

The Magicians

The Terrible Phantom
Paradise without Adam
Romance of a Queen
Czech Luminaries
Hidden Narratives
The Nun of the Marriages

Books of Elisa Masselli

There is always a reason
Nothing goes unanswered
Life is made of decisions
The Mission of each one
Something more is needed
The Past does not matter
Destiny in his hands
God was with him
When the past does not pass
Just beginning

Books of Vera Lúcia Marinzeck de Carvalhoç and Patricia

Violets in the Window
Living in the Spirit World
The Writer's House
Flight of the Seagull

Vera Lúcia Marinzeck de Carvalho and Antônio Carlos

Love your Enemies
Slave Bernardino
the Rock of Lovers
Rosa, the third fatality
Captives and Freed

Books of Mónica de Castro y Leonel

In spite of everything
Love is not to be trifled with
Face to Face with the Truth
Of My Whole Being
I wish
The Price of Being Different
Twins
Giselle, The Inquisitor's Mistress
Greta
Till Life Do You Part
Impulses of the Heart
Jurema of the Jungle
The Actress
The Force of Destiny
Memories that the Wind Brings
Secrets of the Soul
Feeling in One's Own Skin

World Spiritist Institute

www.ingramcontent.com/pod-product-compliance
Lightning Source LLC
LaVergne TN
LVHW041747060526
838201LV00046B/928